Non-Fiction
291.4082 D292c

10-04

Davis, Elizabeth, 1950-
The circle of life : thirteen archetypes for
every woman /

9000926181

*The Circle
of Life*

D0872592

DISCARDED
Mead Public Library

Also by Elizabeth Davis

Heart & Hands: A Midwife's Guide to Pregnancy and Birth

Energetic Pregnancy

Women's Intuition

Women's Sexual Passages: Finding Pleasure and
Intimacy at Every Stage of Life

The Circle of Life

Thirteen Archetypes for Every Woman

Elizabeth Davis and Carol Leonard

CELESTIAL ARTS

Berkeley / Toronto

Copyright © 1996, 1997, 2002 by Elizabeth Davis and Carol Leonard
First published in 1996 by Viking Penguin, a division of Penguin Books USA Inc.
First published in paperback in 1997 by Viking Arkana

All rights reserved. No part of this book may be reproduced in any form, except brief excerpts
for the purpose of review, without written permission of the publisher.

Grateful acknowledgment is made for permission to reprint the following copyrighted works:
Excerpt from *Women Who Run with the Wolves* by Clarissa Pinkola Estés, copyright © 1991 by
Clarissa Pinkola Estés, reprinted by permission of Ballantine Books, a division of Random House,
Inc., and the author. Excerpt from *Sent by Earth* by Alice Walker, copyright © 2001 by Alice
Walker, reprinted by permission of Seven Stories Press. Excerpt from *Women's Rituals: A Source-
book* by Barbara G. Walker, copyright © 1990 by Barbara G. Walker, reprinted by permission of
HarperCollins Publishers, Inc. Excerpts from *Motherpeace* by Vicki Noble, copyright © 1983 by
Vicki Noble, reprinted by permission of HarperCollins Publishers, Inc. Excerpt from "Women's
Moontime—A Call to Power" by Brooke Medicine Eagle, *Shaman's Drum,* spring 1986, reprinted
by permission of the author. Excerpt from *The I That Is We* by Richard Moss, copyright © 1981
by Richard Moss, reprinted by permission of Celestial Arts, PO Box 7123, Berkeley, Calif. Selec-
tion from *Magical Rites from the Crystal Well* by Ed Fitch, copyright © 1984 by Ed Fitch, reprinted
by permission of Llewellyn Publications, PO Box 64383, St. Paul, Minn., 55164.

CA

Celestial Arts
PO Box 7123
Berkeley, California 94707
www.tenspeed.com

Distributed in Australia by Simon and Schuster Australia, in Canada by Ten Speed Press Canada,
in New Zealand by Southern Publishers Group, in South Africa by Real Books, in Southeast
Asia by Berkeley Books, and in the United Kingdom and Europe by Airlift Book Company.

Library of Congress Cataloging-in-Publication Data

Davis, Elizabeth, 1950–
The circle of life : thirteen archetypes for every woman / Elizabeth Davis and Carol Leonard.
  p. cm.
Rev. ed. of: The women's wheel of life. 1996.
Includes bibliographical references and index.
ISBN 1-58761-160-0
1. Women—Religious life. 2. Goddess religion. I. Leonard, Carol.
II. Davis, Elizabeth, 1950– Women's wheel of life. III. Title.
 BL625.7 .D38 2002
 291.4'082—dc21   2002003868

Cover and text design by Elizabeth Stromberg

First printing, 2002
Printed in Canada

1 2 3 4 5 6 7 8 9 10 – 06 05 04 03 02

0926181

*To the women gone before us
who have sacrificed or lost their lives
trying to transmit this knowledge.*

Contents

Acknowledgments

We wish first to thank our mothers, Marian Elinore Fogel Drake and Louise Leonard McKinney, for never failing to encourage us to be ourselves, and for offering support and guidance with regard to this project. And to our children, Orion Davis, Celeste Davis, John Shebalin, and Milan McAlevey, our thanks for powerful experiences of birthing, tender experiences of love and nurturing, and ever deepening communication.

We must also thank our mentors in midwifery, including Tina Garzero and Dr. Francis Brown, for teaching us both the science and mystery of the birth process. And we most gratefully acknowledge our women's circles, our sisterhood of sacred outlaws and tattooed wimmin, for providing inspiration, insight, and humor.

In this book, we identify a new phase in a woman's life cycle that falls between motherhood and old age. This formerly hidden face of the goddess, the Matriarch, seems to have emerged spontaneously in numerous women's groups and circles. In the spring of 1992, after painting a mural of four seasonal aspects of women's lives and naming the Matriarch as queen of autumn, Carol began presenting information on this heretofore missing phase in her workshops, articles, and interviews. In 1994, the We Moon Calendar contained a mention of the Matriarch in an article signed by Musawa. The article also placed Amazon and Priestess stages adjacent to that of the Matriarch, and identified a "blood sisters" stage in women's lives. Although we've adopted these terms with gratitude, we locate the Blood Sister stage differently.

We specifically thank those authors whose work we have cited repeatedly and who provided fundamental context for our own research: Vicki Noble, Alan Bleakley, Barbara Walker, Judy Grahn, and Starhawk.

Above all else, we extend our deepest gratitude to the larger circle of women who agreed to be interviewed for this project— our sincerest thanks to all of you.

Preface

The timing of revising this book could not have been better. It has been eight years since the original manuscript was written, and today women are exponentially more passionate about circling together and better prepared to do it. Young women seek the wisdom of their elders; older women are inspired to teach the young. This is truly a burgeoning time for women's wisdom!

In fact, interest in every aspect of Carol's and my work—our midwifery care, healing practices, workshops, course work, and publications—has also increased exponentially. The hardest part of revising this book has been the fact that we can barely keep up with the demand for what we do and what we know. And yet we have revised with relish, delighted to find ourselves older and wiser, and more capable of articulating the subtle aspects of what these archetypes mean and how they are connected. We are in our fifties now, and so understand full well the later stages in the Circle: archetypes of Sorceress, Crone, and Dark Mother that were rather elusive in the first exploration.

And both of us have expanded our circle work. In addition to my Sister Circle, I've circled and played with the Wild Darlings, and am newly invited to join an established and socially conscious women's circle, the Owl Eagle Lodge. My midwifery classes have always met in a circle; now I've been asked to lead workshops on the Sacred Circle by students and their friends interested in learning what it takes to create a circle and make it last. And Carol has established a birthing home and midwifery school, right on her land in New Hampshire! Everywhere we go, even in business and board meetings, we circle. The circle is a metaphor for what women know and what they value—egalitarianism, truth, synergy, and wisdom.

The most exciting part of reworking this book has undoubtedly been adding the new chapter, Creating Your Own Circle. This chapter carries the wisdom of what we have learned, and we hope it imparts our excitement and passion for circling in a way that proves contagious. Along these lines, groundbreaking work is taking place through an organization called The Millionth Circle,[1] spearheaded by author Jean Bolen. Her work is loosely based on a story by Ken Keyes, Jr., who in his book *The Hundredth Monkey* shared the amazing discovery that monkeys geographically isolated from one another inexplicably began identical new behaviors at more or less the same time. (In particular, they all started washing sweet potatoes before eating them.) Following up on Keyes's research, theoretical biologist Rupert Sheldrake postulated the Morphic Resonance Hypothesis, which accounted for a similar effect in birds and animals. The premise of The Millionth Circle is simply that if more women circle, more will follow, and hierarchical paradigms now dominating our culture will inevitably be undermined.

This is a long-term goal, but for the short term, the Circle holds some solutions for women's immediate wants and needs. Put simply, scores and scores of women have come to realize that there is no turning back, that the work will only increase, and that if they must accomplish more and more in life, they need more too— more respect, more power, more sexual freedom of expression, more equality in their primary relationship, more opportunities to advance their own work, more quality health care and education for their families, more honest representation by a government that demonstrates conscience for the needy and reverence for the Earth, and more support for all the above. Women are waking up to the fact that no one else is going to do this work for them, nobody at the top will provide rescue. We're also aware that the struggle of realizing these goals, the grit and glory of the journey, are just as important as the final objectives. But—bottom line— these goals can only be met in concert with others.

For example, in terms of keeping our health, having a circle of women friends has been proven to help us live better and longer. The famous Nurses' Health Study from Harvard Medical School showed that the more friends women had, the less likely they were to develop physical impairments as they aged, and the more likely they were to lead joyful lives. The results of this study were so significant that the researchers concluded that not having at least one close friend or confidante was as detrimental to a woman's health as smoking or carrying extra weight![2]

Similarly, a study at the University of California at Los Angeles showed that women need each other to successfully manage stress. Until now, research in this area has been predicated on the typical male response of "fight or flight." In contrast, researchers Klein and Taylor found that women under stress release a cascade of brain chemicals that causes them to bond with other women, in what they termed the "tend and befriend" response.[3] One of these triggers is the hormone oxytocin, sometimes called the "love hormone," which is released with sexual foreplay, orgasm, and breast-feeding. Oxytocin has also been shown to counter human depression. Unfortunately, the calming response of oxytocin does not usually occur in men because testosterone—which men produce in extra high amounts when under stress—reduces its effect.

With so much evidence pointing to how women need women, many a post-feminist has wondered just exactly how men fit into the picture. Men are in our lives, and we love them—we love our sons, we love our fathers, we love our brothers, we love our husbands (the good ones, at least) and know that the Circle stands for inclusiveness. In fact, women have asked repeatedly about a Circle of Life for men!

I recently found a wonderful passage addressing this issue in a book by Diedre Badejo, titled *Osun Seegesi: The Elegant Deity of Wealth, Power and Femininity.* In it, Badejo explains that according to the goddess Osun, the power of woman

> remains independent of male dominance and . . . evolves autonomously. . . . [W]omen and men possess their own separate sources of power, which are interwoven into the complex fabric of existence. . . . [T]he balance between these gender-based sources of power keeps the world advancing, and is the objective of gender reciprocity which, in the words of the late Professor Sterling Brown, "keeps a people coming" . . . a feminist can be for women without being against men . . . imbalance and disharmony affect the entire social composition. What Osun wanted me to say is that women are powerful in and of themselves, and that power exists to ensure our continuity, and that controlling our lives and our destiny is a joint effort not to be diminished by male dominance or female antagonism. In short, Osun wants to negotiate a truce, and bring the Town of Women back to the community of men and women so we can ensure our survival and growth.[4]

What a simple and elegant statement on the relationship of male and female power! Woman's power evolves autonomously, exists to ensure the continuity of community, and should not be diminished by male dominance *or* female antagonism. Let us take a giant step back from blame against the male gender, and begin to focus on revitalizing our own feminine power and wisdom. We can do this, and according to the passage above, *must* do this for our survival.

I do think it is critically important that as women circle for power and support, they also begin to articulate their political views and spirituality to the men and boys in their lives. I recently started constructing an altar at each turning point of the year, and have made it a point to bring my husband and sons to sit at it, if only briefly. I try to bring ceremony to every family occasion. And I find that my students are increasingly intent on sharing their intimate, woman-to-woman learning experiences with their male partners, less with the expectation that these will be fully understood and appreciated than to communicate the depth of intimacy of which women are capable. As the passage above points out, this is the province, the "Town of Women," that the greater community sorely needs.

And as we do our work and come together, the worldwide Web of Women becomes more evident with each passing day, our diversity generating a multiplicity of threads, glistening with our accomplishments. There certainly is no end of work to do! Wishing you blessings along the way—and may our threads interweave with purpose and joy.

—Elizabeth Davis

Introduction

This book results from many years of research and long contemplation of women's mysteries by me, Elizabeth Davis, and my coauthor, Carol Leonard. Although we live on separate coasts, powerful parallel experiences brought us together to formulate *The Circle of Life* and introduce the new archetypes of women's experience it puts forth.

Carol and I are both midwives, teachers and practitioners of women's spirituality, and mothers of children born at home. We both remember our first conversation, poolside at the first national conference of the Midwives Alliance of North America. We were both board members, and I had been chosen the keynote speaker of the event as I had recently written the so-called bible for practicing midwives, *Heart & Hands: A Midwife's Guide to Pregnancy and Birth*. After some political chitchat, I confided to Carol some uncertainty about my forthcoming speech. She ventured a few ideas and opinions that I spontaneously incorporated into my address, which was received with a standing ovation.

This was an interesting bonding event for us, our first experience of sharing ideas. But an even stronger bond was our mutual passion for midwifery. We each had had nightmarish childbirth experiences in the early seventies; both of us were isolated, strapped down during delivery, and denied immediate access to our babies. And we had informed ourselves enough while pregnant to have wanted and expected more, making our disappointing experiences doubly painful. Had midwives been more widely available back then, we both would have gladly chosen to give birth at home.

As we met other women who had experienced abuse and degradation while giving birth, we became activists. I went on to have another child, born at home. Carol found herself being called to births by women unwilling to submit to hospital procedures, and got training from an old country doctor in rural New Hampshire. In a few years, when my children were a bit more independent, I too found an apprenticeship, with a traditional midwife in San Francisco. Back then, assisting home birth was an act of courage, as licensing was unavailable for non-nurse midwifery practice. Nevertheless, we had learned of "direct-entry" midwifery's importance in Europe and the rest of the world and were determined to make this option available for women in the United States.

Little did we know how formidable the resistance would be! When midwives moved into the political arena to fight for the right to be licensed, they were repeatedly foiled, often harassed, and occasionally arrested. This was especially true in California, where I led the struggle—though a liberal state in many ways, California also has the strongest branch of the American Medical Association. I soon learned that enacting midwifery legislation was not dependent on demonstrating the safety or cost-effectiveness of midwifery care, but was entirely a matter of power and politics. Carol had better luck in New Hampshire, where she spearheaded a successful midwifery certification campaign in 1982. But it took ten more years, and seven legislative attempts before our efforts in California finally paid off.

As trying as the political process was, it strengthened both of us dramatically. We were pushed out of our idealistic nests, and forced to fly in the face of the medical monopoly's old guard. We were also moved to develop and articulate the ideological under-pinnings of our faith in the struggle: we believed in birth as a rite of passage, with the midwife a skilled but humble assistant. The more we developed expertise in prenatal care, the more we under-stood our services to be secondary to women's care of themselves. The more we witnessed women taking their power in birthing, the more we saw self-determination as crucial to self-esteem and genuine acceptance of motherhood. The more we studied birth customs and practices in other parts of the world, the more we came to believe that desacralization of birth is at the root of numerous problems in our culture, to wit, the continual disem-powerment of women and the erosion of the family. We identified our task as nothing less than restoring the importance and dignity of birth to society at large.

It seemed the only way to do this was to curtail our busy mid-wifery practices and spend more time teaching and consulting. Then fate stepped in and changed the course of both our lives. Carol suffered the sudden death of her husband, an obstetrician with whom she had collaborated for many years. Her shock was so deep that her attempts to recover changed her life profoundly. She observed a year of silence, moving out of her house and into the woods on her property. She then went to Kripalu Institute to study healing, where she learned trance and breathing techniques. She began using these skills (and the lessons learned from her time in the woods) to work with chronically and terminally ill women. She also formulated and began to offer a workshop called "Women's Ordinary Magic," teaching women how to develop healing skills for themselves.

I revised my midwifery text and went on to write *Energetic Pregnancy,* a book about personal growth through childbearing. Having learned firsthand the central importance of empowering women to be their own authorities, I wrote yet another book, *Women's Intuition,* intended to help women acknowledge their body-based, instinctive ways of knowing. Soon I was presenting intuition workshops, along with making a steady stream of appearances on the childbirth lecture circuit.

Carol and I reconnected in 1989, when she came to San Francisco and guided me through my first trance breathing experience. That event is recounted later in the book; suffice it here to say that it changed my life. I began to meet monthly with a Sister Circle of dear friends, and was invited to participate in nightlong singing prayer ceremonies with some very powerful women. Carol came west again, this time to present "Women's Ordinary Magic" to a group I had organized. The shared experience was so dramatic that we decided to coteach this workshop at an upcoming midwifery conference. It was then that we first discussed the prospect of writing this book.

But we were continually drawn back into the political aspects of midwifery. Carol was the first midwife from the United States to visit and teach in Russia; her testimony on Russian birth atrocities was written up in the Congressional Record. I did research for the State of California on alternative birthing methods, consulted at the national level on midwifery legislation and education, and became president of the newly formed Midwifery Education Accreditation Council (MEAC).

Ultimately, however, we came to realize the limitations political activism put on our work. Not that we were disillusioned—our focus had simply changed. Over the years, we had expanded the context of our work to include the spiritual dimensions of women's transformation. We became curious about how women's rites of passage—not only childbirth, but also menarche and menopause—were celebrated in other times and other cultures. We studied the goddesses—archetypal female mythological figures—of bygone eras. And we were soon convinced that the best way to assure women their reproductive rights was to resacralize the entirety of women's lives, not just the act of giving birth.

We realized that honoring the Blood Mysteries of menarche, birth, and menopause was crucial to this process. We came to see these biological turning points as initiations for women, part of a psycho-spiritual life cycle. *The Circle of Life* emerged from our studies as a symbolic representation of the passages and transformations that occur in all women's lives. We started with the Blood Mysteries as cardinal points on the Circle, each representing a certain phase of life. As we looked at various configurations of women's archetypes, our thirteen stages emerged to fill out the Circle and this book was born.

As we outlined the manuscript, we knew that we would need input from a variety of women at different ages and stages of development. We agreed to do interviews and research together. We decided that I would write the text, with Carol contributing sections on the Blood Rites.

Our interview format was simple enough. Once women were introduced to the thirteen stages, they were free to locate themselves anywhere on the Circle, to tell a story about a particular stage, or to go through the stages for us one by one. We made it clear that the stages were not necessarily sequential, that women may move not only forward, but also backward and crosswise on the Circle. A key question emerged: "Was there a particular experience that brought you from your previous stage to the one you're in now?" This helped us establish lines of demarcation between stages, and identify more completely the unique qualities of each. We also asked women to speak of their experiences with the Blood Mysteries, to describe how they felt and how they were treated at menarche, during childbirth, and at menopause. Younger women were asked to envision Blood Rites in their future—how did they hope to give birth, or celebrate their menopause transition?

We did approximately one hundred interviews, with women from a variety of socioeconomic and ethnic backgrounds, aged eleven to ninety. Time and again, we were moved by the courage and candor of these women in describing their life experiences. Some of their disclosures were stunning and/or disturbing, and many thrilled or moved us to tears. We saw that we would have to include lengthy excerpts in the text in order to do the interviews justice. It is no exaggeration to say that a good many of the book's themes originated with our interviewees; they focused our research and inspired our vision. To every one, we offer our heartfelt appreciation.

No matter what the subject, books have a way of transforming their authors. We sought the broadest possible context in which to understand and empower women, and we feel our lives and work have been profoundly affected by this new paradigm. Step into *The Circle of Life* with us. We are honored and excited to share our revelations with you.

—Elizabeth Davis

CHAPTER 1

The Goddess and the Mystery

No woman today needs to be told that Reason has long been defined by men as the only legitimate way of acquiring knowledge—that in our culture, Reason is king. But this is not another book about how men define women, or about how women must free themselves from the clutches of destructive conditioning. This is a book about how women have been defining themselves for centuries, a book about women's intuitive ways of knowing linked to nature, the body, and the mystery of transformation.

Mystery is defined as that which is beyond understanding, that which baffles or perplexes, that which is profound and known only by revelation. When we speak of women's Blood Mysteries, we are referring to certain biological events, such as menarche and childbirth, that are accompanied by changed perspective and the influx of knowledge beyond Reason. We don't know why we change and grow and acquire knowledge at these times, but we do—this is the Mystery. And as we share this knowledge, the revelations linked to changes in our bodies, we reclaim the power and wisdom inherent in being women.

Menarche is a prime example of how mystery has accorded women power and respect. Before the advent of science, women's menstruation was virtually incomprehensible, particularly to men. How could women bleed thus, and not be injured? This must be magic of some kind: this ability of women to bleed and yet be well. Long before conception was understood to require fertilization, women were thought to generate life simply by withholding their menstrual blood in an autonomous process unique to females. Sex was not connected to conception. Instead, women were "stirred by spirit," then retained their blood, gestated, and brought forth new life. Thus menopause was viewed not as a loss, but as an increase of power—older women retained their wise blood permanently and so transcended the cycle of death and rebirth; they became like the source of creation.

But when Christianity recast women's bodies as evil, the source of Original Sin, the womb ceased to be a sacred temple and the Blood Mysteries were no longer acknowledged. And as science deconstructed human beings into a set of physiological functions, medical technology was developed with the express purpose of ministering to the body alone, healing it of disease caused, as often as not, from divorcing it from spirit. Now we have tools to "aid" the birth process, medications to "ease" menstruation or override the effects of menopause, surgery to extirpate women of their wombs. We seek to tame and dominate the forces of nature: we plant crops that deplete the soil, we raze our forests and pollute our waters. This would be unthinkable in a world that reveres the feminine and recognizes the interconnectedness of all living things.

This is not to deny that technology has its benefits—contraception has been a boon, and women's lives have been saved in complicated childbirth or pathological gynecological situations. But we have lost the Mystery. Reclaiming women's Blood Rites as spiritual turning points is the foundation of revealing new, empowering archetypes for women, and rediscovering those most ancient.

What, exactly, are archetypes? Jean Bolen, author of *Goddesses in Everywoman,* defines them as "powerful inner patterns . . . dominant forces within us"[1] strongly linked to myth. Joseph Campbell calls myth "depersonalized dream."[2] Jean Houston, author of *The Possible Human,* adds, "I have always thought of a myth as something that never was but is always happening."[3] Within myths are characters that express singular aspects of our existence and potential. These are archetypes, alive in human imagination since the beginning of time.

The purpose of familiarizing ourselves with archetypes is to better understand our behavior, our responses to certain situations in life, our deepest longings and desires. Archetypes are universal, yet gender-specific. *The Circle of Life* brings together female mythological figures and archetypes from numerous cultures, renaming and placing them in the context of contemporary life. It is noteworthy that the most ancient goddesses of India and Egypt are shown upright, of fierce or powerful countenance. Goddess figures of Greece and Rome are reduced to sitting, kneeling, or bending over. And in this century, goddess figures generally recline. The more the body has been circumscribed by Reason, the more women's mysteries have been feared and suppressed, and the more we have images of women that are austere, suffering, or degraded.

The most basic goddess figures actually embody all of the Blood Mysteries at once. The Indian goddess Kali was virgin, mother, and elder wise woman simultaneously, as were the Celtic Cerridwen, Sumerian Astarte, and Egyptian Maat. Each of these triple goddesses combined the sweet innocence of the Maiden, whose rite is menarche, the nurturing qualities of the Mother, whose rite is childbirth, and the wisdom of the Crone, whose rite is menopause.

In this book, however, we introduce a new phase in the women's life cycle, which falls between motherhood and old age. For just as women's ways of knowing have been culturally devalued, so too has the time been ignored when women hit their stride with this knowledge. Women in their late thirties and beyond have struggled in recent years with the confining imagery of the triple Goddess, trying to find a place for their mature abilities, growing independence, self-directed questing, and recollection of youthful aspirations. Some have yearned so much for the stature and authority of "elder" that they've taken the title of Crone before reaching menopause!

Enter—the Matriarch. Who is she, and where do we find her? She is us, when childbearing urges begin to wane, when careers are well established and a sense of mastery comes upon us. Not yet in menopause, still beset with worldly responsibilities but longing for something more, the Matriarch rekindles the passions and dreams of youth, and may pick up broken threads of spiritual pursuits with new intensity and direction. She is the Clan Leader, overseer of her personal domain. Contrary to cultural stereotypes that cast the Matriarch as harsh, stern, and aged, she is in fact an elegant woman no longer young but in full possession of her sexual power, magnetically attractive. She is aesthetic, bringing beauty and harmony to her environment. She weaves her sensuality, her ability to work hard and well, and her deeply passionate love of self and others into one gorgeous tapestry. Having learned much about life's rhythms of ebb and flow, she develops an increasingly powerful sense of timing, which compensates for the inevitable loss of youthful energy. She utilizes power with grace, and reveals the unseen aspects of growth and change.

This new face of the Goddess came to Carol in her process of painting a mural in the early spring of 1992. She wanted to represent the four seasons with four interacting, dancing goddesses. The trinity of Maiden, Mother, and Crone was easy: to represent spring, the joyous Maiden tripped lithely through the first flowers; in summer, the beautiful, fecund Mother carried a basket of blooms; in winter, the silver-haired, windswept Crone held a sprig of holly. But what for fall—the autumn of a woman's life? Painting her way through uncertainty, Carol created an image of a queenly woman, draped in rich robes of deep red and gold, holding a basket of harvest goods. When she introduced the Matriarch in a workshop several months later, all the women in their middle years unanimously said, "Yes!" and breathed a collective sigh of relief.

It is no accident that the title *Matriarch* comes from the word matriarchy, for in this stage women manifest their queenly essence and natural leadership abilities. Why, then, is the Matriarch historically absent from the Goddess trinity? In terms of our life cycle, a longer lifespan and the later onset of menopause (the average age is now fifty-three) have combined to open wide the window between childbearing and old age. And too, women today are finding opportunities, unprecedented since ancient times, to exert influence and effect social change. All of this seems synchronous with the resurgence of women's spirituality, which demands powerful avenues of expression befitting the Matriarch.

Or perhaps the Matriarch has always been with us, her face merely hidden from view. Throughout history, in diverse cultures, the Dark Mother, black madonna, or destroyer aspect of the Goddess has been recognized as the keeper of the gate between life and death. This aspect is naturally linked to the dark or new moon, and should logically be the stage of the Crone, the wise elder woman past menopause. But in the usual configuration of the Goddess trinity, the Maiden is represented by the waxing moon, the Mother by the full moon, and the Crone by the waning moon, with the dark phase omitted altogether. Was the Crone at some point moved from dark to waning moon, that women's knowledge of the fourfold mystery might be concealed? And was this a deliberate decision of a matriarchy under fire, or a corruption perpetuated by a growing patriarchy? Whatever the answer, if we acknowledge a fourth phase of the dark mystery for the Crone, we open the time of the waning moon to the Matriarch.

Particularly in the West, darkness has been equated with evil, wickedness, uncleanliness, and wrongdoing. But in many parts of the world, especially among non-Christian, nonwhite peoples, darkness is simply the complement of light; one is seen and the other unseen. If there is any definition of evil at all, it occurs with the imbalance of the two aspects. Consider the yin-yang symbol of numerous Asian cultures, a circle half black, half white, with a little dot of the opposite color on each side and both halves swirling together inseparably. The dark is the great void from whence life springs, the underpinnings of existence, the energy between substance, eternity, home.

And although the concept of triple Goddess, or trinity, has been with us from the earliest ages, there are numerous spiritual traditions that recognize a fourfold divinity. Native American traditions honor the Four Directions—East, South, West, and North—and call upon the ancients, the Grandmothers and Grandfathers of each sacred direction, for guidance and support. In our hemisphere, these directions (as listed above) correspond to the seasons of spring, summer, fall, and winter (in the Southern Hemisphere, summer is in the North and winter in the South).

The Earth-based religion of paganism (from the Latin word, *pagani,* meaning country dweller) features celebrations at both equinox and solstice, as well as at the cross quarter days found midway through each season. These eight cardinal points in the pagan wheel of the year are linked to ancient agrarian and pastoral festivals that signaled people to plant, harvest, form sexual unions, initiate the young, and honor the dead.

Other systems also feature four aspects. Astrology works with four elements—air, fire, water, and earth—as signifiers of personality and mission in life. The tarot works likewise with four major arcana—the swords, wands, cups, and pentacles—which link directly to the astrological elements cited above.

On the wheel of the year, the four seasonal, cardinal points form a cross, a symbol seemingly at odds with the Goddess trinity. Yet in tracing the derivation of the cross, we learn that it was not shown in Christian art until 600 C.E. and was, in fact, a pagan symbol long before the birth of Christ.[4] The cross is generally thought to represent male genitalia. In Egypt, however, the male cross was combined with the female orb to compose the amulet of sexual harmony. And the Celtic cross also features a ring encircling the arms, expressing the union of opposites.

The circle signifying the female brings to mind the symbol of *vesica pisces,* a pointed oval shape found in the ancient Sheila-na-gig figure carved repeatedly in the stonework of old Irish churches. This squatting, naked goddess displays her vulva, sometimes drawing it open with her fingers in a diamond shape. Similar are the temple door statues of Kali in India, where visitors lick a finger and touch the vaginal opening, or yoni, for luck. (The oldest figures have holes worn deep in the yoni from so much touching.) Surely, the four-sided diamond is a more anthropomorphically correct representation of the vaginal entrance than the triangle, which appears to be based on the *mons veneris* (pubic mound)—that which is readily seen, versus the unseen yoni, hidden, dark, and mysterious.

With the Matriarch added to the trinity, the four faces of the Goddess find correspondence to the four seasons. The Maiden's time is spring: she is budding in her body and in her sexuality. Her moon is waxing, equally dark and light, as she balances her purity with eagerness to share herself with another. This is the time of first blood, of flowering into womanhood.

The Mother's time is summer. Her moon is full: a metaphor for the fertile egg, the fullness of her body in pregnancy, her full breasts and open arms as she welcomes new life. Her rite of passage is childbirth, an initiation that gives her a glimpse of the opposite side of the life cycle—the time of wisdom and transformation represented by the dark moon.

The Matriarch is the queen of autumn, reaping the rewards of hard work and sustained effort. At her peak, her moon is equally light and dark as she balances her power in the outer world with a growing fascination with what is beyond. She remembers the ancient rite of blood bonding, finding her greatest strength in an intimate circle of sisters, the matriarchy.

The Crone's essence is reflected in winter, a time of deep introspection, of contemplating what lies dormant. Linked to the Winter Solstice, a time of endings and new beginnings, the Crone makes peace with her life and comes to terms with death. She has passed through menopause and is revered for the wisdom she has accumulated from many years of watching the wheel turn.

These, and other archetypes on the Circle of Life, are intended to rekindle memories of a time when feminine energy was revered as the source of community well-being. When survival depended on being in harmony with the seasons that food might be grown and harvested in a timely fashion, when cycles of birth, death, and rebirth in nature were the basis for human affairs, women had their own authority and exalted place in society simply by virtue of being themselves. They established the first calendar, marking time via the menstrual cycle. Preliterate women cut notches on sticks to establish lunar months; the ancient Mayans and Chinese women developed lunar calendars over three thousand years ago.

The lunar calendar has thirteen months, in contrast to the twelve-month Julian calendar we use today. It has been suggested that the Christian church promoted the use of the Julian calendar to eradicate the Goddess-oriented, earth-based religious beliefs of paganism. To this day, the number thirteen is considered unlucky; no high-rise office building or hotel admits to a thirteenth floor. But in our system, we hold to the sacred thirteen by identifying the same number of stages in women's life cycle.

How do the thirteen stages fit with the four prime faces and phases of the Goddess? We soon identified three stages within each phase, periods of initiation, integration, and transformation. For example, the Matriarch is accompanied on either side by Amazon and Priestess. Women enter the powerful autumn of their lives by declaring their independence as Amazons; they integrate and utilize their newfound power as Matriarchs; they go on to transform themselves as Priestesses to prepare for the next phase of winter and wisdom.

Rather than placing these stages in a linear, rungs-of-a-ladder sequence, we believe they belong in a circular pattern, with death ushering in new birth as in the natural world. And although we saw the stages as flowing somewhat consecutively, we also realized that we had revisited certain stages in our lives numerous times (the Lover, for example) or had leaped ahead intuitively to more mature stages in times of inspiration or pressing need. Our Circle of Life required a means to facilitate movement among the stages. This means became the thirteenth stage.

The thirteenth stage, we felt, belonged in the center. But we went further, drawing this central aspect out among the other twelve like glue or connective tissue. Now we had a web pattern that supported movement not only sequentially around the Circle, but crosswise, or back and forth. There could be no better name for this thirteenth stage than that of Transformer, medium of change. The Transformer archetype adds the dimension of space to the Circle; we experience her as "stillness behind motion, when time itself stops, the center which is also the circumference of all."[5]

Once the Circle was in place, we noticed striking complementary patterns between stages positioned directly opposite each other. For example, the Amazon and Daughter are clearly connected, in that the Amazon draws heavily on her girlhood freedom to recreate herself as an independent adult. The Midwife and the Dark Mother are both gatekeepers, one of life, the other of death. As we discovered that these complementary relationships existed in every case, we realized that we could better describe the stages by pairing them together. The opposites were integral to one another, and formed a sum greater than its parts. Simply going around the Circle and describing stages in order seemed too linear an approach, and one that would not reflect the average woman's experience.

The round shape of the Circle expresses the unique way that women learn and grow. Constructing knowledge "bricklayer" style from distinct bits of information is a typically male approach, whereas women tend to encircle an area of inquiry, considering it from many angles and viewpoints before moving to the center or heart of the matter. This is woman's way of knowing, drawn from the nature of our existence: our monthly cycles, our ability to gestate young, our bodily experiences of growth, healing, transformation. We see patterns in our own lives, and likewise seek patterns in our interactions of work, love, and relationships. We know the magic moment when things "gel," when the answer is suddenly distilled, when the mist lifts and turbulent waters grow calm and clear. We believe in what Zen philosophy terms the "sudden school"—realizations so sweeping and unexpected as to appear irrational, but to us, gifts of the Mystery.

Our interviewees corroborated this fluid and nonlinear approach to life in the way they articulated their experiences on the Circle. Many commented that certain stages intrigued or repelled them, drew them back repeatedly or mystified them utterly. We consider the Circle to be a blueprint of women's potential, not a series of directives. It is not necessary to experience every stage on the Circle to find fulfillment in life. Nor should the archetypes be taken too literally—passing through the stage of the Mother does not, for example, require one to actually birth a child, but may well involve the conception and delivery of a project or other mode of expression at the heart of one's identity. Neither are these stages rigidly age linked, least of all, the Crone. Women may spend years after the actual cessation of menses exploring roles of Priestess and Sorceress before feeling ready to accept the charge of Cronehood.

Although we venture our opinions regarding the challenges and joys of each of these stages, we know that only you, the reader, can bring this book to life. You hold your own keys to the Mystery! We encourage you to use *The Circle of Life* to look deeply into your own experiences and validate them, to find your own truth and share it with others. Trust yourself to assimilate intuitively whatever you need to know. Take what works for you, and don't worry about the rest.

CHAPTER 2

The Thirteen Stages
of Women's Lives

Every stage of the life cycle has its joys, lessons, and opportunities. In this chapter, we present each stage briefly in chronological order to give you an idea of the characteristics of each archetype. In later chapters we will provide examples of women revisiting certain stages or forging ahead to explore those most suited to their needs, as we discuss the archetypes in complementary pairs.

The Daughter

The first stage is that of the Daughter. This archetype expresses the purity of a young girl's soul from infancy to pubescence, as yet unfettered by adolescent hormones or social pressure to mate. In this first stage of life, the Daughter has a one-on-one relationship to her essence; she has not yet abstracted herself to meet others' expectations. As such, she is a joy and inspiration to women of all generations, who do well to guard her integrity of being while beginning to educate and prepare her for life.

Her moon is ascending, the light crescent. Her time is the month of February, when days begin to grow longer. She likewise grows visibly stronger day by day, regenerating cells, surging with possibilities, reveling in the joy of life.

It has been said somewhere in modern psychology that we have only to look at what we loved most to do at the age of seven or eight to know our life's work or mission. Think back on your favorite activities of girlhood—what gave you the greatest enjoyment? Were these solitary pursuits or group pastimes, and how did you feel while involved? Those of us fortunate enough to have grown up unburdened by premature responsibility or tragedy will find that reviewing these years reveals the ever young and determined Daughter still living inside us. Take the example of a woman in her thirties who suddenly remembers her talent for costuming neighborhood kids at every backyard play or performance and decides to pursue professional theatre, or that of the post-menopausal woman who impulsively buys a red convertible—reminiscent of her first flashy roller skates or bicycle—just for the freedom-loving fun of it.

The Daughter's quest for individuation corresponds to the pagan holiday of Imbolc, otherwise known as Candlemas or Saint Brigit's Day. *Imbolc* is a Celtic word referring to Earth's belly or womb, where the new year quickens. This celebration of resurging life, of seeds and bulbs stirring in the ground, has modern correspondence with our Groundhog Day, when omens for the coming growing season are said to occur. February 1 was originally a festival of pagan Rome, honoring Juno as virgin mother of Mars. In the Celtic empire, the triple Goddess figure of Brigit was likewise revered for her virginal purity and power. Finding her impossible to eradicate, Christianity canonized her as a saint; Saint Brigit's Day ironically became known as the Feast of Purification of the Virgin, or Candlemas.

Imbolc was traditionally a time of initiation, when daughters were brought to the wise ones of their communities for ritual acknowledgment and consecration to the Goddess. Quite unlike contemporary notions of religious training, this initiation was done in a spirit of playfulness, honoring the precious enthusiasm of youth.

The Maiden

The next stage is that of the Maiden, the pubescent or adolescent girl who experiences menarche, the first Blood Mystery. Her moon is first quarter, equally light and dark, mirroring the balance of day and night at the vernal equinox, her holiday. (Note the connection between the old Northern European term for menstruation, *oestris,* and that for equinox, *oestre*.)

The Maiden expresses the kindling of life in her budding body and budding sexuality. And yet, like her complementary opposite, the Matriarch, she is in charge of herself, beholden to none other. She may explore her sensual self and have first sexual encounters, but she remains the "virginal lover," her integrity impenetrable.

Although the moon of the Maiden indicates balance, this may also be a time of great conflict, with struggles between growing urges for independence and anxieties over the impending responsibilities of adulthood. If her menarche is honored and celebrated, the Maiden is better able to integrate the desire to hold to girlhood simplicity with a longing for more adult explorations.

We enact the Maiden whenever we bring virginal innocence to a new enterprise. As we embark on an adventure, set out to travel on our own, or take some risk in our professional lives, we may invoke our Maiden aspect to help us blend vitality with purity of intent.

The manner in which the menarche transition is experienced has much to do with the degree of confidence and independence a woman finds in subsequent stages of adult life. (The next major opportunity for transformation and rebirth occurs in the stage of the Mother, with the Blood Mystery of childbirth.) If menarche is celebrated in a way that establishes a Maiden's place in her community and strengthens her relationships with her peers, she will readily find support for her growing autonomy in the forthcoming Blood Sister stage.

The Blood Sister

The archetype of Blood Sister is explored in our culture furtively, at best. The Blood Sister is in her late teens or early twenties, may or may not be sexually active, and seeks other sisters to entrust with the sharing of life experience. Her stage is that of female bonding. It is filled with crucial opportunities to overcome culturally conditioned competitiveness and jealousy.

The Blood Sister's moon is more light than dark, signifying her increasing extroversion and emergence into society. She experiments boldly with unique modes of self-expression in dress and body adornment. Open heart and open mind combine with wildness and a sense of invincibility to generate powerful connections with her peers. These close ties help clarify her purpose in life, and motivate her continued explorations.

It is distressing how our society frowns on the mutual expression of affection among women, when in Europe women freely hold hands or walk arm in arm in public. Even with the recent media trend of "lesbian chic," homophobia persists, causing us to censor these natural and spontaneous bonding behaviors. This is a shame, as shared affection not only helps young women buffer the trials and tribulations of dealing with the opposite sex, but can ease their own struggles of maturation.

The culturally acceptable alternative to expressing physical affection is intellectual camaraderie or, as often appeals to Blood Sisters, exploration of radical thought. Thus feminist demonstrations and campus marches, apart from their political function, are potent Blood Sister bonding rituals. Dedication to mutual empowerment now leads many women in their early twenties to circle with others on a regular basis, exploring diverse aspects of their womanhood.

However bonding may occur, the stronger and deeper it is, the more Blood Sisters are able to give selflessly to one another. Later in life, when we come to the aid of a troubled friend, a woman who has suffered the pain of loss or is seriously ill, we are playing the role of Blood Sister. Or when we ourselves feel depleted by sadness or despair, have little left to give and yet find it hard to accept support, Blood Sisters are the ones who come to our rescue, who take us for what we are and help us hold on to what we have.

The Lover

The stage of the Lover is associated with the celebration of Beltane on May 1, a pagan holy day notorious for wanton sexual behavior. However, Beltane was originally observed with the practice of sacred fertility rites. The Maypole is the classic phallic symbol, with entwining ribbons signifying the glorious way the female encircles the male.

This celebration occurs when days get noticeably longer and brighter, when "spring fever" reaches a peak. The "Bel" of Beltane is a northern version of Baal, the Canaanite word that means lord. Tane comes from a Celtic word, *tienne,* meaning fire. Traditionally, this festival is initiated with a bonfire, and all-night merrymaking and mating follow.[1]

In women's life cycle, this is the time we search for a mate, when hormonal urges (not necessarily rational considerations) cause us to desire conception. The challenge for the Lover is to figure out how to hold her power and place in the male/female dance, a task made doubly difficult in a culture that offers women only grudging autonomy in marriage and childbearing. Women partnered with women must face prejudice and discrimination at least as formidable as those struggling to work it out with men, particularly if they desire children.

However, the Lover is the least age-linked of all the archetypes—take the example of a woman in an elder-care facility that finds herself falling passionately in love as if for the first time. On the other hand, some women are Lovers to their work and will do anything for the pleasure of that connection, even if it means sneaking away to make phone calls and do business while on vacation. "When sweet desire weds wild delight," we do the timeless dance whereby all of life is renewed.[2] Love kindles our essence of being; we can't control its prompting or its course. The challenge is to surrender fully yet hold onto our uniqueness.

In Greek tradition, the sacred marriage of *hieros-gamos* unites man-as-god with woman-as-goddess. This mythic dimension of love holds deep fascination for Lovers of any age; all try to find some context for the stunning miracle of true affinity. The signifying goddess for women in this stage is Aphrodite, whose moving force is pleasure in union.

Love may lead to impregnation and gestation. But whenever we conceptualize a creative project and give ourselves passionately to its development, we enact the Lover archetype. Impassioned lovers wrestle as one to procreate; impassioned artists and creative women wrestle likewise with their muse, or other source of inspiration.

This stage correlates to late morning when sunlight permeates all, stimulating growth and enhancing the beauty of nature. In the Lover's lunar phase, the moon is nearly full. Thus Lovers are perpetually hopeful and filled with the promise of wonderful experiences yet to come, magic just over the horizon.

The Mother

The stage of the Mother is life at its zenith. This is the time when women meet the Great Creatrix, and merge with the divine matrix of life through the second Blood Mystery of childbirth. No matter how birth transpires—whether naturally and spontaneously or with numerous interventions—the experience reaches deep to the roots of a woman's identity, transforming her utterly. The prime lesson of this Blood Mystery regards surrender and control; it is the paradoxical discovery that only by letting go do we gain mastery. For women who cannot (or choose not to) have children, or for those at other points in the life cycle, this discovery may occur with the first fully passionate commitment to a creative work, particularly if the only way to complete it runs through uncharted territory. Birth gives us an opportunity to stand at the gateway or portal between worlds, and learn beyond forgetting the ultimate source of our power and creativity.

The round, full moon of this stage mirrors the fertile egg, the fullness of the pregnant belly, the rounded vaginal opening at the moment of birth, the ripeness of a project come to fruition. The time of year associated with this stage, high summer, brings the grace of long days and all-pervading warmth to comfort and inspire us in this challenging, demanding period.

Summer Solstice brings the victory of light, but also marks the point when darkness returns and introspection begins to increase. We watch our children grow or our artistic efforts begin to bear fruit, and slowly, imperceptibly we turn inward to more deeply understand our own creativity. Opposite the Mother we find her complement, the Crone, who at the nadir of the moon and the year nurtures society by virtue of self-containment, drawing all to her wise self. This contrasts sharply with the Mother's outward focus on family members or creative projects.

Mothering is presence. It is modeling behavior or ideals worth emulating because someone important is watching, and you want to be at your best. Sometimes we wring our hands and know we can do nothing, nothing to force maturation or completion. Starhawk describes the basis of motherhood as "a love so complete that all dissolves into a single song of ecstasy that moves the worlds."[3] In the highest sense, Mothers nurture by holding and tending, with total faith and remarkable forbearance, all that is germinal in themselves and their loved ones.

The Midwife

The stage of the Midwife may be otherwise known as that of the teacher and facilitator, she who has known firsthand the transformation of birth (be it the birth of a baby or her own creative self) and is now ready to help others through the same process. We all remember some wonderful teacher who helped us discover our most heartfelt ideas or greatest talents, then encouraged us to take wing and fly. This is the role of the Midwife.

Characteristic of the Midwife is the ability to trust, to take the leap of faith, to suspend rational and logistical thought for a walk on the wild side, relying on intuition or other nonlinear ways of knowing. Thus Midwives make manifest what is unseen or unexpected, and so may appear to those unfamiliar with their ways as miraculous in their abilities. It is noteworthy that during the Inquisition and the subsequent period of history known as the "burning times," the prime targets for torture and death were midwives. Healing by way of nature, possessed of intuitive insight, and aligned with the wisdom of the body, the Midwife posed (and continues to pose—see chapter 10) a formidable threat to the patriarchy.

Out of respect for women's ways of knowing, the Midwife is often expert in womancraft, herbology, massage, or other healing arts. Yet Midwives are also found in the most entrenched corporate and/or political situations. It is the enabling manner in which the Midwife works with others that distinguishes her.

In the business world, Midwives may be agents or publicists who decide, on a hunch, to back the work of a struggling artist or other newcomer. Nurses who use intuitive healing techniques unauthorized or unrecognized by their superiors are likewise playing the role of Midwife. Any professional woman who ferrets out and supports the most life-affirming, elemental needs of her clients is a Midwife.

The Midwife extends what she has learned of mothering—lessons of love, responsibility, faith, and transformation—to those beyond her biological circle. How might you enact the Midwife archetype? When you feel like you'd go to the ends of the earth to support growth in a protégé, even though it means putting yourself on the line, you are Midwife. When you prod a client to go deeper to get at the truth of a troubling situation, you are Midwife. When you take responsibility for the safety and well-being of a friend in a major life transition, you are Midwife. When you call upon the greatest powers you know to guide you in crisis counseling, you are Midwife.

The Midwife's time is early afternoon. As the day wanes, women may perceive their mortality for the first time. This may trigger confusion, disorientation, feelings of loss and fear of the unknown, even as the phase of nurturing gives way to that of power. The Midwife's face-to-face encounter with the forces of creation unite her irrevocably with the Dark Mother, her polar opposite and complement who is mistress of the death rites. Seeing the Implacable One in her work is both the Midwife's burden and her blessing; it prepares her to assume power in a comprehensive, compassionate way.

The Amazon

The next stage is that of the Amazon, initiator of the Matriarch phase. The Amazon feels the pressures of mothering, teaching, and nurturing begin to lift, and suddenly finds more time for herself than she has had in years. Her children and/or career are off to a good start, and she is free to be more self-directed, to pursue new modes of self-discovery (or recovery, as the case may be).

The Amazon finds strength in her own right by reanimating her original nature and integrity of purpose. She rekindles the intensity of her complementary archetype, the Daughter, and returns to an independent sense of herself, pre-Lover and pre-Mother. Feeling the freedom and wildness of earlier stages, she may reexplore mind-altering, consciousness-expanding techniques (with ecstatic birthing or creative experiences as her foundation). A spectrum of life experience allows her to place these explorations in a broad sociopolitical context, and make real use of her revelations.

A genuine biological shift from the hormones of reproduction to testosterone-related androgens may bring an Amazon woman's "outlaw" aspect to the fore. As she grows increasingly self-confident, and decreasingly concerned for what others may think, she becomes openly confrontational. Bringing her hard knocks as mother and nurturer to bear in the workplace, she resents patriarchal constraints and rebels against inadequate child care, inequitable wages, the "glass ceiling." Unfettered by "good girl" restraint, she initiates change with a powerful, albeit explosive, blend of traditionally male and female characteristics. Learning to integrate and assert these parts of herself effectively is key to her forthcoming mastery as Matriarch.

Women enact the archetype of Amazon at other points in the life cycle, as well. A young woman on her own for the first time, keeping her own apartment and feeling so proud of herself, is tapping into her Amazon aspect. Or an older woman freed from an unhappy marriage may reexplore her Amazon side with wild exploration of relationships outside socially acceptable limits. Regardless of age, any woman who chooses to be independent for the sheer pleasure and satisfaction of being able to follow her own rhythms, instincts, and creative impulses embodies the Amazon archetype.

The seasonal celebration of this stage is Lammas, an ancient summer festival falling on August eve and honoring the Goddess of the Grain (Ceres, Ops, Demeter). The Amazon reaps the first fruits of self-development, whereas, in the forthcoming stage, the Matriarch realizes the full harvest of maturation. The Amazon's moon is yet more light than dark; she is still extroverted in focus, though her dark, introspective power is growing.

The Matriarch

The Matriarch is the director of her family, head of her clan, who assumes leadership by virtue of her maturity. Her stage is initiated by the autumnal equinox. In Celtic pagan culture, this holy day was called Mabon, in honor of the wise and highly independent fairy queen, Mab. Mab's legends date from prepatriarchal times, when queens chose and invested their own kings.

The Matriarch reflects this autonomy and authority; she is utterly secure both in herself and in her social position. Having found appropriate outlets for the intense passions (and excesses) of her Amazon period, she is remarkably calm and collected. She discriminates between the thoughts and emotions she wants to express and those she had best keep secret, in order to guard her privacy and know herself more deeply.

As with her polar complement, the Maiden, the Matriarch's third-quarter moon is equally light and dark. She has finally overcome her awkwardness at juggling inner realities with outer expectations. Nevertheless, in this time of seeming equilibrium she may experience new challenges and conflicts, for the Matriarch reaps what she has sown, for good or ill. As her waning moon darkens, she likewise looks inward for her errors and omissions, with increasing need for resolution. This draws her to the forthcoming stage of Priestess, when she will shift her worldly focus to more spiritual concerns.

The Matriarch experiences the Blood Mystery of blood bonding, exploring menstrual power and synchrony with her female cohorts. As she discovers and begins to share the visionary power of her moon time, she discerns the support she will need as Priestess to go more deeply into the Mystery. The sisterhood of blood bonding is central to the Matriarch's evolution; it is her source of emotional strength, ever more critical as her physical strength is waning. (For more on blood bonding, see chapter 3.)

We are Matriarchs when we bring forth the mature expression of our worldly wisdom, when we win awards for our accomplishments, when we see in the world around us the results of our labors, and when we still have the energy to keep all running smoothly. A young woman, mature beyond her years and busily directing community service projects with aplomb, is expressing her Matriarch aspect. Or a woman in later life, retired yet deeply drawn to some enterprise that evokes her most cherished beliefs and natural leadership abilities, may replay the Matriarch role.

The Matriarch in you seeks to have maximum impact so that ripples from your work can spread the farthest. The reins are in your hands, but you hold them sensitively and responsibly. No matter your age, if you assume leadership in an empowering, noncompetitive way, you are acting as Matriarch.

The Priestess

Chronologically, women in the Priestess stage are premenopausal— they begin to experience some degree of hormonal instability with concomitant surges of heightened emotion and insight. As her moon grows dark, the Priestess surrenders material concerns to spiritual explorations. Lingering warmth in her month of October, combined with days not yet short, make this time conducive to reflection and soul searching. The Priestess is a joyous student of the Mystery: she is in service, a handmaiden.

Ultimately, the Priestess finds she must shed her skin in order to truly wield power—a process that can be disorienting, and not a little painful if subject to outside scrutiny and criticism. Thus she desperately needs support from other women, just as she did in the earlier, complementary stage of Blood Sister, and will hopefully find a circle of sisters to help her take the leap of faith into the Dark Time. With two steps forward and one step back, as in the gradual process of birth, Priestesses can help each other cross from the phase of power to that of wisdom by culling transpersonal aspects of their experience.

This period coincides with the end of fertility and, as hormones shift, less biologically motivated child rearing. Particularly if childbearing was delayed and she has still young children, the Priestess may feel conflict between urges for spiritual exploration and the still-pressing duties of motherhood. This dilemma is frequently compounded by socially induced guilt for placing her personal interests on a par with family obligations. It is no wonder she needs support from women willing and able to understand her concerns.

The Priestess fuses the solidarity of sisterhood with loving discrimination. She not only seeks to confirm her peers, but to help them transcend outmoded patterns of behavior. In other words, she gives the same frank feedback she would like to receive. Whenever we counsel a friend determined to know the truth about her shortcomings so as to better understand her situation, we may invoke the Priestess, particularly in a group context with each participant candidly sharing her own piece of life's puzzle. (There may also be ceremonial or ritualistic aspects to problem solving in this stage; women enacting the Priestess may utilize sacred objects or symbolism to help focus their inquiries.)

You are Priestess when you ask for group input on a personal dilemma, when you pull a group together to aid someone in distress, when you rely on women's wisdom to inform your activities or guide you through troubled waters. Sometimes younger women leap spontaneously to the wisdom of Priestess, counseling another with wisdom at their core of being. As Priestess, we serve what we seek, we are humble, we long to be purified and revealed for what we are.

The Sorceress

The Sorceress is the "madwoman" linked chronologically to the menopause transition; she is highly introspective yet surging with energy. Whereas the Priestess yields to the Mystery, the Sorceress takes command as medicine woman or shaman.

It's not easy to find many Sorceresses in our modern-day culture. This is because the Sorceress's power is tremendously strong; it is the mysterious force of transmutation otherwise known as alchemy. In the complementary stage of the Lover, the physical union of male and female foreshadows the Sorceress's ability to merge the male and female within herself and release alchemical forces. Way more than some intellectual exercise, this is fusion enabled by love, a love so great, wise, and universal that it is virtually unstoppable. Not the personal, conjugal love of early years, but love wedded to spirit and the realities of earthly life: love beyond hope or illusion. The Sorceress learns that the alchemy of *hierosgamos* is ultimately the alchemy of life, death, and eternity.

The holy day associated with the Sorceress stage is Samhain, the first of November, just preceding All Soul's Day and the Day of the Dead on November 2, when the veil between worlds is said to be thinnest. The Sorceress explores the sacred gateway between this dimension and others, she steps out of time and becomes the seed of her own rebirth. Her moon holds the last bit of light as dark crescent, and her time is evening.

One of the Sorceress's best-known goddess representatives is Medusa, considered evil and fearsome for her power to turn men to stone. Yet Medusa's head teems with the serpents of wisdom; she is revered in ancient traditions as "mother of all gods, whom she bore before childbirth existed."[4] She represents the Sorceress's ability to tap the forces of creation in her communications and actions. Far from being wild or out of control, she is highly directed and serious about her work. Her pathway narrows, her choices become clear. When we see with the eyes of the Sorceress we are in sync with the Mystery; we know exactly what to do in any given situation.

Anyone coping with life-threatening illness, hardship, or disability who nonetheless manages to transmute feelings of fear and anxiety into unconditional love enacts the Sorceress. Sometimes the Sorceress is triggered in women at an early age by a serious accident or other calamity. We access the Sorceress when we face our deepest fears, or find ourselves in situations where survival depends on being all of one piece, firmly united within ourselves. Whenever we feel a sense of being drawn and dedicated to a certain course of life, that our steps are clear before us, that we're exhilarated yet grounded and will go the distance, whatever it takes, we embody the Sorceress.

The Crone

The Crone's stage is that of the dark moon, a time of latency and retreat. Her direction is north; her totem in Native American tradition is either the bear, signifying hibernation, or the eagle, signifying wisdom derived from the overview. The Crone comes to terms with endings; she is at peace with herself and yet has work to do. Like her polar complement, the Mother, she is a caretaker, but of society. She nurtures with the wisdom stored in every cell of her body. Her Blood Mystery is menopause completed.

Her seasonal celebration is Winter Solstice, when days are shortest and darkness reaches its peak. She sees clearly the power of the Dark, and weaves the cord that will sustain her through the death transition. She stirs the Sacred Cauldron where gestate the seeds of rebirth for the next round of life.

The goddess Hecate is the classic Crone figure: wise, prophetic, active, protective. Her name is derived from *heq,* tribal matriarch of predynastic Egypt who commanded the *hekau,* or "Mother's Words of Power."[5] Hecate's symbol is the frog—dormant below mud in winter, it also symbolizes the fetus. In addition to being wise, Hecate is known as the trickster, with a remarkable sense of humor and irony. She is traditionally worshiped with gifts or offerings set out at a crossroads, in acknowledgement of the wry and humbling twists of fate that can reset one's course abruptly or provide answers to seemingly insurmountable problems. The trickster aspect of the Crone is linked to another December festival, that of Saturnalia, which antedates the Roman Empire. In this weeklong celebration, societal constraints were suspended, courts adjourned, and schools closed. Overseen by the Lord and Lady of Misrule, this was a time for pranks, practical jokes, and carnival.

We act the Crone when we storytell to make a point, when we put some humorous twist on a troubling situation, when the big picture is our foundation in problem solving. If you have ever chosen to stand back and let someone fall into his/her own trap or get caught up in his/her own words, you've got a little Crone in you. At any age, when we feel at work on the loom of existence, when we sense the warp and the woof of life and align our activities accordingly, we know the wisdom of the Crone. Crones counsel by example, they model behavior for society, as Mothers do for their young.

The Dark Mother

The Dark Mother's stage is that of impending and actual death. She is the Queen of Shadows at the end of desire, at the end of life's pursuit. In transiting to Dark Mother, the Crone becomes reaper, the Implacable One who feeds on old life that new life may grow. Like her polar complement, the Midwife, the Dark Mother stands at the portal between life and death, but with different responsibilities. Whereas the Midwife facilitates this transition for others, the Dark Mother must take her own private journey into the unknown. Her way is filled with the sorrow of leave-taking, but if she meets death consciously and deliberately, she finds release and transformation.

The Dark Mother is scorned in this culture, due to our over-riding fear of death. Yet elsewhere she is recognized and honored. In India she is Kali the Destroyer, who puts an end to that which has outlived its usefulness. She is fierce, passionate, and devouring. The mythic god Vishnu respectfully called her "both mother and grave."[6]

In the time of the Dark Mother, we surrender to the turning of the unbroken circle, moving from darkness toward the light. The Dark Mother's moon is the slimmest early crescent, symbolizing rebirth. Her month of January is the time of year when days begin to grow longer and light returns, though imperceptibly at first.

The Dark Mother's scythe (as reaper) is a symbol of her uncompromising truthfulness and frank disregard for the opinions of others. She is the woman of the fell gaze who clarifies herself and those around her, down to the bone. She expresses what is really essential in life, a distillation of meaning and purpose elusive to women in their younger years. But she does not speak of this truth, or teach it; it is simply what she has become. As she feels the dissolution of her body, she has nothing left to lose and her spirit is freed.

We explore the Dark Mother whenever we take a great leap into the unknown, particularly when the leap is unavoidable, beyond our control. Like birth, death comes when it will, we can do nothing to stop it. The Dark Mother must deliver herself, ready or not. When we experience the sudden loss of a loved one, when a major relationship ends abruptly, when the normalcy of day-to-day life is shifted completely by accident or terminal illness, whenever we must somehow rise to the occasion of ensuing transformation, we come face to face with the Dark Mother.

The Dark Mother also comes into play when we are forced to relinquish outmoded beliefs, surrender the caretaking of our young so they can become independent, or take a business-related risk in order to survive. Faith in our ability to recreate ourselves, or be recreated by life, is key to accessing the wisdom of the Dark Mother.

The Transformer

Holding the center of the Circle and flowing out between each stage, the Transformer is the Source, she whose name cannot be spoken. The Transformer is the great Cosmic Womb, the means of regeneration through birth, death, and rebirth. In the Circle of Life, she is fiery molten core, superstructure of existence, and medium of evolution all in one—the Sacred Cauldron, the pot of blood in Kali's hand.

The Transformer is actually on a different plane than the other archetypes. She is the Void, still and boundless, where all is possible, all is potential. Through her, time is suspended as the Dark Mother transforms to infant Daughter and passes through the portal of life, the cervical os of the Cosmic Womb. Meanwhile, somewhere on the earthly plane a groaning, sweating, heaving woman explodes in emotion as a little baby slips from her body and into her arms, gazing up at her with timeless wisdom.

This is the essence of the Transformer, from whence life comes and whence it shall return. As Dark Mothers we stand at death's door; once we cross over, the Transformer is our refuge, our time-out, our opportunity to rest and regroup. When our earthly life ends, she guides us through a process of molting, shedding the skin of our past, burning the dross so that we may emerge reborn. One thing becomes another in the womb of the Mother.

Whenever we cross the threshold of a major life transition, we pay the Transformer a visit, particularly at times when we're shocked into surrendering all vestiges of identity. The Transformer may seem elusive, but we can access her wisdom with specific tools and techniques, as discussed in chapter 4.

To bring these archetypes to life, we will provide in-depth examples of how women experience and manifest them. A word of caution—many of the accounts you are about to read may seem extreme or be somewhat shocking. Try to keep an open mind as you peruse them, and remember that our culture has so stifled women from being in their fullest power that wild experimentation may be the only way for some to recreate these archetypal roles. We consider our interviewees to be models of courage, women on the edge of our collective potential. But you must find your own ways of fleshing out the Circle's archetypes in a manner that works for you. Find your own edges, use the words of these women to inspire you to play them out, and have compassion for yourself, whatever your place in the Circle.

CHAPTER 3

Blood Bonding

Before we go on to explore the archetypes in depth, we must consider the Blood Mystery of the power phase—blood bonding. In each of the four phases in the Circle of Life, the Blood Mystery is the vehicle for embodying the lessons of that period in an integrated, fundamental way. And just as the Matriarch is newly identified, so is her rite of blood bonding.

In essence, blood bonding means using the power of menstrual blood to clarify ourselves and unite with others. We have already touched on ways in which our culture discredits or degrades the Blood Mysteries of menarche and birth; now we must go further, and seek to understand basic menstrual taboos and their derivation.

In ancient times, menstrual blood figured powerfully in creation myths and cosmology. Hindu theory held that the Great

Mother created life by thickening her substance into a curd or clot, which crusted over to form solid matter. Thus She produced the cosmos; in similar fashion were women thought to gestate young. Indians of South America claimed that all life was made of "moon blood," a belief echoed in old Mesopotamia, where the Great Goddess supposedly made humankind from clay suffused with her menstrual blood. The Koran says man was made of "flowing blood" by Allah, who in pre-Islamic times was the Goddess of Creation, Al-Lat. Even the Roman creation myth cited lunar influences as necessary to the inception of life.[1]

Further, numerous gods were thought to be dependent on menstrual blood for their very lives, not to mention their powers. Hindu goddess Kali-Maya, mother of all creation, invited the gods to "bathe in the bloody flow of her womb"; if they accepted and, "in holy communion, drank of the fountain of life and bathed in it," they rose to the heavens, infinitely blessed. Norse god Thor was said to have reached enlightenment by bathing in a river filled with the menstrual blood of giantesses, primal matriarchs. Odin was said to have derived power by stealing and drinking "wise blood" from the cauldron in the womb of Mother Earth. Indra (of India) obtained immortality in similar fashion by stealing Soma, a sacred fluid produced by the churning of the primal sea known as Kali's ocean of blood. (Another version of this myth says the goddess Lakshmi gave Indra the Soma directly from her body; he drank and became wise and powerful.[2])

Egyptian pharaohs became divine by drinking *sa* (blood of Isis), the hieroglyphic sign for which is the same as that for vulva. In Persia, the ambrosia of immortality was called *amrita,* or "fluid of the moon," sacred blood. In Celtic Britain, to be "stained with blood" meant to be appointed king by the Goddess, yet a king could become divine only by drinking "red mead" from the fairy queen Mab.[3] Mab's annual celebration falls at the autumnal equinox, suggesting that the power of menstruation and blood bonding is integral to the Matriarch phase.

Envy and fear of women's "magic blood" have also led men to imitate menstruation. Perhaps the most classic example is the act of subincision, practiced in New Guinea, Australia, the Philippines, and Africa. This drastic operation involves slitting the underside of the penis, so when placed upright on the abdomen it resembles the vagina. Sometimes blood is caused to flow periodically from this wound, known as "man's menstruation." According to Phyllis Chesler, the slash in Christ's side and his bloody crown of briars are allusions to menstrual magic of earlier spiritual traditions.[4] Male bloodletting rites such as circumcision and the Native American Sun Dance are further examples. Even the ritual paraphernalia of the priesthood suggests imitation of women in order to obtain their magic—the wand was originally used by women to mark their menstrual cycles, and the ceremonial robe is traditional woman's garb.[5] As Paula Weideger notes, "Obviously menstruation is not universally believed to be a curse, although it may be that it is universally envied."[6]

On the other hand, there are numerous examples of extremely repressive menstrual taboos; in fact, the list seems endless. The Talmud says that if a menstruating woman passes between two men, one will die. The Brahmins maintained that a man who lay with a menstruating woman should suffer as severe a punishment as that for the most heinous crimes. In Vedic mythology, Vishnu copulated with the goddess Earth when she was menstruating and thus conceived monsters who nearly destroyed the planet. Zoroastrians upheld this belief, saying that any man who slept with a menstruating woman would beget demons. Persian patriarchs claimed menstruating women were poison and belonged to the devil; the glance of a menstruating woman was as feared as the glance of a gorgon, like in effect to that of Medusa.[7]

To this day, Orthodox Jews refuse to shake hands with a woman, for fear she might be menstruating. Pliny said that a menstruating woman's touch could blast crops, break mirrors, sour wine, rust iron, dull knives, and any man who lay with a menstruating woman during a lunar eclipse would surely die.[8]

Christianity upheld these patriarchal superstitions. In the seventh century, the archbishop of Canterbury forbade menstruating women to take communion (a genuine irony, as we shall see in a moment). From the eighth to the eleventh century, numerous laws denied menstruating women any access to church facilities. A Scottish medical text of this period stated:

> Oh! Menstruating woman, thou'rt a fiend
> From which all nature should be closely screened.[9]

Even as recently as the sixteenth century, medical authorities believed that demons were produced from menstrual flow.[10] Although peasant traditions and beliefs were somewhat more positive regarding the power of menstrual blood, our culture has deep roots in what Luisah Teish has termed "hemophobia."[11] Phyllis Chesler draws a direct correlation between cultures that are most warlike or violent and those most terrified of women's wise blood.[12]

Then again, Vicki Noble reminds us that menstrual blood was the only blood on any altar until women were dishonored and their power ignored.[13] A woman in the Matriarch phase states boldly:

> "I like saving my blood. I always have a little blood on hand. It's in the freezer. I joke around that if I ever had to sign anything serious, I would sign it in blood. I find if people look in my freezer and say, 'What's that?' and I say it's my blood, they are afraid of it.

I've noticed that. Even when it's frozen in a jar, probably just a couple of tablespoons, people are really afraid of it. I think that's great! They fear it. They fear our power. I am so tired of our power being abased and oppressed."

Consider the composition of menstrual blood. It contains the unfertilized ovum, carrier of genetic material for the next generation. No wonder prepatriarchal cultures associated it with enlightenment and visionary strength! Testament to this is the omphalos stone of Glastonbury; it is a large, egg-shaped rock with a depression in the center, which priestesses of old would straddle to collect their menstrual blood, even as they gave voice to the word of the Great Mother as her oracles. (Christian monks at the Glastonbury Abbey later turned the stone into a candle holder.) Menstrual blood is often alluded to as a flower yet to bear fruit, but containing the soul of the future. In India, when a girl first menstruates she is said to have "borne the Flower."[14]

The very color of the menses is thus considered a powerful charm. The Maori rendered objects sacred by tinting them red, whether with dye or actual menses. Australian aborigines used red ochre to paint themselves and their ceremonial effects, declaring the ochre to be real menstrual blood. Andaman Islanders are known to cover the bodies of their sick in some red substance thought to be a cure for any illness. In Greece and southern Russia, Easter eggs (classic womb symbols) are painted red and laid on the graves of the dead to rejuvenate and strengthen them. In fact, burial customs from Paleolithic times have involved anointing the body with red as a key to rebirth. Both red clay and the red ore hematite were seen as the blood of Mother Earth, her holy menses.[15]

Thus was menstrual blood considered a most precious fluid with limitless magical potency, used for various purposes of consecration and preservation. Contrast this to the way our society would have us feel about our blood—that it should not be touched and must be hidden away, that it is messy and inconvenient, that it is ultimately valueless. How would we feel about ourselves if our blood was considered sacred, and how might we utilize its power for deepening our connection to the Earth, ourselves, and to each other?

Many women we interviewed told of collecting their menstrual blood to nourish their houseplants or gardens. Some used cervical caps or diaphragms emptied into watering cans; others soaked cloth menstrual pads or tampons in similar containers. All reported that their plants thrived, and that the ritual has great psychological benefit. Hear what Brooke Medicine Eagle says in this regard:

> Let me speak for a moment of women's moon-time blood and its power. This blood has been shown to be among the (if not *the*) most nurturing, bio-energizing substance on earth. When placed on plants, they are deeply nourished. In our native ways, during our ceremonies of planting and nurturing our crops, we had moon-time women move among the plants and give away their blood. Always, our women gave away this wonderful blood in an honoring way. They sat upon the ground and gave away directly, or bled upon moss and later placed it upon the earth to nurture and renew.[16]

Another woman with a different orientation has similar views:

> "At a recent conference on the status of the planet, a major point of concern was our diminishing topsoil—we have about five years of topsoil left—and that we need to stop growing so much food and start growing topsoil. We need to give back more than we've taken for our own lives, and let our intuition tell us which plants to cultivate. I see women giving their blood to the earth as a way to do this.

"I think it's crucial that we re-create our Blood Rites. When we collect our blood, we foster a relationship with our place in nature—but we become the place, there is no separate us, no reality separate from nature. When we give our blood to the earth, we create an opening for distinguishing domains we don't ordinarily access, we integrate the idea of 'other' and become the tree, the plant."

This is the Gaia hypothesis, that the Earth is a self-creating and self-maintaining live organism, not just some conglomerate of minerals and water. In contrast to androcentric belief systems, ecofeminism maintains that human life is of no greater or lesser value than that of animals, rocks, trees, or plants. This is because all living things are considered interdependent and in delicate balance.

"Giving my blood to the earth makes me feel proud to be on the land, grateful to be on the land, and these feelings are commensurate, they come from the land, they come from me, they go back and forth. I feel my own gratitude and I feel the gratitude of the land; I feel my own respect and the respect of the land. The land gives me my life, and I contribute to the life of the land."

Blood bonding to the earth serves as the foundation for more complex blood bonding, whether to friends, lovers, or one's own power:

"Just as I was about to move from a place I had lived for many years, my inner voice told me I needed to save my menstrual blood. And I thought, 'That's interesting, how do I do that?' So I worked out that I'd use a sponge inside a diaphragm, take the diaphragm out and squeeze the sponge into a container, which of course I had to carry around in my purse because you never know . . . so here I was carefully putting my purse down wherever I went so it wouldn't fall over. When I completed this, I asked what I was to do next because here I had this vial of menstrual blood and it was strong—it didn't smell bad, but it was strong. I had collected some beach stones for runes, and I got that I was to place some on those runes, and then mark my territory, mark around the building where I had been, just a little bit each place I had been, to say good-bye. I think that was the purpose; I don't really know, I just did it. It was interesting to be that intimate with my blood, not to just let it go. It really altered my relationship with menstruation, with that rite that happens every month for us, the beauty of it and the strength of the blood, and you know, I just don't discard tampons in the same way anymore. Most cycles, I make some effort to do some bleeding into the earth, to return to that really strong connection between the menstrual blood and the Mother that birthed me."

Blood bonding between women has only recently been researched. In 1971, using her dormitory living quarters as ground for her experiments, researcher Martha McClintock demonstrated that women who live or work closely together tend to cycle together.[17] In 1986, Stanford researchers confirmed menstrual synchrony and found it to be pheromone-related. (Pheromones are substances produced by our glands that become airborne, much like those produced by a cat in heat, to attract or influence others of our species.[18]) But experience teaches that continuous contact is not always necessary for this synchrony to occur; I watched it develop between my sister and me with just weekly contact over a period of months.

Yet another explanation for menstrual synchrony is that of entrainment, defined by drummer Mickey Hart as "the quality of two similarly timed beats to link up and become synchronized in each other's presence."[19] Nondigital clocks behave this way and so, says Judy Grahn, do menstruating women. In her wonderful book *Blood, Bread, and Roses,* she reveals how women in tribal cultures "bonded through entrainment by their common flow of blood, including birth blood, and so created an increasing complex of rites."[20] She notes that in certain cases, the interactive rhythm of menstrual periodicity was deliberately cultivated by the use of emmenagogues (menstrual-inducing herbs) and other cycle-regulating substances. She also has numerous references to the use of mind-altering substances to heighten the psychic effects of menstruation and menstrual rites.[21]

As women synchronize their menstruation they not only enhance physical and emotional changes common at this time, but at other points in the cycle too. Dramatic variation in the content of our dreams when ovulating or menstruating may reflect a cyclic range of moods. According to Ernest Hartmann, author of *The Biology of Dreaming,* women typically report dreams of eggs, jewels, fragile things, or sex with their beloved at mid-cycle, while their dreams immediately before and during menstruation involve sex with strangers, violence, dark intrigue, animals, things breaking apart, and death.[22] In my women's circle, I have noticed not only that our blood times have become aligned, but that the nature of our interactions, and even the topics we select for forthcoming meetings, reflect the feelings and concerns of that point in the cycle. For us, the bond of blood links us strongly to one another, whether we're menstruating or not, as well as reinforcing our indi-viduality. Depending on the time of the month, we share our tender, ovulatory longings for union, or our intense passions and visionary perceptions when menstruating. Our entrainment enables us to go deeper in knowing ourselves than we would otherwise go alone.

And in many indigenous cultures, women have been isolated when menstruating. The menstrual hut symbolizes separation from the ordinary concerns of daily life. Sometimes this has been by choice; other times, cultural taboos have removed menstruating women from the rest of society. Judy Grahn speculates that in Neolithic times, females may have been isolated in order to protect the rest of their tribe, sent literally up a tree so that the odor of their blood, sure to attract predators, would not endanger the lives of other community members.[23]

But in patriarchal cultures, the real reason menstruating women are considered taboo is their volatile combination of forthrightness and unbridled libido. This forthrightness has now become legendary: I'm reminded of a dinner party where we were joking about PMS and I, about to start bleeding myself, piped up and said, "Well, that's the only time we really tell the truth." As regards libido, Mary Jane Sherfey, author of *The Nature and Evolution of Female Sexuality,* contends that taboos dictating seclusion and avoidance of sex during menstruation rose directly from a need to suppress "women's inordinately high drive and orgasmic capacity" at this time.[24] Expert Dr. Alfred Kinsey states:

> [T]he human female, in the course of evolution, has departed from her mammalian ancestors and developed new characteristics which have relocated the period of maximum sexual arousal near the time of menstruation.[25]

Authors Penelope Shuttle and Peter Redgrove elaborate:

> It is as though the mating signal of genital blood has been wrenched from its former position at ovulation, to a new position at menstruation—as though this evolutionary step meant that sex was now to be used for something other than reproduction.[26]

Returning to menstrual isolation as a choice, we find that in cultures that honor the feminine, menstruating women usually elect to retreat, at least for the first few days of bleeding. Relief from their regular duties has purportedly been more than offset by the special contributions menstruating women have made to their communities. For example, Native American tradition holds that the coming of the white man was foretold by the women of the "moonlodge" (place of menstrual isolation). The Greeks believed menstruating women had power over the earth's fertility, thus menstrual isolation was thought to ensure a good harvest. It appears that women's ability to weave and utilize magic is increased exponentially when they bleed in unison. Thus blood bonding strengthens not only women themselves, but important aspects of community life.

How has blood itself been used in this process? Sometimes women have painted their bodies with it in symbolic designs. It has been suggested that menstrual blood was the original cosmetic; in cultures where women chose isolation at the blood time, they painted their mouths with it to warn their men to stay away. Judy Grahn reports that in Australian aboriginal society, women would let their blood run down their thighs to deliberately engender menstrual synchrony.[27] One woman we interviewed spoke of marking herself with her blood, touching chakras she wished to activate or bring into harmony. In a circle, women may spontaneously select a symbol—the spiral, the circle, the Celtic cross, the ankh, a crescent moon—and mark themselves in unison with some mutually agreed upon intention. As previously described by one interviewee, blood can also be used to sacralize some object or location. Like any primary element—earth, water, air, or fire—blood has sympathetic power, meaning that a small amount can serve to call upon its grand essence. If we want to call the rain, we do a ritual with a bit of water; if we want to call vision and foresight, we use a bit of menstrual blood.

"In my women's circle, we use our blood in several ways. Sometimes we collect our blood, and when we meet, we mix it together in a chalice and then anoint one another with it. We also have a menstrual wand, a wooden baton, and each month, whoever is to lead our next meeting will take the wand home with her and when she's bleeding, will paint it in some way—the wand is covered with blood now [laughs]. As she opens the next circle, she speaks of what her blood time and cycle were like that month, and we often find a common tone of ease or difficulty in our time apart. We're just beginning to explore what we can do with this power."

Although the danger of blood-borne disease discourages this today, menstrual blood seems also to have been ingested in a ritualistic way in former times. We've already explored the mythological basis for this: those fortunate enough to drink from the Creatrix find wisdom and immortality. The word "eucharist," or communion, was derived from Charis, goddess of sexual love whose blood was held sacred. Barbara Walker surmises, "Medieval churchmen insisted that the communal wine drunk by witches was menstrual blood, and they may have been right," citing the example of the legendary Fairy Queen of Elphame, who bade her initiate Thomas Rhymer, a fourteenth century poet-seer, to drink of the "bottle of claret wine . . . here in my lap."[28] In common English usage, claret was a synonym for both blood and enlightenment.

Our current fascination with vampire lore is undoubtedly based on the taboo of drinking blood, which has been exacerbated by the AIDS epidemic. In numerous myths, vampires required not only blood but lunar influences to sustain them; they were often called forth from slumber by the moon. Author Dion Boucicault's vampire instructed his students to carry his body to a high mountain that the first lunar rays might touch and restore him; the Greek word for vampire means literally "flesh made by the moon."[29] The connection between menstrual blood and vampire lore seems obvious enough, but only in lesbian erotica (such as the anthology *Daughters of Darkness*[30]) do we find it explored in any depth.

Nevertheless, one woman we interviewed stated:

> "I love oral sex when my partner is bleeding. No, love is not strong enough—I adore the taste of her blood; it compels me, drives me into a frenzy and draws me down deep; it makes my scalp tingle, it is home beyond home. There is definitely a kind of bonding in this that is more than emotional—it's fundamental, elemental, very strong. An old Caribbean proverb says, 'When a woman loves another woman, it is the blood of the Mother speaking'—that's what it's like for me."

What about women blood bonding with men? I have been repeatedly surprised in my research on sexuality at how men continue to refuse to make love to their menstruating partners, enforcing the old taboos. This aversion is obviously rooted in the notion that menstrual blood is unclean or somehow defiling. Unfortunately, most men also remain unaware of the power of women's blood— it has been so effectively neutralized that sex during menstruation is viewed as messy, nothing more.

And yet, men hunger for blood. Hunting for sport is little more than an updated bloodletting rite, replete with ritualistic elements. Blood lust is also expressed in the graphic violence and bloody images that permeate our media, far more attractive to men than to women. Alan Bleakley, author of *Fruits of the Moon Tree,* conjectures that "the need for men to engage in bloody warfare is an issue of unresolved and projected menstrual distress," and suggests an antidote derived by "sharing of the menstrual rhythm, through women initiating men into its mystery."[31] How is this to be done? Bleakley sums up his view of the process:

Set up a positive prophecy: if the period is looked upon as a time when a woman's creative power is at its height, and this can be helpfully and supportingly engaged with by the man, then the energy of the period that is often turned to depression may be transformed into energy available for creative effort. The man enriches his experience in this process . . . he becomes appropriately more open, softer . . . and releases new directions for development. The man can then usefully respond to the woman's cycle, and there are gains for woman and man, rather than separatism, as denial of one or the other's power. The man attains his symbolic wound (the opportunity lodged in his vulnerability) and releases the power of his inner woman, and the woman resolves the potential distress of her own "wound" by releasing its healing energy.[32]

In tantric traditions, the power of this alchemical approach has been formalized through specific sexual practices. Tantra holds that women have more spiritual energy than men; thus men can achieve enlightenment only by emotional and sexual union with them. For the Great Rite, the two essential ingredients are *sukra* (semen) and *rukta* (menstrual blood). The following description serves to illustrate many points of discussion thus far:

> When the semen, made molten by the fire of great passion, falls into the lotus of the mother and mixes with her red element, the conventional mandala of thought enlightenment is achieved. The resultant mixture is tasted by the united father-mother (Yab-Yum), and when it reaches the throat they can generate concretely a special bliss, the bodhicitta. The term "secret initiation" comes from the tasting of this secret substance.[33]

One of the most common symbols of the alchemical union of male and female, yin and yang, semen and menstrual blood, is the *vesica pisces*. *Vesica pisces* literally means "vessel of fish," its image being two interlocking circles that overlap to create a pointed oval in the center, which forms the yoni or vulva of the Goddess. This ancient yonic symbol was called *pisces* on the observation that female genitals smell like fish. (Christians later tipped the fish horizontally to symbolize Christianity.)

In the beautiful gardens of Chalice Well in Glastonbury, England, the famous pools of the *vesica pisces* are found. These two shallow stone pools were constructed according to the gematria, or sacred geometry of the symbol itself. One pool's source is a spring known as the Blood Spring, with waters bright red from iron deposits. The spring flows at a steady rate of one thousand gallons per hour—its water represents the blood of birth and menstruation. Thousands of people in search of cures for their ailments come every year to drink and bathe in this water, long considered to have healing properties. The other pool is fed by a second perennial spring known as the White Spring, which emerges beneath the powerful Glastonbury Tor. This spring flows at a fluctuating rate of between five and seventy thousand gallons per day—its water, chalk white from limestone deposits, is honored as the semen of the male. The two waters meet in the center pool in an alchemical mix of red and white, menstrual blood and semen—a sacred fusion of the male and female principles. According to Glastonbury legend, this holy well represents the vulva of the Great Mother from whom we are born into this world.[34]

Considering the intensity of women's sex drive immediately before and during menstruation, it is no surprise that menstrual blood has long been considered an aphrodisiac. Madame de Montespan used it to inflame the ardor of her lover, Louis XIV. Gypsy lore held that a woman could win any man's love with a potion of her menstrual blood. And according to Tibetan tradition, menstrual blood mixed into a man's food or drink is the easiest way to subjugate him.[35]

It seems crucial that we use the power of our menstrual blood with clear and loving intention, and create rites that hold sacred the mysteries of blood bonding. Power is dangerous when untempered by wisdom, and women exploring the power phase of the Circle of Life may encounter potent lessons in this regard. Fortunately, each stage in this phase also bears inherent constraints to power's abuse: for the Amazon, curiosity and wanderlust generally preclude obsession with power; for the Matriarch, cross-generational responsibilities and obligations tend to discourage power's misuse; and for the Priestess, the experience of descent teaches her to surrender power so as not to disturb the precarious balance of life and death.

Blood is life; our menstrual blood is the life of the future. We must use it fearlessly and proudly to find the relationship between fate and power, unique to each of us, that leads to wisdom.

CHAPTER 4

The Role of the Transformer

The Transformer is the source of all, the context of life. She represents the most basic and fundamental ground of our being, the very essence of our ability to grow and change. In the Circle, Transformer energy flows from the center and between each stage, making it multidimensional rather than linear and locked. This gives us the freedom to traverse the boundaries of any stage at any time. Thus a woman may be in the stage of the Amazon chronologically but may dip back and revisit the Lover stage emotionally as she nurtures a new romance. Or a woman immersed in the actual responsibilities of Motherhood may leap forward intuitively to express her ideals in the broad social context of the Crone. One woman we interviewed stated, "The more you move around on the Circle, the better you get at being in the Transformer."

The keys to transformation reside within us. We can open our minds to the possibility of dramatic shifts in life, but our hearts tell us when it is time. We may not understand the mystery of transformation, but we can learn to recognize the signs—feelings of boredom, detachment from creativity or sense of direction, the dead-end malaise that trumpets the need for something new. And when the window of change begins to open, we feel it as a literal opening in the heart, accompanied by rapid-fire cognition and imperatives to act.

Cultural constraints dramatically impede this process. Most industrialized nations are addicted to change but terrified of transformation. In the United States, consumerism riddles our media— we are constantly bombarded with new products, services, and options impelling us to change our looks, our lifestyle, our very beliefs and principles on a whim. All this exploits our idealization of youth, and so we make changes (or purchases) in hopes of being revitalized, more attractive, young again. Yet this sort of change is little more than substitution, exchange, replacement of one thing for another—the opposite of transformation, which renders the new.

At the heart of transformation is the paradox of surrender and control. To control means to order, structure, force, or mold to certain expectations. One can dictate change, but not transformation. Transformation is beyond our control, and is best met with an attitude of surrender. Control-based change is isolating and fragmenting, but transformation integrates and moves us to a state of awareness that is universal, timeless, and potentially ecstatic.

So why do we resist transformation? Underlying our cultural penchant for control are Judeo-Christian beliefs that separate mind and body, that espouse self-restraint and self-denial to the exclusion of personal growth. Letting go to "let God" is acceptable; letting go to oneself is considered the height of self-indulgence, pure hedonism. Transformation that incorporates the self is suspect, as are those who feel comfortable in its boundless state. This comment from an accomplished woman in her seventies serves to illustrate:

> "On the Circle, I can go as far as the Crone—I'm approaching Dark Mother intellectually but I'm not there physically. Where do I really live? If I were to define myself with one word, it would be curiosity. Now where does curiosity fit into this Circle? In the Transformer, I'd guess. Being a musician, I think that's where I live, though I step into the world every now and then to other points on the Circle. My curiosity leads me to encounter people with views opposing mine—not because I want to argue, but because I want to learn. And there's an enormous difference—sometimes I am seen as confrontational when I'm really just curious. People defending religious or political beliefs have a terrible time with this; they get polarized and label me this or that. But I'm not any of those things, it's just my curiosity.
>
> "I also have a lot of the trickster in me. Sometimes I trick myself out of a certain frame of mind, and don't see until later what I've done. Being flexible is more important to me than anything else—it's the source of my music, my creativity."

Consider transformation in the world of nature. The snake periodically sheds its skin: an act that cannot be commanded but is inevitable nonetheless. Transformation of caterpillar to butterfly is even more dramatic and likewise incontrovertible, encoded in the DNA. As part of the natural world, we women also experience certain biological changes that transform us whether we like it or not—these are our Blood Mysteries.

The Blood Mystery of childbirth is a climactic event that illustrates the agony and ecstasy of transformation. Predictably, most childbirth preparation methods in the United States emphasize control of the process through mastery of various breathing and relaxation techniques. Pregnancy itself is viewed not so much as a transformative period in a woman's life as the means to have a child; consequently, most of the attention goes to the baby's welfare. The psychological and spiritual changes of women in this transition are considered extraneous, if not ignored altogether. But there is no getting around the fact that labor is major life event with a sharp learning curve: no sooner has a woman found a workable tool or technique for coping than she finds it no longer applicable, so letting go must occur again and again. Being fully present to her experience, facing fear and moving through it, working with the process rather than against it enables her to cope with and transmute labor's intensity. In surrendering, she merges with ancient, biologically encoded rhythms and is herself reborn.

Transformation at its most profound always involves great difficulty at the beginning. This is because if we are to be taken apart and put back together again in new form, the experience can never be what we expect. Disintegration of the known must occur in order for the unknown to take shape. As Demetra George says, "Nothing new can be reborn until something old first dies."[1] Sometimes the death of a loved one, a natural catastrophe, or other major loss catapults us into the arms of the Transformer; other times, we hedge the edge, struggling with the inevitable leap. But repressing the call of the unknown leaves us bereft of the magic and miracle of our own existence: directionless, passionless, dry. No one has more beautifully described the symptomology of holding back than Clarissa Pinkola Estés, in *Women Who Run with the Wolves*:

> Feeling frightened, halt or weak, without inspiration, without animation, without soulfulness, without meaning, shame bearing, chronically fuming, volatile, stuck, uncreative, compressed, crazed.
> Feeling powerless, chronically doubtful, shaky, blocked, unable to follow through, giving one's creative life over to others,

life-sapping choice in mates, work or friendships, suffering to live outside one's own cycles, overprotective of self, inert, uncertain, faltering, inability to pace oneself or set limits.

Not insistent on one's tempo, to be self-conscious, to be away from one's God or Gods, to be separated from one's revivification, drawn far into domesticity, intellectualism, work, or inertia because that is the safest place to be for one who has lost her instincts.

To fear to venture by oneself or reveal oneself, fear to seek mentor, mother, father, fear to set out one's own imperfect work before it is an opus, fear to set out on a journey, fear of caring for another or others, fear one will run on, run out, run down, cringing before authority, loss of energy before creative projects, wincing, humiliation, angst, numbness, anxiety.

Afraid to bite back when there is nothing else to do, afraid to try the new, fear to stand up, afraid to speak up, speak against, sick stomach, butterflies, sour stomach, cut in the middle, strangled, becoming conciliatory or nice too easily, revenge.[2]

In fact, fear plays an essential role in transformation, serving as a catalyst. Yaqui shaman Don Juan teaches that fear is one of our natural enemies, for if we don't go out to meet it squarely, we can't progress.[3] Fear registers in the body, it takes us out of our minds, out of abstraction. Considering the trouble we tend to have in trusting and listening to our bodies, it's no surprise that such phrases as "numb with fear" or "paralyzed with fear" riddle our language.

Yet fear is an ally, if we but make it so. The process of becoming afraid is really that of discovering that our experience and beliefs cannot decode a new situation—our reality is shifting and we have no control. Fear is the harbinger of growth, heralding the need to step outside the confines of what we've known as true. When a relationship is ending that we thought would last forever, the context for all of our relationships changes. When an occupation we believed to be our life's work loses meaning and we long for something more, our social identity is dramatically altered.

Fear is our ally in that it alerts us, energizes us, keeps us awake. In teaching student midwives, I've come to believe that one of my most critical tasks is to help them form a healthy relationship to fear. I've discovered in my own work that when life-threatening situations arise, I have a choice—I can panic, scatter my energy, and look for a way out, or I can embrace my fear and use the sheer force of it to enable me to act with intent. My own imaging technique for handling fear is to tuck it under my arm and hold it close to my body; I make it my partner. To further illustrate, note that what we say to women in the throes of hard labor—"Just let go, go right through it, don't fight it, trust the process, you can do it"—are fully applicable to us as birth attendants, particularly in handling emergencies. In contrast, I've had ample opportunity to watch hospital personnel fight against fear in threatening situations, exacerbating the crisis as no one steps forward to do the obvious until precious moments have already passed.

The antidote for fear is courage, which springs from the heart. Opening our hearts when afraid can be a euphoric and exhilarating experience. Even daily encounters with minor fears, as signaled by subtle changes in our bodies, give opportunity to practice bravery. Luisah Teish observes that fears tend to come in waves or sets, and express deeply conditioned patterns of behavior.[4] For example, once we become aware of certain stumbling blocks in a relationship and trace these back to their roots, we may experience more fear, more holding back until a deeper understanding provides the courage to go on.

As we face our fears repeatedly we become more flexible, more comfortable with the Transformer, as this woman in her forties relates:

"Fear is no longer frightening to me. I think this has been a process of having enough experience to feel safe, to know I'm not going to perish. I have faith, I know about descending into the darkness, I know about coming back up, I know about the spiral, thinking I've gotten through some issue then coming around to it again, but in a more powerful place. I have faith in this process—I look forward to it."

Beyond day-to-day struggles with fear, major life crises like the death of a loved one, sudden dissolution of a primary relationship, or catastrophic accident or illness may disorient us so utterly that we are pushed beyond our boundaries will or nil. At these times, there is a critical (though generally unacknowledged) role played by adrenaline. Helen Palmer, authority on intuition, uses the image of a lion in the middle of the road to illustrate how shock and terror can enable us to cut through cognitive response to inner power and clarity.[5] Whenever we feel mortal fear, we are moved to these basic resources for our survival.

Fear opens the way between worlds, lifts the veil between this and other dimensions for a moment, or sometimes for an extended period of time. As we explore these thresholds, we may need to cross and recross repeatedly in order to die to what we have known and complete our transformation. One woman we interviewed placed herself in the stage of Transformer and tearfully claimed she was stuck there. She felt herself unable to progress from her current role as Blood Sister to that of the Lover, due to a history of extensive sexual abuse. As she hovered between these stages, she began to see the Transformer role as means for completing her crossing.

Yet another woman described how she had spent the better part of a year in the Transformer's realm after the violent death of her husband, emerging every once in a while to find footing in her own chronological stage of Midwife moving toward that of Amazon. Thus experiences of loss and withdrawal may be punctuated with periods of reintegration, which lead one gradually back to ordinary life. This process is well described in the *I Ching* hexagram of Return/The Turning Point:

> The powerful light that has been banished returns . . . but this is not brought about by force. The idea of return is based on the course of nature. The movement is cyclic and the course completes itself. Therefore it is not necessary to hasten anything artificially. Everything comes of itself at the appointed time. This is the meaning of heaven and earth.[6]

It is no accident that the Transformer shares the number thirteen with the Death card of the tarot. In the Waite/Pamela Coleman-Smith deck, a skeleton astride a victory steed carries a black banner emblazoned with the white rose of life. In the Motherpeace/Noble-Vogel deck, a lively, molting snake encircles skeletal remains. Both portray death and life as "shifting poles of the same phenomenon, a revolving door between the worlds."[7]

In the words of Joan Halifax, the challenge of transformation is "to open the mystery by becoming it, to transcend death by dying in life, to pierce duality by embracing the opposites, to reunite the fractured forms."[8] "Dying in life" is the process of descent, which takes us deep down to the core of our being. For this reunion of self with greater Self, we must go alone; Jean Bolen uses the image of a solitary traveler entering a forest at its darkest point.[9] Thus directionless and bereft of our usual defenses, we encounter our archetypal fears, our warring, opposing aspects. As we begin the work of ascent, we reunite these "fractured forms" and pull the pieces of ourselves back together again. Once done, light appears at the edge of the forest and we are free to leave.

The dark forest of transformation is also a place where visions occur, where images come to mind to guide us on our way. Certain symbols and imagery have been associated with transformation throughout antiquity. We may find them in our dreams, our waking reveries, our art, or in the world around us. By paying close attention to these symbols and the context in which they appear, we gain a sense of direction and meaning in the otherwise unsettling experience of transformation.

One such classic image is that of the *butterfly*. Transformation from caterpillar to butterfly consists of four stages, each with metaphorical meaning:

1. The egg stage—inception, the ground of being.
2. The larvae stage—the impulse to recreate.
3. The cocoon stage—developing the new, gestating.
4. The butterfly stage—emergence, coming out in the world.

The egg stage signifies a return to the womb, to the Transformer as Great Mother. This is the still point, the moment of utter darkness upon entering the forest, the pause before the first steps are taken. The larvae stage is the inhalation, the inspiration to begin again, the impetus to move and overcome inertia. The cocoon stage is the tangible face of change, the recreating activity, the first step (and all steps thereafter) through the shadowlands. The butterfly stage is rebirth, reemergence, coming out of the darkness recast, renewed, and revealed for all to see.

The image of the butterfly is frequently associated with immortality. In Christian symbology, it connotes resurrection. In Celtic traditions, it signifies the soul as eternal. Butterfly motifs are also found in Mycenaen artwork (1500 B.C.E.), representing the Great Mother in all her previous and future incarnations. These images are reminiscent of the Minoan double axe, which signifies the Great Mother's ability to continually recreate herself.

The *snake/serpent* represents transformation through transmutation. In its cyclic molting, it routinely renews itself without changing its essential nature. It embodies the mystery of death without decay—the startling revelation of bright, fresh skin is the snake's expression of the power to transmute old to new.

In the Garden of Eden myth, the serpent offers Eve knowledge of good and evil. This is the essence of transmutation: the wisdom to take that which is harmful or has outlived its usefulness and change it into something life-giving and good. According to Jamie Samms and David Carson, the snake teaches that "all things are equal in creation, and that which might be experienced as poison can be eaten, ingested, integrated, and transmuted, if one has the proper state of mind."[10] The challenge here is to suspend judgment and engage the truth of our situation, no matter how difficult or grim, as foundation for discovering genuine alternatives. Only by seeing ourselves without any illusion can we embrace the possibility of what we might become.

The snake is also a symbol of sexuality, passion, vitality, and procreation. It represents the ascent of Kundalini (the sacred fire) up the spine and out the crown chakra at the top of the head—an experience of unification, enlightenment, and physical ecstasy. To fully own and incorporate one's sexuality as a mode of transformation is to unite body and spirit in a sacred way.

Cross-cultural references to the snake as gatekeeper of the life/death mystery are abundant. Hindu serpent mother Ananta the Infinite embraced the gods in death, rekindling them for life. Chinese serpent goddess Mat Chinoi nurtured angels in her belly, who in turn received the souls of the dead. Kadru, snake goddess of India, gave birth to the immortals, the Nagas, who guarded secret teachings. Egypt's serpent goddess was Mehen the Enveloper, who enfolded the Auf-Ra (Phallus of Ra) nightly as he traversed the underworld. As regards her use of sexuality to affect the fates of men, Cleopatra was known as the "Serpent of the Nile."[11]

For women, the snake symbolizes the integration of sensuality and wisdom. Dancing in the darkness, moving gracefully and powerfully through the badlands and lush forests of desire, we are at one with the Great Mother in all her fecundity.

The *phoenix* also represents purification. Crushing nothing on which it alights and eating nothing but dew, it is considered both regal and ethereal. The Mayans call it Quetzal, the long-tailed bird of freedom and good fortune. To the Chinese, it is Feng-huang, a spirit bird embodying both male and female characteristics, solar and lunar energies.[12] In Peyote traditions it is a symbol of resurrection, rising from the ashes of the sacred fire.

Sometimes we experience the way of the phoenix through sudden death or loss. Other times, when there seems to be no end to equivocating some decision, we become the phoenix by deliberately taking a plunge into the unknown. This archetypal "leap of faith" recurs in fable and folklore worldwide; hero or heroine bravely charges into some life-threatening situation and enters a timeless dimension where seemingly anything can happen. The act of surrendering to one's fate, pulling out the stops to one's passion is transformation phoenix-style, culminating in glorious flight.

As one young woman explained:

"My experience of transformation has been far from a gentle metamorphosis. It's been more like leaping from tree to tree in the midst of a raging fire, with the wind blowing like mad and whipping all around me. Once in a while there are lulls, and I'm in the eye of the storm, gliding and soaring ecstatically."

Becoming a bird in a trance or visionary state has long been considered a sign of spiritual death and rebirth, or particular paranormal ability. Sacred serpents were said to have licked the ears of Trojan prophetess Cassandra, that she might understand the language of birds and receive their visionary messages. Many cultures believe that the soul takes flight to other realms at the time of death. One woman we interviewed, in the midst of an abrupt divorce, described herself as having "fallen over the edge, flying with nowhere to land." She also spoke of "spending time in dimensions other than ordinary reality," and described this experience as "satisfying like sex." Jean Bolen echoes this in depicting the dark forest as a "place where you withdraw from the ordinary world and go into a kind of magical realm that has scary parts and also clearly has elements in which you become more whole."[13]

When it is time to reemerge from the darkness, we do. Of this turning point, the *I Ching* suggests that "everything should be treated tenderly and with care at the beginning, that the return may lead to a flowering."[14]

As mentioned earlier, the key symbol of the Transformer is the Sacred Cauldron, portrayed in numerous spiritual traditions as a magical vessel wherein inspiration and reanimation occur. In Babylon, the cauldron was under the control of Siris, the fate-goddess who stirred the waters of regeneration. The Egyptians called the rekindling cauldron of life the "Lake of Fire." The Welsh goddess Branwen was keeper of the "Cauldron of Regeneration" in which the dead could be resuscitated overnight. The spherical cauldron and its swirling contents universally represent "cyclic recurrence, as opposed to the patriarchal view of linear time."[15] In the earliest civilizations, the cauldron represented the Great Mother as Creatrix—a parthenogenic view of creation at odds with both the Genesis myth and the Big Bang theory. Her domain was dark, fluid, and filled with potential, much like the uterine environment.

This image of the Transformer as the great Cosmic Womb may be the most comforting of all. Just as the human womb draws the fertilized ovum into itself, the Transformer takes us in when we are ripe for change, and in need of nurturing and protection. She is the safe haven, the place of solace beyond thought and action. She draws us as a black hole draws matter and inverts it, turning us inside out and releasing us on the other side, redefined and reformed.

The elemental contents of the cauldron, the water and fire, mix together as life blood. This is the holy wine in the sacred chalice, said to reveal truth to the seeker. The chalice or Holy Grail is yet another symbol of the Transformer—as portrayed by myth, a magical and elusive expression of her gifts to us.

Besides abstract symbolism, most ancient spiritual traditions incorporate hands-on tools for transformation. These include oracles such as the tarot, the *I Ching,* and the runes, said to foretell the future or predict outcome based on apperception of one's current situation. We can use these tools to become knowledgeable regarding patterns of human existence; they serve as symbolic maps for our personal growth and development, they comfort and inspire us with archetypal images and expressions of power and beauty.

Certain practices like yoga, Tantra, meditation, breath work, and trance work may also be used to deliberately invoke or enhance transformation. Many indigenous cultures further rely on ritual celebrations and rites of passage to cast the challenges of birth, maturation, and death in a more eternal context. When we enact these ceremonies in our own circles or communities, we overcome one of the greatest fears in transformation—being lost and alone. What a blessing, what a gift these tools are for us!

As in all else, the right tool must be chosen to suit the need. It's important to stay flexible in appointing our tools, and to avoid using the same one over and over, especially if it doesn't seem to be working anymore. Because every tool has its particular applications and limits, it's wise to maintain a diverse, well-stocked toolbox.

Tarot cards are one such spiritual tool, said to contain teachings of a formerly oral tradition dating back to the earliest civilizations. The initiation schools of ancient Egypt, the secret doctrines of the Druids, Mayans, and Arctic peoples all maintained a view of the life cycle involving symbolic stages of death and regeneration. When it became dangerous to express such knowledge verbally, visual images were created to preserve what words could not. We do not know who developed the original tarot, but it can be traced back to the Saracens, who brought illustrated cards to Spain in the late fourteenth century. Gypsies migrating from Hindustan also brought cards to Europe; their "game of man" was called Faro (from Pharaoh) because their cards featured Egyptian figures and symbols.[16]

Our modern-day playing cards are based on tarot suits of wands, swords, cups, and pentacles (or discs), corresponding to clubs, spades, hearts, and diamonds. Notably absent from our deck are the twenty-two major arcana, tarot's key pictorial images. Arcana is derived from *arcan,* which is Latin for chest or container; in alchemical terms, it is a vessel in which a remedy is produced, much like the cauldron of the Transformer.[17] The major arcana are the power cards of the tarot, configuring the human experience with titles such as Temperance, Justice, Death, the Lovers.

Laying out the cards in particular spreads can serve to break down and define various aspects of a situation so we may better understand it. We learn most from the tarot (or any means of divination) when we concentrate not so much on our problem or concern, but on the point inside us from whence it springs, the heart of our inquiry. It is best to begin by suspending both desire and disbelief, yielding to the "dark forest" or causal substance of the Transformer wherein all may be known apart from ordinary time constraints.

Tarot is uniquely applicable to situations where we feel blocked, unable to separate prevailing influences from our true destiny. It is especially wonderful in that it reveals a trajectory based on the card we choose to begin the reading, known as the significator. This can be any card in the deck, denoting person, state of mind, or pressing concern. Around the significator we lay out additional cards that help us understand the foundations of what we are experiencing and what is likely to come.

My favorite spread is the Celtic Cross in that it is simple and easy to read. The significator is placed in the center, then the rest of the cards are shuffled three times, cut three times and restacked. Lay the top card over the significator; the next, crossing it; the third, directly above it; the fourth, directly below it; the fifth, to the left of it; the sixth, to the right of it; the seventh, to the far right near the base of the spread; the eighth, directly above the seventh; the ninth, above the eighth; the tenth, above the ninth. Here are the place meanings:

1. What covers you—pervasive influences at the moment.
2. What crosses you—conflicting influences.
3. What crowns you—the ideal, which may or may not be made actual.
4. What is beneath you—that which has already occurred, the foundation of the inquiry.
5. What is behind you—influences passing away.
6. What is before you—influences just coming to bear.
7. Yourself—your attitude or self-image in the matter.

8. Your house—environment, family, and friends.

9. Hopes and fears—conscious and unconscious projections.

10. What will come—the result, the culmination.

Any deck may be used with this layout. My personal favorites are the Waite deck (emotionally evocative images), the Crowley deck (powerfully energetic, Egyptian images), and the Motherpeace deck (round cards, matriarchal symbology). You too will find your favorite; even so, it is useful to cross-reference other decks for the meaning of an especially intriguing or challenging image. I particularly like Noble's treatment of the minor arcana (suit cards) in that she decodes the numerology first, and then addresses its interpretation in a given suit. For example, she reveals all fives as representing struggle, then explains that the nature of this struggle in cups regards emotional loss, whereas in swords, humiliation and mental defeat. Eights signify change, but in wands indicates a need for passionate risk taking, whereas in discs, a goal of right livelihood.

Tarot reading may be simplified by drawing a single card, or perhaps three to represent past, present, and future. As this woman relates:

> "Each year on my birthday, I draw three tarot cards to be my guides for the coming year. I check in with them periodically to see what they have to say about the ever-changing *now.* Invariably they give clues, point the way, or clarify something I am missing.
>
> "This year, I laid all the cards out on the Balinese temple scarf that houses them in their black velvet bag, and at noon I smudged them, wrapped them up again, and walked down to the labyrinth on my land. I walked round and round, spiraling in with the intention to choose cards that would best guide me through the coming months and truly help me see. When I reached the center of the labyrinth, I sat down in the warm winter sun, laid out the scarf,

and took cards in hand. I use the Stormrider tarot, created by my friend Requa Tolbert. The first card I drew was Pattern: 'What the mind adores . . . wave, circle, spiral, branching, tessellation. The path in the wilderness, the crack between the worlds.'

"Near the end of each year, I review and write about my cards. It's been a year of seeing patterns that aren't working and making some moves to break them. The little blue crack between the rocks, the light of day, the end of the tunnel, are all patterns that have called me out of a low-level depression into brighter days. Patterns can be so seductive, so sweet, so safe in their familiarity. The pattern of a house I could walk around in the pitch black and not bump into anything. A house I have touched every inch of with my hands—painted or wallpapered, or at least cleaned. But now the pattern of living in the same place for all of my adult married life has become claustrophobic and I find myself screaming, 'I don't want to do this anymore!' Of course, this has *nothing* to do with being menopausal, or both girls grown, or gray joint-aching cold California winter, or my friend Deborah sending outrageous email accounts of her year-long adventure in Mongolia, or my dear friend leaving her body (talk about breaking patterns!). Oh no, *nothing* to do with being a gypsy at heart, a gypsy who hasn't moved the wagons for a long, long time."

It is crucial to learn to recognize the urge to merge with one's oracles, to hit on the right moment when curiosity and receptivity run high. Sometimes it is hard to accept what we see, and the temptation to erase and do it over again is great. This may be a time when it's best to put the cards away, and set aside the imagery for a while until it's not so painfully vivid. On the other hand, a profoundly affirming reading may be savored by keeping the cards in order atop the deck, ready for review at any moment. Other times, the images don't sink in so easily and the spread can be left out to return to periodically.

It can be interesting to have a trusted friend read your tarot. You choose the significator, shuffle, and cut the cards, but your friend lays them out and interprets their meaning for you while you sit back and listen. This can be a powerful bonding experience, creating deeper intimacy between you.

The *I Ching,* or *Book of Changes,* is the great "break it down" of oracles, clarifying and illuminating the precise nature of a given situation or dilemma. In contrast to the tarot, the *I Ching* focuses on current or impending change, and how a specific course of action or frame of mind may work for good or ill. To employ this oracle, three coins are thrown like dice, and depending on the combination of heads or tails, either a solid or broken line is derived. Six throws generate the six lines comprising the hexagram (or reading). Should all heads or all tails turn up on a throw, we call that a changing line, and will find a special interpretation for it in the text. Additionally, each changing line transforms to its opposite—if broken, it becomes solid, or if solid, it becomes broken. This creates a new hexagram, which describes what is likely to occur if we enact the directives (or persist in the errors) our changing lines have indicated. There are a total of sixty-four hexagrams; within these, eight elemental trigrams:

1. The creative—heaven.
2. The receptive—earth.
3. The arousing—thunder.
4. The abysmal—water.
5. The gentle, penetrating—wind.
6. The joyous—lake.
7. Keeping still—mountain.
8. The clinging—fire.

The combination of two of these trigrams within each hexagram creates visual and energetic imagery, as does the placement of each—which is above and which is below.

The *I Ching* is said to predate written language, although numerous Chinese sages and political leaders have added to the commentary over the years. The first such contributor was said to be Fu Hsi, a legendary figure representing the era of hunting, fishing, and the invention of cooking. However, the eight trigrams have names that cannot be found in any Chinese dialect; thus the original work may be of foreign origin.[18] Although the book has been used for street-corner divination for centuries, it is considered first and foremost a book of wisdom. Were we only to read the hexagrams, contemplate the images they engender, and consider the appended judgments for each, we would learn far more about human nature and the human condition than might reasonably be expected from a single book. Used judiciously for personal illumination, the *I Ching* is truly one of the greatest allies available to us.

Although the most reputable and best known translation is by Richard Wilhelm and Cary Baynes (with a foreword by Carl Jung), some women object to its consistently sexist terminology. An alternative is *The Quan Yin Book of Changes* by Diane Stein. I have personally consulted the *I Ching* for almost thirty years now, and I have found that especially in times of duress when objectivity is lacking, the value of its guidance is inestimable.

The *runes* are a Nordic divination tool derived by Odin, spiritual truth-seeker who voluntarily hung himself from a tree for days that he might find enlightenment. During this ordeal, he saw patterns among the branches that suggested twenty-five cross-hatched shapes, now marked upon stones that can be randomly selected to describe various life situations or spiritual challenges. In times of turmoil, the runes are blessedly positive and affirming, healing and comforting in their effect. One does not need great courage or for-titude to consult the runes; they grant the broadest and most for-giving interpretation of human foibles and difficulties. Perhaps this is due to the great sacrifice and anguish of Odin in discovering them; as hanged man, he paid the price that the runes might be a balm for human suffering.

Rune is derived from the Gothic *runa,* meaning "a secret thing, a mystery." According to Ralph Blum, author of *The Book of Runes,* the ultimate purpose of this oracle is to render us car-tographers of our own destiny: "Just as the Vikings used the runes to navigate their ships under cloudy skies, so now you can use the runes to modify your own life course. A shift of a few degrees at the beginning of a voyage will mean a vastly different position far out at sea."[19]

The simplest way to use the runes is to draw one stone only. There are spreads that give more in-depth readings, but a single rune will do. The tactile aspect of using the runes, shuffling through the bag of stones until one makes itself evident and is chosen by feel, is grounding in and of itself. And the markings look like ancient hieroglyphics, readable in a way that transcends the linear nature of the contemporary language. Symbolizing experiences of breakthrough, wholeness, defense, constraint, initiation, partner-ship, harvest, the runes arouse precognitive, primal memories, and an appreciation of the fabric of nature from which these symbols are derived.

It is noteworthy that many of the rune casters of the Teutons and Vikings were women. The anonymous author of *Saga of Erik the Red* (thirteenth century) vividly describes a mistress of runecraft:

> She wore a cloak set with stones along the hem. Around her neck and covering her head she wore a hood lined with white catskins.

In one hand she carried a staff with a knob on the end and at her belt, holding together her long dress, hung a charm pouch.[20]

The runes are deceptively simple in that they engender a childlike immediacy in our perceptions. Whenever we feel the need to hone in and eliminate the clutter of extraneous information, the runes can do the trick.

All these tools have one thing in common—they serve to elicit a state of *trance,* which shifts our consciousness beyond ordinary linear perception. A trance state is generally defined as one of complete mental absorption somewhere between waking and sleeping; it is deep musing, rapture. The word "trance" and the prefix "trans-" are identical in root, from the Latin meaning to cross, convey. Our language renders additional meanings of crossing over, going beyond, altering, as in the words transfer, transform, transmute. In fact, any word with the prefix "trans-" connotes some aspect of Transformer energy, which is both medium and mechanism of change.

We can deliberately invoke the Transformer by choosing to enter a trance state. We need not wait for mortal fear or life crisis to push us to the brink. Trance states deepen and sustain the Transformer's influence; they set the stage for her continuing input.

Another way to elicit the Transformer is through a *vision quest,* in which the seeker isolates her/himself from daily responsibilities for an extended period of time in hopes of receiving inspiration and guidance. The vision quest is of Native American derivation, and traditionally involves going to some remote location to fast or otherwise purify oneself before prayerfully invoking whatever spirits, allies, or deity one knows and trusts. This process is otherwise known as retreat—the perfect solution for chronic weariness, sadness, or longing. In this time of separation, we may descend deliberately to the underworld, to beckon transformation directly. And in the process of return and ascent, we may reweave and reconstruct our reality. Here is one woman's experience:

"For my fortieth birthday, I decided to go on a vision quest to honor the beginning of the second half of my life. I took this quest quite seriously, as I was warned by a wise friend that when I opened to lessons they would come rushing in, and there might be some hard ones. I didn't really know what to expect—I was a city girl and not used to sleeping in the woods, so I knew it would be challenging, to say the least.

"I went into a dark, unknown forest near the coast of Oregon. I walked until twilight, until I found a perfect circle of pine trees with an indentation in the center the exact size of my body, like a nest. I laid down naked in this spot, which was comfortably lined with pine needles and moss. I closed my eyes to pray for guidance and to ask permission from the pines to share this sacred space.

"As my breathing slowed, an ominous feeling crept over me—a paranoid feeling that quickly became a full-blown panic attack. My heart was crashing against my ribs, and my eyes flew open to see the largest pine looming above me as the exact twin of the tree where my dear friend, with whom I had much unresolved sexual stuff and anger, had taken his life a few years earlier. I felt claustrophobic, and as I clawed the earth to get out of the hole, my fingers closed around a twelve-gauge shotgun shell, the same as my friend had used. Holy shit! I hadn't bargained for this! My anxiety turned to nausea. I was frozen with fear and felt as though I was sinking into the earth and my nest was becoming a grave. I think I may have actually lost consciousness for a while; my lips and extremities were numb from hyperventilating. But then something gentle started flowing through me—a warm pulsing in my body that felt almost electric, the Earth, soothing and comforting, healing me. I felt like I was sinking into her soft body, her womb. I cried tears of surrender and bliss.

"My body became the Earth. As I stared up at the Milky Way, I died—died to all the sorrow and guilt I had felt, to old ways of being. New teachings came flooding in, until finally I dozed off. When the birds started to sing above me, I slowly, stiffly crawled from my nest and made my way to the shore. The fog on the water made the landscape prehistoric, mists from more primitive times. I cried for the beauty and the love I felt, and I cried in exultation at my rebirth."

In contrast to the above account, vision quests more commonly take place under the guidance of an experienced facilitator. The process is structured, so that the experience is seldom as disorienting as the one described above. Vision questing may last for ten days or more, but can certainly be modified to require less time away from work or other daily obligations. Just dropping what we are doing to take a long drive or a hike in the country can serve a similar purpose. Teacher and philosopher George Gurdjieff repeatedly advised his students that one of the keys to staying awake (conscious) in life was to take in new impressions. He was particularly fond of travel and was known to take off by train, destination unknown, for the express purpose of deconditioning himself.

Travel is our modern-day attempt at vision questing, particularly as more of us forsake a formal itinerary for offbeat experiences on the "back roads." In preference to rushing around, seeing all the sights and hitting all the hot spots, we can experience what author Ed Buryn terms *vagabonding*.[21] Vagabonding, akin to wandering, is nomadic exploration without certain course or direction. One woman we interviewed told of an extended transitional period in her life when she moved continually—she still had a home but spent very little time there, going from one friend's sofa (or guest room) to another, taking out-of-town jaunts and enjoying unusual experiences (rather like the woman who related earlier that she had nowhere to land, and liked it that way). Vagabonding is both metaphor for and means of transformation, whereas conventional travel is little more than a relocation of habitual patterns and inhibitions, intensified by the stress of moving around. No wonder we often return from vacation exhausted! In contrast, vagabonding tends to be rejuvenating because it is interactive and challenging. It helps us develop flexibility and engages our capacity for change.

Vagabonding requires that we become itinerant, learn to alternate work (concentration) and play (relaxation) as we embrace the pleasure principle as change agent. Vagabonding has its risks in that frustrating and seemingly negative experiences on the road can feel alternately like obstructions or golden opportunities to change direction—affording us a crash course in transmutation. This is snake medicine, whereby poison is ingested and rendered harmless, even nourishing. In short, vagabonding offers a highly condensed opportunity to identify deeply ingrained patterns of behavior, so that we may rescript our personal mythology.

The same can be said for sexuality as a mode of transmutation and transcendence. In chapter 8, we explore the alchemy of sex and the sacred marriage of masculine and feminine, as expressed in the philosophy of *Tantra*. Barbara Walker defines Tantra as "a system of yoni-worship, or female-centered sex-worship," founded thousands of years ago by the Vratyas, later to be known as the sacred harlots. The main tenet of Tantra is that women hold the spiritual center; thus men must unite with them both sexually and emotionally to achieve enlightenment. Although many have heard of the sacred Tantric rite of coitus reservatus known as *maithuna*, Tantra may also be practiced by consciously prolonging sexual intercourse so that desire builds to ecstasy, with ejaculation permitted. Early Gnostic

Christians called this *synesaktism,* or the Way of Shakti. Literally translated, Shakti means "cosmic energy," and is also the Indian word for yoni. A Shakti was spirit-wife, female guardian angel both incarnate and immortal. Final union with Shakti was said to occur at the moment of death.[22]

One woman we interviewed was actively engaged in Tantric practice involving both her partner and a larger circle of intimates. Here are some of her comments:

"Tantra has you look at every drop of your stuff, if you stay with it long enough. One of the things that has brought us so much closer in the last two years is that my husband has grown tired of the games men play—though he sometimes plays them himself—and is connecting with me more on a soul level, seeing me separate from a male definition. He is looking more for feminine perspective; we both are. All this has meant that I've had to let go of cultural bias, how close I can get to myself and other women. In Tantra, I like the ritual space of working with other couples and being able to get past gender, seeing us as androgynous so it's not so much male-female polarity, but the male and female in every person and to what degree they're balanced or unbalanced. It's just easier with women, especially since most men are not as much in touch and don't honor their female side."

Another woman in her fifties spoke of her experience in learning to be sexual with herself:

"I was separated from my partner, estranged really, and when I was saddest I felt most like I wanted to come in touch with myself as a sexual being—when I couldn't get any higher on wine or whatever, then I felt, well, let's go to my sex. And that made me feel much, much better, because I was touching myself, not numbing myself, coming alive instead of being dead. When I discovered this,

I got a sense of being able to take better care of myself in life, as well as sexually. To watch myself evolve a dialogue with myself, to watch myself become a better, more sensitive lover to myself, was really an interesting process. 'Cause it's like—what do I really want to hear . . . what would I really like someone to be whispering when I come?"

Along with emotional revelation, many of the physiological perks of sex—release of tension, trance breathing, total relaxation—can be found in movement therapies like yoga, tai chi, and other martial arts, not to mention various athletic activities. Any of these can be done in a meditative frame of mind, with an eye to transcendence.

Trance dance is another such option that deserves special mention. Throughout the ages, women have evolved various forms of dance to facilitate transcendence, whether alone or together. Indigenous styles of African dance, Celtic circle dance, belly dance, and Hawaiian hula have magic in their movements. Resonating with the unique sounds of traditional music, feeling our bodies take postures surprisingly subtle, graphic, or out of the ordinary, we can readily enter trance and find our way to ecstasy.

In Goddess-loving cultures, dance was an integral part of life and a primary way to raise energy for art, enterprise, or healing. But dance did not always follow a definite form; often, it was spontaneous movement in response to profound emotion or passionate intent. This sort of dancing is what I personally know best; it is what I do when nothing else will serve to release some tremendous sadness, anger, or joy welling up inside me. Sometimes I light candles and create ceremony, sometimes I dance naked near a mirror—it enhances my trance to watch the inflection of my movements. The more I witness, the deeper I go.

Certain indigenous cultures still feature what anthropologists call "possession cults," in which elder women transmit knowledge to young girls by bringing them into healing circles. Where patriarchy predominates, this process is veiled by the pretense that these girls are possessed by evil spirits and must be delivered by women with experience. The main feature of this widespread practice is "ecstasy," as everyone in the circle takes on the invading spirits and dances them out again for healing. These celebrations of women's ecstatic power are accepted by the men of these cultures because they both fear and respect magic, and concede certain privileges to women for their apparent facility with it.[23]

Another component of trance dancing is *trance sounding*—letting any tone, word, song, call, or scream that arises surge out in response to movement. Sounding is itself a vehicle for entering trance; it is a classic component of certain types of meditation. The sounds we make spontaneously when making love, when in great sorrow or pain, when giving birth or witnessing great beauty, represent our deepest capacity to feel. As we release similar sounds in trance, we link to the essential human experience and get in touch with our ground of being

Yet another avenue for transformation is *breath work*. Trance-inducing breathing practices are found in numerous cultures, and are integral to various spiritual traditions. Trance breath work changes body chemistry; it alters the oxygen and carbon dioxide ratio in such a way that consciousness is altered as well.

There are many approaches to breath work; I will mention two. The first, known as rebirthing breathing, is a slow, deliberate pattern of circular breathing, with no pause either on inhalation or exhalation. The breath is continuous, round. This technique induces deep relaxation, and a fine and subtle state of mind. It is a refreshing practice, deeply integrating and excellent for developing concentration. Practitioners report gentle and positive experiences with this breathing technique. On one occasion I did it with a lover, and had visions of two snakes twirling round a staff in perfect synchrony, coming face to face with each exhalation. I later read in an alchemical text that twin serpents wrapped around the staff of life are a symbol of egalitarian sexual interaction.

The second breathing method, which produces more dramatic results, is similar to both the Kundalini breath of fire and the holotropic technique popularized by psychotherapist Stan Grof.[24] This practice involves forced inhalation with brief, spontaneous exhalation, which leads to hyperventilation and the release of DMT (a biochemical substance known to induce visions) in the brain and spinal column. Occasionally, muscle spasms occur. The first time I tried it I experienced great pain in the exact area of one arm that had given me trouble when I was Rolfed years earlier, only now I was able to get to the root of my trauma. Nonverbal revelations were transmitted throughout my entire body; I felt I was being reimprinted on a cellular level.

It is helpful to have a guide or partner for this work, particularly the first time. The two of you can take turns—one does the breathing while the other bears witness. When it is your turn to keep watch, refrain from touching your partner even if she yells or cries out; these are normal reactions to the intensity of this work. Your touch, no matter how sensitive and well intentioned, can prevent or interfere with her breakthrough. If breakthrough does occur, you will notice a spontaneous change in breathing and countenance, with deep physical relaxation and ecstatic demeanor.

My first experience with this work was a turning point in my life. I had been feeling directionless and insecure with my activities but didn't know why, didn't know what needed to be changed. When I began the breathing I felt nothing but agony, and kept trying to find a way to escape or get through my pain. When Carol (who guided me) suggested I ease up, I learned a lesson life has handed me repeatedly, that the direct way is not always the shortest or the best. Once I surrendered, I broke through to a visionary realm. I was in the body of an animal—I could feel myself running across rugged terrain incredibly fast and very surefootedly, and it dawned on me that I had become a wolf. (This was long before *Women Who Run with the Wolves* had been published.) Eventually, I came to a clearing where a council was taking place, and a half circle of wolves gathered to face me. One came forward to me and brought her face close to mine. She did not speak, but told me of my fate with her eyes and reassured me of my place in life. About this time, Carol quietly suggested that I might be meeting a totem animal, and after a few deep breaths I managed to utter, "I already have!"

The second time I practiced this breath work was in a large circle of women, after a day of preparatory ritual. My experience was completely different, not as visionary as before but more ecstatic. Carol was once again my guide, and later reported that I had levitated! All I know is that I felt totally fulfilled, in a state of highly sexual yet spiritual transcendence. I reached a point with the breathing where I could slow it way down to savor the ecstasy more fully, then pick up the rhythm again to go further, higher. My prime revelation was that I had learned how to die—I understood how I could transcend pain and embrace the transformation of death.

After my first experience, I read up on the wolf as totem animal. I learned that she represents the teacher; one who is loyal and caring, yet wild and roaming with curiosity. Several months later, a Native American woman came to study midwifery with me, and commented at our first meeting that I walked with a wolf by my side. Another time, when I lay in the afterglow of a wonderfully loving and playful sexual encounter, I had visions of wolf cubs rolling and tumbling together. I also called the wolf into all-night ceremony on one occasion, and she came to me and to all that were present.

There are many other tools and practices for transformation. Native American Medicine Cards, or the Sacred Path Cards (of similar derivation) are powerful divination tools. Art therapy, hypnotherapy, trance journeying, ritual drumming, or singing can also serve to facilitate transformation, as can numerous spiritual practices and disciplines. Perhaps the key is in the toolbox; if we can learn to recognize when a tool is old and worn, we can refurbish or replace it with something else. Different tools become useful at different points in the lifecycle. Geared as we are to finding a single mode of expression and sticking to it, we must, paradoxically, work hard at being playful with our options, childlike in trying the new.

CHAPTER 5

The Daughter and the Amazon

On occasion, I participate in an all-night singing ceremony with a group of women friends. Frequently, I find that I form a special bond with the woman sitting directly opposite me. This is undoubtedly due to direct eye contact over an extended period of time, but too, it often seems that we bear complementary messages for each other, or perhaps our polarity within the circle evokes these.

Similarly, archetypes opposite one another on the Circle of Life are strongly connected. The earlier stage bears seeds that will mature in the latter, and the latter stage taps the earlier one for source energy, remembrance, and rejuvenation.

The Daughter and the Amazon, for example, have much in common. Both represent the initiatory energy of their respective phases—the Daughter expresses innocence at life's inception, while the Amazon re-creates her original, independent self as foundation for her power period. Both experience rapid, surging growth—the Daughter in a literal, physical sense, the Amazon through psychological maturation. Their head-over-heels lust for life is fueled by fiery passion; both are nearly insatiable in their longing for new experiences, new sensations, and new, exciting relationships. The sheer wildness of these desires tends to provoke others to repress them, particularly during the Amazon phase, when society interprets the freedom quest as an adolescent regression. Amazon women may indeed appear immature to the uncomprehending, as they shoot off their mouths, act out in public, experiment boldly with dress and speech, and take new, perhaps even younger lovers. Yet these are simply ways to reconnect with the essence of the Daughter, her high-spirited intelligence, playfulness, and autonomy. As one woman, age forty-five and self-identified as Amazon, stated:

> "I'm very much into the 'virginity' of holding on to myself. I may have relationships with men or women, but holding to myself is important to me right now, and a hard one to hang on to when you have love affairs. You have to constantly call it back—it's a conscious thing, for me anyway, and it doesn't happen easily."

Both Daughter and Amazon soon discern that which gives true nourishment, so imperative is their need for continual regeneration. The Daughter needs food, exercise, adequate sleep, and plenty of play in order to thrive. The Amazon needs focus for her passions, in order to elicit the intensity she requires. In this regard she is less experimental than intent, seeking connections that sustain her, holding on to these as long as they serve, then moving on. Thus we associate the Amazon with the warrior archetype; she has single-minded concentration, she enlists her deepest resources for survival and will fight to the death for freedom.

A classic example of the Amazon warrior is Joan of Arc. She claimed to have received a vision of her mission at the "tree of the Fairy-ladies," a power site for members of the French Dianic cult.[1] Dianic cults were found throughout Europe in the fifteenth century, and were in fact feminist groups focused on goddess worship. At first, Joan of Arc was glorified by the Catholic Church for her heroism, but was later burned as a heretic. I believe many women have cellular memory of the burning times, which has encoded caution against fighting for our freedom. We are further intimidated by cultural constraints that would keep us forever mothering—if not our own children, then society at large. Perhaps this is why so few women find the courage to go beyond the nurturing phase of the life cycle, fearing ridicule, loss of position, or punishment more severe.

> "Right now, I feel like I'm re-searching who I am *not* as a mother. And since I'm not with my children's father, I have a lot of freedom that way. I'm coming into my power, not caring what society thinks. To a certain extent I care—I still have children in public school and I have to have credibility in the community. There's a role that I play in society and I want my role to be acceptable, but also, I *choose* what I show. I know how to hide what needs to be hidden and show what needs to be shown—these are my choices, not society's choices."

Vicki Noble ties the Amazon to the tarot card of Chariot, "Winning One's Own Way."[2] She too links Virgin and Amazon, in their shared imperative to focus less on relationships than on their own work. In the case of the Daughter, this involves individuation from the mother and for the Amazon, separating the self from the mothering role. A woman in her late sixties recalls:

"I think of my Midwife time as that when I went back to teaching, when I left my smaller arena and went on to a more social arena. I cared very much about those little kids I was working with—very much. As a Mother I had no feeling of power, not that it was a feeling I missed, but when I began to work and have success I did start to have power feelings, which probably peaked in the years when my ability was recognized and I was made a Master Teacher. This was the beginning of my Amazon stage, when I really began to feel pride and satisfaction and some sense of accomplishment in myself. There was another factor too—I was still good-looking then, and the combination of knowing that I was good at what I did and was also good-looking, with all these men around me at my mercy [laughs]. . . . Yes, I can relate to the Amazon. It was quite a feeling, a new feeling for me. I think this is why the forties are fabulous—you have this great sense of personal power and worth and self-esteem."

Finding true self-worth may require time out, a break with the past. Again, this is greatly at odds with society's expectations—how dare a woman prioritize time for herself? This account from a woman, age forty-eight, serves to illustrate:

"I worked in the system for two years and then I said, 'I'm not doing this anymore, it isn't serving me or anyone.' I took some time off and went traveling, and during this time, my father died. We had an incredible karmic relationship, very tumultuous, and when he died I felt released, liberated. That's what catapulted me into the Amazon. I started a private practice, a holistic health practice. This was definitely my Amazon time—I was in a relationship, but it was not my focus. My focus was on creating something in my work that was *vastly* different than what was available. It was immensely satisfying and also a huge headache."

And from another woman, age forty-three:

"I was old when I was young; I never had the time I have now. Now when I drive around and I'm free and I don't have to be any place at three in the afternoon and can keep on working or do all the social stuff I want, I feel like the teenager I never was. I'm not into mothering right now because my children have gone to live with their father and I'm free to do what I want: use my power for what I want to do. I've been mothering for twenty-five years. . . . I'm not sitting around carving pumpkins anymore. My business is supplying fifty-eight stores with a line of botanical products. This is feeding me, not just financially but in terms of feeling successful.

"I kind of feel like a guy. I drive around in my car getting coffee and donuts to-go, then on to some store to show my line and set up a new account. I walk out thinking, 'Gee, I feel like a guy!' Maybe I'll have the kids on the weekend and maybe I won't. I don't have to be a mother. I feel very male. Original integrity of purpose, that's what I'm doing. *My* purpose. This is all new to me. Exciting. Interesting. Sometimes scary. There are probably only five other women in the business and we all gravitate to each other and talk.

"Also, I'm pissed these days. I represented myself in court during the divorce, and I felt like a second-class citizen; I didn't feel like I got equal time in there. This last hearing, I felt that they were outright condescending to me for representing myself. Women in the courthouse are not treated like white males are. I don't know where all this Amazon energy is going to take me—I like the freedom, but then I think of my experience as a woman and mother over the last two decades, and I get angry."

Amazons were powerfully portrayed in both Greek and Roman art. In his writings, Herodotus linked them to the transitional period between matriarchal and patriarchal times. These women found meaning apart from men; they tended to separate into all-women tribes. One contemporary notion is that the Amazons chose this lifestyle by default, being either too unattractive or unstable to sustain a heterosexual relationship. Yet artistic representations prove the opposite case—Amazons were elegant, powerful women of so much strength, vision, and intensity that they were probably unsuited to the domestic life of their era. The classic Amazon goddess is Artemis/Diana, who represents female autonomy and self-reliant physical prowess. Portrayed as a ruthless huntress, she sought the destruction of gods who had presumed too much on their power or privilege. Yet she was equally diligent in nurturing that which could not fend for itself, life fragile or new. To the beasts and little children she was Queen: strong, tender, and beautiful.

Another Amazon figure is the fictional Eowyn, from J. R. R. Tolkien's *Lord of the Rings* trilogy. Disappointed in love, bereft of the man she believes to be her intended, she falls back on herself and finds strength in defending her homeland and kin. There is an unforgettable scene near the end of the trilogy when, utterly desolate and tottering with injury and exhaustion, she deals a final blow to the forces of evil. Free of both hope and despair, concentrated only on the moment, on meeting this consummate challenge with everything she's got, she is the quintessential Amazon.

Eowyn's descent to her core resources is the mature counterpart of Persephone's descent to the underworld. The standard version of the Persephone myth tells that she was raped and abducted by Hades, when in fact Persephone was known as the Queen of the Underworld long before Hades entered the picture. Charlene Spretnak has thankfully reconstructed a pre-Olympian version of Persephone's journey, based on the pre–Indo-European belief system of Greece combined with Egyptian mythology. She concludes that the rape of Persephone was a late addition to the myth, a reference to the occupation of Greece by patriarchal tribes. In her version, Persephone was compassionate and highly sensitive not only to new life, but to the souls of the newly dead, and thus quested for the underworld of her own free will. In mortal fear, Persephone's mother, Demeter, tried to discourage her daughter; when she departed regardless, Demeter withdrew her life-giving force from nature and the first winter ensued. Persephone's work with the dead was complex and emotionally rending, but she survived and reunited with her mother, whose joy spontaneously brought the return of springtime.[3]

So may the Daughter, recently come from the Transformer herself, make a similar descent without fear and of her own volition. She remembers the previous stage of Dark Mother, she who opens the portal of death, just as the Amazon remembers the lessons of the Midwife who shows that surrender, not force, is how we discover the strength to give birth.

Here is one woman's experience at age thirty-eight:

"I'd just had my fourth child, and was getting back into my career. Somewhat impulsively, I decided to attend a conference on intuition, a topic definitely outside my field. I was also at a point in my personal life where something needed to change, some new me was trying to emerge. In one of the workshops, I did an extended, guided visualization I later identified as a Persephone quest. We were led in trance to descend deep into the earth, through rock tunnels and a series of gates. At each gate, we removed some article of clothing that represented an aspect of ourselves in the outer world, getting more and more basic as we went. At last, naked and pure, we were brought to meet a guide at the very bottom. For me, this was an old woman, ancient and haggard. I never will forget the rustle of her garments and how the dim light reflected on the folds of her sleeve as she reached to pull from her robe a rose, perfect dewy fresh, the softest pink, luminescent. 'The flower of my girlhood,' I realized, and felt it one of the greatest gifts I'd ever been given. Even now, when I need guidance I cannot find anywhere else, I go to her—I know now that she is always there."

Implicit in the Amazon taking her power is reconnection with herself as Daughter. Another woman concurs:

"I was the youngest of four, and I was pretty and bright and cheerful and everybody loved me. Maybe in my case, maybe because I had that early affection from my mother and strong regard for myself as a mother, I was able to enjoy and accept the powerful feelings and experiences I had later in the Amazon stage."

Sometimes we return to the Daughter later in life simply to have a little fun. Have you ever found yourself longing for the simplicity of girlhood activities, tempted to get out the crayons or watercolors, go horseback riding or roller skating after many years? A woman in her forties relates:

"I had my children later in life; my youngest just turned four. When we play, I often find myself remembering games and activities I had long forgotten, moments of joy and satisfaction buried deep in my memory. I especially remember coloring for hours, taking great care with my work and being much more concerned with the process than the result. Reexperiencing these memories has changed my self-concept—I really am a playful person, I just forgot how to be that way!"

On the other hand, a less than optimal childhood can stimulate premature Amazonian tendencies:

"As for my Daughter time, I never felt like I came from my mother's body. It's interesting—I was reading about Athena, how she was born from the head of Zeus. I related to that—I didn't get much mothering growing up. I don't remember those little daughterlike things I've tried to supply my girls. My mother was going to give me up for adoption—maybe she should have. The mothering I did get was from my grandmother, but there were all these weird power trips between my mother and grandmother, and my grandfather was very controlling and macho. I was sad to feel all this stuff at such an early age. And my grandmother sheltered me, cloistered me almost. She home-schooled me for a while, but when I finally went to public school I walked home and said, 'I'm out of here.' So that was the start of the Amazon for me."

And from another woman, age seventy:

"I just remembered something that happened to me when I was six or seven. My father took me down to get school shoes. He was very particular about the fit of my shoes because he had been a shoe salesman. Apparently I had my mind set on some patent leather shoes and that wasn't what he had in mind. So I came home with a kind of oxford or saddle shoe. I didn't like the shoes, so I filled up the bathtub with water and put the shoes in the tub.

"I don't really feel much different now than I did then, except I'm a little freer. I don't feel much wiser—just *freer*—being able to do what I want because I don't have the responsibility of a family; I'm on my own. I don't feel terribly connected to my children right now; everybody seems to be doing their own thing—they don't seem to need me. I certainly don't have the connectedness a lot of my friends have, being with their grandchildren all the time, having them in their life all the time. I don't live that way. Maybe that's a selfish thing? I feel if they needed me, I'd be there but everyone seems to be pretty independent.

"I've been on my own since I was eight and my mother died. I guess I'm an Amazon, pretty much on my own. Maybe that's why I don't have any great need to be in the middle of the family, surrounded by family. I'm no Crone—I'm not ready to hang up my cleats yet or my cowboy boots. I'll do my Croning Rite at the nursing home!"

Sometimes, though, the Daughter needs deep healing in order for her Amazonian counterpart to seize the reins of her own existence. Usually this involves an experience of descent in order to recontact the Daughter and heal her at the site of injury, or wherever her growth was curtailed. A woman in her mid-thirties relates her own passage:

"Right now, I feel like I'm both four and forty. I'm remembering who I was when I got here, before I was socialized, coming back to little girl places that are primal and playful.

"My crossover to Amazon happened in nursing school last year. I was confronted with such patriarchal energy that I could no longer survive as a nurturer—no one would accept me that way, it was not allowed in any context. Things got to be so extreme that I couldn't waver—I either had to give up my power, or assume it. A lot of what I was dealing with was repression of women and women's sexuality, the annihilation of women in birth.

"At the same time, I was shaking off the bonds of how I was defined as a nurturer in other parts of my life. I got annihilated as a Daughter; my innocence was ripped off by my brother putting his penis in my mouth, and I minimized this, compared it to going to the dentist—uncomfortable, but life goes on. And my mother's denial forced me to nurture her *and* my brother. I do like giving, but in this case, it was the only vehicle I was allowed for controlling my own destiny. Nurturing is not power, it's a gift; you have to give it freely, and if you're not giving it freely but are using it to get propelled to where you need to go, it doesn't work. Having my spirit broken in school brought up weird, repressed shades of my mother that catapulted me into the Amazon and back to the Daughter.

"I came here a primal being, with Dark Mother energy all around me. I was fascinated at an early age with sexuality, birth, creation, tide pools, cleaning fish—anything having to do with unveiling. I think most little girls are like this until they're socialized. When my innocence was ripped off, I never progressed to the stage of the Maiden. Now I feel like I have enough power to own my pain and not blame it on anyone else—now, if I deny my maidenhood, it's my own responsibility."

We can derive broader context for the above account by reviewing the holy days of both Daughter and Amazon stages. Imbolc, or Saint Brigit's Day, is a time for Daughters to be initiated in the way of the Goddess (and for older women, a time to rededicate to their highest ideals). Lammas, holy day of the Amazon, celebrates the first harvest and, in a spiritual sense, reveals how well the self has weathered the challenges of maturation. To a large extent, the way in which a young girl is initiated as Daughter determines these first fruits—whether she will harvest her power with strength and certainty or with confusion and regression.

For the Amazon, fruits of self-determination, inspiration, and freedom suit her for a special kind of leadership. At her best, the Amazon is inspired to be truly herself, and as such, becomes truly inspirational to others. She leads by purity of intent, rekindling her innocence as Daughter. She encourages forthright self-expression in everyone she meets, in every situation she encounters. She urges others to take their power as she has, to the benefit of all. Unlike leadership in the nurturing phase, which laments imperfections and seeks to repair that which is troubled or broken, leadership in the

Amazon phase is simple and direct, based on taking action and moving on to the next challenge.

I recall one of my songs in an all-night ceremony some years ago, a song of sadness for women in pain all over the world, for women who were (or who let themselves be) repressed. As I sang, another women in the circle returned with, "Free your sister, free yourself," which became a refrain in the moment (and for me personally in the months that followed). Several stanzas later I added, "And it's the easiest thing," as it dawned on me that being truly myself, being authentic, was my only hope of helping others. As the traditional Charge of the Goddess (commonly used in ceremonies in her honor) states:

> You who seek to know Me, know that your seeking and yearning will avail you not, unless you know the Mystery: if that which you seek, you find not within yourself, you will never find it without.[4]

Both the Amazon and Daughter are headstrong, spontaneous, and outspoken. This may get them into a considerable amount of trouble—particularly the Amazon, who is alert to shock value and will put herself on the line to prove a point. Yet the Daughter is decidedly more vulnerable due to her youth and innocence. How many of us remember speaking out some obvious truth or insight in our early years, only to be hushed by someone in authority? Numerous studies have shown that our education system consistently favors boys: they are called upon more often in class, and standard teaching methodologies are geared to male problem-solving methods. This does not stop little girls from piping up with intuitive or perceptual assessments, only to be ridiculed for being unable to explain how or why they know what they know. In this regard, the goddess Athena is lodestar for the Daughter and Amazon alike, embodying wisdom not only of mind, but also of heart. Her shadow aspect is Medusa, whose snake hair represents nonintellectual ways of knowing, as does the owl, mistress of darkness and Athena's close companion. Athena further represents the Amazon (and the Daughter fighting to be heard) by virtue of her surname, Pallas, which means storm or battle.

According to Christine Downing, author of *The Goddess: Mythological Images of the Feminine,* "Athena is not a virgin in order to be alone, but in order to be with others without entanglement." And she is "androgynous . . . not a goddess of procreation, but of creation."[5] It is on this basis that the Amazon often forms deep bonds and friendships, even intimacies, with women, regardless whether she has had this sort of experience before.

Thus she is similar to Artemis, who Zsuzsanna Budapest gives voice in her book *The Grandmother of Time:*

> I am on fire. I am in love with all lovable creatures of the world. . . . Raised by a she-bear on the mountains, you can imagine that I am wild and love to roam. . . . I am possessed by a hungry, grown-up kind of love. I am yearning for my mate, my she-bear lover. . . . I give courage to women, and self-knowledge. My strength comes from loving myself, and there is enough to give you some too.[6]

The shifting sexual needs and desires of Amazon women may be due in part to hormonal changes characteristic of this period, which typically occur between the ages of thirty-five and forty. About this time, estrogen and progesterone levels begin to decline, while androgens (testosterone-like substances secreted by the adrenal glands) begin to increase. Androgens move us to be more assertive, sexually and otherwise. As our reproductive hormones diminish, we find ourselves less interested in partnering for procreation than for self-realization and personal growth. This may lead to more autonomy in our relations with men and to greater intimacy with women.

EARTH MYSTERY SCHOOL

For the past several years, I have offered a summer camp for young women aged seven to fourteen, called the Earth Mystery School. This school is based on the ancient mystery traditions of instructing young girls about their power and "otherworldly" abilities before they reach the age of conforming to consensus reality and become "adult." Ironically, the original mystery schools for young women were converted to convents with the Christianization of Europe.

Camp sessions run for two weeks. The final night, scheduled around the full moon, includes a sleep-over and performance for the girl's female relatives.

When I first met with my women friends to plan curriculum, we all simultaneously cited *freedom* as our ultimate goal for the girls. The purpose of the school is to foster spiritual emergence, to celebrate the feminine and the goddess within. We felt it imperative that young women see their femaleness as sacred and holy, the feminine principle as divine and the art of womancraft as wholesome and empowering. We wanted to emphasize the feminine in order to contribute to a healthy balance of male and female energies and activities in society.

The first year we presented goddess traditions and ceremonies, focusing on a different heritage each day. We included Native American, African, Greek, Celtic, and lunar goddesses, plus the Gaia hypothesis. Daily arts and crafts activities involved clay work, bead work, shamanic mask making, wreath making, basket weaving, the making of spirit dolls and simple musical instruments, and the construction of a Medicine Wheel. We led guided visualizations to find totem animals, taught yoga practices, led natural history walks, did circle and African dancing, healing-touch bodywork, and storytelling, and performed a full moon ritual on the final night (featuring a not-too-hot sweat lodge).

The second year, our curriculum revolved around the holy days on the Wheel of the Year, including the Sabbats and their respective ceremonies. We made flower crowns and May wine, medicine bags, group tribal drums, and dream catchers; practiced chanting and drumming; and studied herbal lore. The last day included swimming, sailing, and another nighttime performance. The girls choreographed a very beautiful and moving rendition of the video *The Burning Times* danced by torchlight. There wasn't a dry eye in the house!

Our theme last year was "Healing Ourselves, Healing Mother Earth/Women's Ways of Knowing." Daily activities included making herbal necklaces, paper and sacred shields, identifying and pressing flowers, word weaving, the study of ecology, and trance work. Each girl chose a green ally and goddess to research for the final evening's performance. We studied the chakras and their colors, and surveyed the healing arts of polarity, meditation, art therapy, herbology, and homeopathy. This was a fairly demanding curriculum, and we were a little concerned that the younger girls would get restless during the long periods of silent concentration, but they were great! We also interspersed lecture times with strenuous physical activity like archery, to release a little wild energy. On their last night, the daughters dressed as their goddesses (they actually became their goddesses) and performed a dance they called "The Many Faces of SHE." Earth Mystery School works because it combines powerful knowledge with outright fun.

Directing and teaching at the school has been a very special privilege for me, as I had the honor of attending many of these young women when they were born and now am able to help midwife them into their power at the brink of Maidenhood. It is a great gift to see these young women vibrant and confident, with a very healthy attitude about themselves and their place in the world.

Women in other communities have started similar summer school experiences for their daughters. This is a positive way to impress upon growing girls their natural beauty and strength so they will take these things for granted, rather than have to struggle until their mid-forties to find out how great they really are.

—C. LEONARD

Amazons come to know the third Blood Mystery of blood bonding as they recognize the power of menstruation and their profound connection to other women because of it. Particularly if women live, work, and circle together, their cycles may synchronize and lead them to discover new emotional and psychic dimensions of the blood tide:

"Recently I was asked by my lover how I felt about my blood and I just said, 'Well, I'm crazy about it.' I wasn't crazy about it when I was fifteen—but now I am. There are times when I want to paint my face with it; I just *love* my blood. I think it's the whole miracle of the cycle, the connection with the moon, with the tides. I love all that about it—it's a beautiful color, I like the smell of it, and I feel there's something really magical and mysterious about it. I'm excited that my lover is interested in it. I feel like it has this incredible power that I want to do something with before menopause. I know that eventually I won't have it anymore, so I want to do something to honor it."

The wildness of the Amazon years is prompted by our culture's disregard for menarche and childbirth as rites of passage, our separation from the natural world, our lack of ritual celebrations that honor women's traditions, and our sweeping desacralization of life in general. The hallmark of this period is the determination to get beyond normal definitions of reality to find both freedom and support. The Amazon stage is one of rebirth; it is the first stage in the second half of life, the beginning of truly self-determined adulthood. To fully embrace the potential of this time, women must transcend social constraints that would keep them forever in nurturing roles. This may involve a return to the experimentalism of young adulthood, rekindling interests in philosophy, spirituality, alternative healing, alternative lifestyle, altered states. In this, the Amazon is similar to the Blood Sister who thrills to the freedom of being on her own for the first time and greedily explores her sensuality, sexuality, power, and intelligence.

A woman, age forty-five, recalls an extraordinary experience with a friend during her Amazon years:

"My circle meets every full moon, and sometimes on the new moon we have a workshop where we trade a skill in womancraft. Some of our work has centered on ritual, deep trance, and intense breath work, and sometimes we have used mind-altering substances to enhance our activities.

"In this vein, one of the younger women in the circle and I decided to do a Coming of Age Rite for her before she was to leave for California. We created sacred space in a quiet, private place in the woods, and used a combination of the methods listed above to trigger our experience. Before long, I became nauseated and grew very anxious—something was happening to me that had never happened before. I felt hot—too hot. My extremities and mouth area were completely numb. I managed to shed my clothes, and crawled down the ravine to the stream below. I began rolling in the mud to cool myself, and as I wallowed, great snorting, unearthly sounds came from me. My face felt heavy and disfigured, elongating, and my nervous laughter changed to guttural grunts. I felt surprise and horror until I realized what was happening: I was becoming my totem, the boar-woman. I went back up the ravine, hooves tapping—I could feel my hard, muscled body under a mat of thick, wiry bristles, and many small pointed teats swayed on my underside as I jogged up the hill.

"When I returned to the clearing, I looked into the branches above and saw my friend there, her legs lazily hanging over a high limb, her head turned as she casually licked her fur with a long, rough tongue. The sunlight gleamed on her thick, coppery mane and she yawned, exposing sharp, scissoring teeth. She sprang down, and we were off together.

"For the rest of the day we padded and trotted through the forest, exploring. Occasionally, the lioness would streak ahead, a blur of russet color, her muscles rippling. I was content to bulldoze the earth with my tusks, and scrape tree trunks in search of fat worms, insects, and snails. After many hours, there came a great rain and wind storm, and we found ourselves, rather disoriented, in a neighbor's field.

"The next morning, I had tremendous pain in my mouth where my canine teeth had elongated, and my friend had lacerations on her feet. But this shape-shifting experience linked us as sisters, bonded us in a way we will never forget."

The Amazon is definitely the trailblazer, the pathfinder. She will stand up and be counted, she will insist on being heard, and she won't take no for an answer. She will valiantly defend all that is innocent, in honor of youth and her own self as Daughter. She will take her pleasure where she finds it—in love, she pledges her heart to those who are true. She will range far and wide to find nourishment for her burgeoning personal power. And she will use this power to assume the more stable role of the Matriarch, drawing on wisdom acquired during her explorations and discoveries as Amazonian wild woman.

CHAPTER 6

The Maiden and the Matriarch

Both Maiden and Matriarch are at the peak of their respective phases of innocence and power. The Maiden realizes the transformation from childhood to womanhood in her blood rite of menarche. The Matriarch similarly transforms the lessons of all previous phases to a new and balanced expression of power deeply rooted in her femininity.

For each, the signifying moon is equally dark and light. The Maiden will wax and the Matriarch wane, but for now both are in perfect equilibrium, perfect harmony. This harmony lends to each an undeniable magnetic beauty. In the Maiden's case, this is the budding of sexual attractiveness, the first flowers of her springtime. For the Matriarch, this is elegance and grace, a fine combination of physical vitality and worldliness, the harvest of all she has worked for and experienced.

Both Maiden and Matriarch are honored at their respective equinox celebrations. The northern European word for vernal equinox is *oestre,* meaning womb. (*Oestre* is actually derived from *astarte,* a Middle Eastern word for womb.) We rejoice when life stirs anew in spring; the earth is again receptive to seed and vital forces surge once more. As the fertility of the earth is kindled, the girl becomes maiden, dancing the potential of regeneration in her sensuality and the flow of her menses. The red of passion and the white of innocence combine in the pink buds and early blooms of this season.

The autumn equinox is the polar opposite, a time when the growing season is over, the harvest realized and seeds collected and borne inward. The coming of fall coincides with the astrological phase of Libra, whose scales signify elements of karma and justice. This day is also called Mabon, or Witches' Thanksgiving, when the last grain harvested is traditionally plaited, to be kept in an honored place and brought into ceremony the following year. The blaze of dying leaves, the sweetness and richness of the final crops represent the Matriarch's potent maturity.

Maturity is a word with negative connotations in our culture. Yet both Maiden and Matriarch find that maturation brings stability and an effortless sort of leadership. The Maiden consolidates childhood integrity of purpose with ripe readiness to step out in the world. She draws others to herself by virtue of her openness, loveliness, and vision, her purity and promise of fertility. Although she is young and may not yet know her work in the world, she knows her natural self and her natural place in the scheme of things.

Of course, there is plenty in our culture to corrupt her tender self-confidence. Any girl who watches television or reads fashion magazines will feel a split between her inner and outer aspects, and will soon be persuaded that the latter is of greater importance.

Even as young as eight or nine, girls begin to agonize over less than ideal physical features and become obsessed with putting together "the look" in every detail. This preoccupation occludes the fragile beauty of this transforming time, taking young women away from themselves and making them more susceptible to domination of one kind or another.

A potent intervention in this regard is proper honoring of the first menses. A general description of the Menarche Rite can be found later in this chapter, but here is a young woman's account of her own experience.

"I remember wanting to get my period because then I'd be a woman and I felt like, 'Wow.' I used to go to these meetings with my mom and the older women would talk about it; it was such a common thing that was always talked about. PMS, you know—they'd kid around about it. When my mom's friends bled at the same time, it was like this really bonding thing between them and I always wanted to be a part of that. And then I got my period—I woke up and I was so excited! I had just started seventh grade I think, and I felt so much older and wiser.

"The Menarche Rite was my mom's idea. She had read about it and brought the idea home to me. At first I didn't want to do it because it was my own private thing, but then I thought . . . it might be fun . . . it'll be fun! My mom and I talked about it and I read lots of books about it and then we started to plan the ritual. I was having so much fun with it. I was really excited about this high-mark rite where I could become a woman and all my closest friends and all the women that had always been closest to me all my life would be there.

"We planned it out on note cards. Everybody had different things that they would do. We set up an altar with family photographs of all the women before me. My mother and I brought flowers. We made a little altar with tampons and pads all over it and candles—it was so beautiful. I had a beautiful silk dress my mother had gotten for me . . . I can't remember if I wore that or the Indian cowrie shell dress first because I was totally in a daze. I just loved it! It was *my* ritual! All the rituals I had been to before were for celebrating the cycles of the Earth, but this one was *my* rite and it was such a wonderful feeling. I felt grown up—part of the circle of women.

"We decided to do this clay thing, although at first I was really shy about my body but then I decided, 'Sure.' It was a neat rebirth thing. We got clay, and the girls who hadn't gotten their periods yet—my little cousins and a couple of friends—covered my whole body with it. It was a mess [laughs], and then Rosie, my older cousin, washed it off with my best friend, Carrie. I took a shower after that because I was so messy. Then we put oils on my body and I just felt so wonderful; my skin felt so soft afterwards. Then I burned my underpants that had my first bloodstains in the fireplace, as a letting go of my childhood—I made that part up myself.

"Now I look at my bleeding as a natural thing and not at all a pain in the ass. Lots of my girlfriends groan and say, 'Oh, God, I've got my period,' like it's a bad thing. I look at it as such a beautiful thing that millions of women have gone through, and the ritual made me feel that way. I have my menarche box at home with all my stuff in it—I'm really thankful for that honoring."

One of the most important effects of these rituals is to counteract media-induced self-centeredness and isolation with the pleasure of sisterhood. When a Maiden finds her place in the community of women, she knows there is always somewhere to go for advice, solace, insight. She has a home in an extended family, even as she begins to outgrow her biological nest. She sees menarche in a life-cycle context of finding love, having children, growing old and wise. Imagine her excitement when another of her girlhood friends reaches maturity and is ready for her Menarche Rite, and it is her turn guide her peer across this magical threshold. These experiences are her foundation for a Blood Sister stage imbued with trust, honor, and love.

> "When I got my period, I was really excited because I knew that I could actually have a baby. My mother was great about teaching me and my sisters what sex was, what happened at different phases of puberty. She gave us books to read, with pictures, so I knew what to expect. I remember I kept looking at my first blood, and I couldn't believe it was coming out of me, that I could actually get pregnant! We didn't have a big celebration, but my mom told me what precautions to take, how to use different types of protection. I remember the smell of the blood. When I was younger, I used to lay my head on my mom's belly and smell that particular smell and I remember thinking, 'I have the smell now!' It was a wonderful experience. I felt much closer to my sisters who were already bleeding."

THE MENARCHE INITIATION RITE

Women have definite physiologic milestones that herald major life transitions. There was a time when these transitions were held holy and served to connect us with the rhythms and cycles of the seasons and the moon. The first of these milestones is the Menarche Initiation Rite, held at the time of a young woman's first menses to honor her crossing from girlhood to womanhood.

In the past it was customary to mark this major change in a woman's life with a special observance or celebration; it was the most essential of all initiation rites. Anticipation of this honoring helped the girl greet her first bleeding with joy and triumph.

In nonindustrialized societies, seclusion is a nearly universal response to menarche. This is not out of fear, but in reverence for the sacred power of menstrual blood. In some indigenous cultures, girls are isolated for several years. Young Dyak women in southeast Asia spend a year in a white cabin, wearing white clothes and eating white foods only (thought to ensure good health).[1] While alone, they contemplate their transformation to womanhood and consider what society expects of them. Elder women visit periodically to teach the art and craft of womanhood, including the responsibilities of sexuality and child rearing. This has enormous impact on their personal growth.

One of the most beautiful examples of menarche initiation is the Changing Woman Apache Rite. In this solemn ceremony, the pubescent girl becomes the primordial Apache mother, White Painted Woman. She then enacts the tale of Changing Woman who, impregnated by the sun, gave birth to the Apache people. On the first day of this rite, the girl is sprinkled with yellow cat-tail pollen to symbolize fertility, and is taught by tribal wise women of the "fire within," her sacred sexuality. The ceremony lasts for four days, in honor of the Four Directions. On the final night, the young woman must dance from sunset to sunrise for the well-being of her people. At dawn, this song is sung to her:

> Now you are entering the world.
> You will become an adult with responsibilities . . .
> Walk with honor and dignity.
> Be strong!
> For you are the mother of our people . . .
> For you will become the mother of a nation.[2]

Although a four-day ritual may seem excessive in the context of our busy lifestyles, its purpose of enabling young women to experience heightened awareness of their new status and power is highly relevant. Menarche rites of today can range from a formal ceremony to a simple gathering of special women friends and relatives for a wonderful meal together. The main idea is to distinguish this milestone event from everyday life. Women across the country are currently recreating these ceremonies for their daughters. But it is crucial that young women themselves participate in the design and content of their celebrations, choosing what is comfortable for them. Here are some suggestions for a memorable event.

The place where the celebration will be held can be decorated with candles and flowers of red and white, red symbolizing blood and life force, white representing innocence, strength, and reproductive health. The young woman may wish to sit at the place of honor, the head of the table perhaps, with her chair decorated like a throne. The centerpiece might be red roses, one for each year she has lived. She may also want to wear a crown of flowers, signifying her flowering womanhood.

To begin, the group can acknowledge and invoke the young woman's Mother-line, all her female ancestors who have crossed this threshold before. This affirms her place in the community of women, her procreative potential, and the natural beauty of her menarche experience.

The body of the rite involves sharing information on menstruation through storytelling and first-person accounts. Each woman present is given the opportunity to describe her menarche experience. Not all of these stories will be joyous; older women are sometimes very emotional as they recall feeling ashamed of their first blood. Yet this creates even stronger intent within the circle to honor the young woman currently engaged in this Blood Mystery. The group can balance feelings of grief with praise for the Maiden's strength, courage, and beauty.

An ancient form of honoring menarche is the Clay Rite, similar to the Apache use of cattail pollen. This is only appropriate if the young woman feels comfortable enough to be nude in the presence of her friends. Those who have not yet started bleeding cover her with wet, red clay, to symbolize her connection to the earth. This can be fun—a playful, messy act of saying farewell to childhood.

If they are in a rural setting, the group may wish to construct a sweat lodge for the young woman, where she may spend a certain amount of time in seclusion. As an alternative, she might spend a night alone in a tent or cabin with her friends close by, perhaps singing or drumming to give her courage. Or she might simply go off by herself for an hour or so to a place of total privacy.

When the period of isolation is to end, several of the older women (or a special relative) go to her with instructions regarding her fertility and responsibilities in the next stage of life. When they are finished, she returns to the larger group. Her friends may wish to form a birth arch at this point, lining up and passing the young woman through their legs until she finally comes to her mother, who brings her out and into her embrace. As with actual birth, there is a moment in this act where time seems suspended—the power of this ritual is tangible.

The "newborn" woman is then washed clean (of any remaining clay) by her friends who have already begun bleeding: thus they welcome her into the adult community of women. She should be dressed in new, beautiful clothing she can treasure for years to come, fussed over and adorned like the Goddess herself!

The group may then make some final comments or affirmations regarding the power of menstruation and appropriate roles for women to play in today's society. Each participant may also wish to confide her own special ways of honoring her menstrual period. To close, the young woman's mother may give her some jewelry, perhaps a family heirloom piece, or anything featuring red stones. She may also want to formally present her daughter to whatever higher power they recognize, asking for protection and guidance.

When the ritual ends, feasting begins. Red foods represent fertility; guests may wish to toast the Maiden with red wine. Perhaps other family members will choose to participate at this point. Men often find it hard to stay away during the ceremony, and are very pleased when finally welcomed to join the festivities. Above all, this ritual should be exactly as the young woman wants it, so that she may discover a new degree of trust in her body and in herself.

If such a formal ritual seems too complex or inappropriate for your family, simple variations may suffice. One mother told her daughter that when she got her period, she could choose any three things to do in celebration. On the first day of her bleeding, this young woman opted for: (1) a shopping trip, (2) total silence from Mom for the entire day, (3) a steak. The last was somewhat controversial for this vegetarian family, but as her mother observed, "Eating a steak was my daughter's ultimate statement of adult decision-making power."

I personally recall my father giving me a dozen long-stemmed roses. It was a little embarrassing because, after all, he was my dad. But it was the most touching and sentimental thing he ever did for me.

Another option is for mother and daughter to go off together to some favorite outdoor place, reconnecting with nature and each other. They may want to go hiking or canoeing, or perhaps just build a campfire together, as long as they spend time alone and make it a celebratory day. The mother could use this time to review her daughter's birth and childhood—what she was like when she was younger and all the great things she has done in her life thus far. She might also share visions and hopes for her daughter's future.

In addition to the aforementioned gift of jewelry, some mothers allow their daughters to pierce their ears on this day, presenting them earrings with red stones. Another precious keepsake is a Menarche Book, consisting of photos of all the women in the family and suitable for passing on to the next generation.

The day could end with the mother drawing a bath for her daughter, perhaps placing flower petals on the water. When it is over, the two can decide how to share the news with the rest of the family (if they don't already know) and whether a party of some kind would be desirable. Again, the most important thing is the young woman's comfort level; if she happily participates in planning a larger celebration, she will joyfully remember it for the rest of her life.

—C. LEONARD

On the opposite side of the Circle, the Matriarch's maturity is based on the sum of her life experience rather than on a single physiological event; she has passed through innocence and nurturing to a point of security with herself and her place in the world. Unlike the Amazon, she is no longer struggling to individuate as a mature adult. She knows her strengths and weaknesses, knows to what degree the enemy is within or without, and can thus move mountains with a fraction of the energy it took in earlier years. The title Matriarch connotes a female leader, a queen. But her methods of leadership are rooted in women's ways of empowerment; she is quick to acknowledge the gifts and abilities of others and is, on that basis, masterful at delegating responsibility. She knows her limits and will no longer take everything upon herself; she recognizes overload as a disservice to herself and to those who love and rely upon her. Besides, the Matriarch is no longer young and must thus conserve her energy by deliberately choosing how, where, and when to allocate her resources.

From a woman, age fifty, who serves her state as a representative:

"The social consciousness of the sixties got derailed for a while, but seems now to be returning. Being in the House of Representatives is a pretty straight job, but my reasons for wanting to do this aren't much different than demonstrating for civil rights before. This is the first time in twenty-five years that I've worked *within* the system to create some change. I used to work in alternative organizations, doing my own thing and setting up my own structure. It's very, very different to have a lot of rules imposed on you—but I'm still active and wanting to change the things I always have. Only now I'm doing it in a very conventional structure."

To a certain extent, the Matriarch must rein in the excesses of the Amazon stage to better concentrate on that which gives her life greatest meaning. In order to do this, she needs to have attained a certain security with the material aspects of life. This does not mean she is without financial worries, but she understands her fiscal responsibilities and knows how to make the most of whatever she has. Frequently, women expressing the Matriarch archetype demonstrate keen executive ability, not only in the administration of their own affairs but in sound management of the concerns of other family members. Women age-linked to this stage may find they have to juggle school-age children's busy rounds of extracurricular activities with their parents' increasing dependency. How to make all of this work with time to spare for her own needs is a both challenge and the realm of potential mastery for the Matriarch.

"I am Matriarch, but I'm drawing on the stages of Amazon and Priestess to figure out what that means. Age-wise I feel more like an Amazon, as well as in terms of my sexuality—I'm newly divorced and exploring, playing the field. But when it comes to my worldly responsibilities as head of my household, owner of several small businesses, political organizer and activist . . . I feel I'm at the height of my power and I'm doing all right.

"The Priestess comes in as insight, an ability to see the spiritual aspects of what I am doing that grows more acute each day. Sometimes I feel like I am being drawn into a higher pattern of meaning that has little to do with my own decision making. This is pretty exhilarating, a blessed thing to me, a saving grace that infuses my responsibilities with magic and mystery. Actually, I am more and more drawn to this magic, which I discern in the way

I take risks and move on, and all the while my higher perspective is saying, 'Yes, yes!'"

Before the Matriarch can move on to the Priestess stage, she must fully realize her harvest, with all its attendant responsibility and significance. "Autumn's grain is spring's seed"—whatever is sown in the time of the Maiden reaches fruition in the time of the Matriarch. Many modern-day Matriarchs are troubled that they never celebrated their menarche or experienced the feminine as sacred in their younger years. Some women have recreated the menarche ritual they missed, particularly if their first menstruation was denigrated or met with shame (for example, the Jewish custom of slapping a girl at her time of first blood). My own daughter, now in her twenties, recalls with amazement that I had the foresight to leave her a box of pads and instructions on what to do before I went off to teach at a conference—she was only ten at the time, and indeed, she started bleeding when I was away. Yet this was more a validation of our connectedness than an honoring of her personal transition.

The wild sexual experimentation of some women on the Amazon/Matriarch cusp is often an attempt to reconnect with the power and prowess of youth, which was suppressed or unacknowledged in the time of Maidenhood. To whatever extent we as elders can enliven the menarche rites of young women in our own communities, we have an opportunity to reweave broken threads in our own psychosexual development. Doing so can provide us a root source of passion that renders our handling of increased responsibilities joyous and insightful, rather than dour and obligatory.

Most of the time, the harvest in a woman's life brings awareness of abundance. The Matriarch often feels extraordinarily blessed, if not somewhat surprised at the richness and fullness of her life as she takes stock. The Amazon stage is merely a burning of the dross, a purification that sets the stage for Matriarchal peace and stability. This is a time to celebrate, to be generous and kind to one's kin. The harvest is meant to be shared; thus as Clan Leader, the Matriarch distributes her wealth to her family members. Not only does she give material gifts but those of time and energy, counsel and guidance, inspiration and support. Above all else, the Matriarch stage is meant for enjoyment—the equilibrium of light and dark does not last forever, autumn wanes and winter approaches. Even in the midst of celebration, the Matriarch begins to surrender her material focus and rededicate herself to the source of life in preparing for her role as Priestess.

This points to another responsibility of harvest time, that of storing for the future. By making long-range plans for her own security and that of her loved ones, the Matriarch demonstrates cross-generational wisdom in the most practical way possible. She stores for her spiritual future too—making note, in the first moments of waking or at any inspirational moment during the day, of her core self beyond worldly preoccupations. Her back-to-essence experience as Amazon lingers in spite of her busy schedule; she clings passionately to the intimation of a time when she will be truly free to pursue her inner directives. Reminders of her subtle aspect, drawn from contemplative reading, listening to music, or making love, intrigue her and foreshadow the pleasure of future explorations. She stores these treasures up for herself.

Yet another aspect of the harvest is realization of failure. Certain crops may not reach fruition—perhaps they were planted too late for the growing cycle, were not cared for adequately or were simply not appropriate for prevailing conditions. Thus harvest time is a time of reckoning, a time for taking stock of what has worked and what has not. From this, we learn what yet needs care and nurturance, how better to cultivate next time around, and what to let go of altogether—as this woman, forty-three, relates:

"I'm the classic superwoman. I have a six-year-old, I'm the mother of a teenager, I'm working full-time, and I'm being responsible as a wife. I'm taking care of everything, and I worry about the state of the world, about politics. I spend a lot of time worrying, and I'm trying to find a place of balance where I'm not in despair about the craziness of life. I try not to be pulled down, I keep trying to find rays of hope.

"I'm also the Matriarch of my intentional community. I oversee work that needs to be done and I oversee the emotional currents of the people around me, checking base, and if someone needs attention I give them a little more attention. Now this is a setup—when I say, 'What needs to be done?' I mean what *I* think needs to be done. I see living in community as the wave of the future, but sharing resources and learning how to cooperate is really quite a challenge. It's hard, dealing with the question of the individual versus the community. Everyone's definition of how much energy to put where is different, and I need to be less attached to mine, so that when others don't live up to my standards I'm not disappointed.

"I'm being forced to assume the maturity of Matriarch by a series of stress-related physical symptoms, and I realize that if I can't be grounded I give no real service to anyone. These are hard lessons, humiliating and distressing. Part of me wants to stay Amazon— I'm a real intensity freak, like 'Dammit, don't make me stop!'—but stop signs are coming up all over the place. What I'm finding is that I'm okay in the outer world, but my family is suffering because I'm not discriminating in what I take on. My family has been helpful in reminding me—my child, by his behavior, my husband, by gentle suggestion, and my teenager, by surfacing when it's quiet in the house, rather than hiding out in his room.

115

"Now I see that I'm so much in the outer world that I can't narrow myself down enough to get into my Priestess, which would really be of greater benefit to all concerned. I would be in a much stronger place if I weren't so scattered."

The tarot card of Justice signifies the Matriarch as judge and juror—not so much of others, but of herself. The classic image of justice is the scales, connoting again equilibrium and harmony. Yet this image is often combined with that of the sword—a symbol for cutting away, cutting back, or cutting free that which has outlived its usefulness.

In the Motherpeace deck, Justice portrays connectedness with nature and all living things as the basis for this discrimination. Illustrator Karen Vogel portrays three figures, the Norns (the three Fates in their Scandinavian aspect), who hold the threads of past, present, and future in their hands. Not only do they spin these threads, they trim and weave the fabric of existence, of destiny. They too are blended in the weave, in such a way that to disrupt the pattern indiscriminately would only bring harm to themselves. Their ultimate goal is to support nature's process of elimination for reanimation's sake. The Greeks called this concept of interrelatedness *themis,* a working principle of just law-making. By Homer's time, Themis the goddess had become the mother of the seasons. Bearing scales and a cornucopia, she "determined the proper time for the fruitful earth's budding and exhaustion, proper times as well for human events."[3]

Another face of Themis is Nemesis, goddess of divine vengeance and retribution. Ovid called her the "goddess that abhors boastful words," the queen of karma and of just outcome.[4] For the Matriarch, meeting up with Nemesis may involve stark realization of errors of excess or omission, less-than-kind treatment of others, abuse of power, lost or neglected opportunities in her past. Vicki Noble's byline for Justice is "Setting Things Right," precisely the task the Matriarch must undertake in order to evolve to the next stage. The only way she can reckon past mistakes is to reflect on how they came to pass in the first place. Mistakes made repeatedly become boldly evident now, and seem irremediable through ordinary acts of will. The Matriarch searches deeply for patterns, and finds it less a matter of eradicating her faults than joining with them, exploring her shadow to find wholeness. This is Priestess work—going beyond the mastery of daily existence to explore transpersonal aspects of growth and healing.

The Matriarch's signifying goddess is Ceres, who rules the grain and harvest. She actually represents the entire Matriarch phase, in that she presides over the Amazon's holy day of Lammas as well as the celestial sphere of influence sought by the Priestess. Zsuzsanna Budapest gives her voice, as follows:

> I am Earth, the most ancient of the prophets.... I have given your kind two million years to develop and learn how to fit into my holy world. I am the only goddess who knows where we are in space at all times. My mantle is the universe. Darkness is my sensor, set on eternity. . . . Every day you are not working for me, you are allowing destruction to be forged in your name. Women must act as my activists. For you, nurturing is automatic, but it is not so instinctive to take the power and responsibility for the world that go with it. Learn it, sister, learn power fast.[5]

Adele Getty, author of *Goddess: Mother of Living Nature,* explained to me in a recent conversation that Native American tradition holds the place of the west as that of the woman; however, the appropriate shield (source of protection and locus of power) to be utilized here is that of the man. She observed that when women place the woman's shield in the west, they have difficulty taking power and feel overwhelmed, indecisive, lost. Perhaps this results from fragmentation in Maidenhood; never having forged a healthy relationship with our femaleness, our relationship to male energy is likewise immature. Whatever the cause, the Matriarch must strive to attain equilibrium of male and female aspects. Her key abilities draw strongly from a balance of intuition and logic, perception and research, faith and preparedness. Sexual explorations in the Amazon stage engender an ability to relate to the masculine in herself and others; as Matriarch, her task is to unite feminine vulnerability with unflinching assertiveness.

> "When I was in my Amazon craziness, I vowed I would do away with missed opportunities and lingering doubts of 'I wonder what it would have been like to go to bed with him?' I was going to check it out as far as I could, as far as possible. Even if half of me was saying no, if part of me said yes I'd investigate until *all* of me said no. No more regrets—just experience.
>
> "After a while, I gave up the idea that men are out to get us. They're out to get what men want—some of that's okay, more than okay—and now I can relate to it. I've got some passionate, forceful part of myself in gear that was silent before. Other things about men and their behavior are still confounding, annoying, and destructive to me. I trust myself to discriminate now, but I'd never be able to do that if I hadn't checked it out."

Women in committed relationships report coming fully into their sexuality in their Matriarch years, feeling a maturity of give-and-take spiced with innovation and risk taking. Many speak of new comfort with sexual practices formerly considered risqué or bizarre. The Matriarch finds the freedom and self-confidence to say, loud and clear, what she likes and doesn't like in bed. When conflicts develop, she knows how separate the opinions and projections of her lovers from her own. All's fair—including inciting revolution in seemingly stable relationships so that deeper intimacy might result. Her magnetism is based on a balance of strength and sensitivity; she is attractive to men and women alike. Some Matriarchs go beyond their established union to explore new intimate relationships; others forge deep nonsexual friendships. The underlying desire is to utilize, rather than repress, the power of attraction in a playful and open way so that all close relationships are enhanced.

This harvest of pleasure leads the Matriarch to explore the transcendent aspects of sexual union. In the search for deep intimacy, she may enter the realm of Priestess as an initiator of visionary and ecstatic sexual experience. (Tantric fusion is no longer a fantasy, though she has yet to realize its full potential.) Particularly when on the cusp between Matriarch and Priestess, women have a foot in both worlds: the light, bright beauty of embodiment touched by dark, mysterious currents that are more than personal.

"I still have a lot to learn about sex. There are times I go deep and really love it, and other times when it's on the back burner, due to stress and fatigue. Usually my husband and I need to get away for a few days, or someone juicy will come into our lives who will spark things. A lot of my sexual fantasies involve making love with other people in a larger circle. I often fantasize when my husband and I make love that another couple is with us, or another man or another woman, just bringing everybody in [laughs]. My husband doesn't do that, but I do. A few times we've actually experimented with this and it's been very exciting for me. I'm really open to bringing this more into my life.

"We have a real strong definition of how it can happen so it works and doesn't get too crazy, so jealousy doesn't interfere. My husband and I made a vow that our relationship comes first and if this feels breached by either one of us, it's not okay and we have to stop. Most of the time our experiences are one-nighters with an old friend, and when it happens it really turns me on to my husband; it's just something I like, even though I don't fully understand why.

"I grew up in the sixties. I experimented a lot and I know where it can take you; it's like opening up Pandora's box, you can end up in some pretty scary places, so I'm really very cautious. Bringing another person in has to happen spontaneously and must feel completely right to both of us. I can't just do it for my partner, or vice versa. It is hard to find the right combination, so it doesn't happen very often. Also, I really trust that if things go too far and I tell my husband to stop, he'll stop—I've said no before, and he's stopped. That's an important commitment we have to each other. We never committed to being monogamous, but I've personally never gone out of our relationship in the seven years we've been married. One reason is that having an affair is so incredibly time-consuming, and everything else in my life is just too important now. There's a certain economy, a very conscious effort on my part. Also, I have a very rich fantasy life and I take time to be sexual with myself. And when I see what some of my friends are doing with Tantra, there's so much I still want to explore with my partner and it's quite exciting. I just hope I don't get too old or too tired before I get my chance—but I know a number of people in their fifties or sixties that have great sexual relationships, so I'm counting on having plenty of time yet."

It bears mentioning that a number of our interviewees skipped over the Matriarch stage in their response to the Circle of Life, or if they spoke to it at all it was merely in passing. Perhaps this is because the title Matriarch bears negative connotations in our society, implying a woman heavily constrained by familial obligations. But other women related strongly to the title of Matriarch, like this one, age forty-four:

> "To me, Matriarch means the lineage of the feminine and something that is intentionally passed along the female line, something of value. Now, this can be property, if that's what you hold valuable. My matrilineal line is very strong. We have a house in Maine that has been passed down mother to daughter, woman to woman for generations. In this house there are portraits of my grandmother, my great-grandmother, and my great-great-grandmother that have always been there; I grew up looking at them.
>
> "I definitely had something passed to me through this matriarchy of what it means to be a woman in the world, but it wasn't very helpful in terms of who I turned out to be. It was about being bright and capable and fitting in and making a home for a man—a woman's value being based on how successful her children are. My mother is an amazing woman, just an amazing woman. She would have been the CEO of any corporation she became part of if she had been a man. Instead, she was the president of every volunteer organization, and she was usually involved in fourteen or fifteen.
>
> "My Matriarch time was about searching for what was offered both within and without my matrilineal line—what is it of value, apart from property and service, that is passed from woman to woman? I immersed myself in women; I lived with women; I worked with women until I found the answers I was seeking. I couldn't move to the Priestess stage until I got this."

At one of my Sister Circle meetings, we decided to bring our female ancestors into the circle, whether by portrait or story of remembrance. It was remarkable to sit together with pictures of our mothers and grandmothers and great-grandmothers all around us, sharing tales of love and guidance, peppered with humor and insight. But even as we brought our ancestors proudly into our circle, we lamented the powerlessness of these women in their time, the misgivings and mistakes that led some to their undoing, the lack of love for self that seemed the common thread. Slowly we began to reweave the tattered tapestry of our feminine heritage into one of great loveliness—to protect us, cover us, and keep us warm as we continue our respective journeys both in and out of the circle.

On another occasion, I was guided in trance to name and invite my female ancestors to come and stand behind me, starting with my mother and going back as far as I could remember. This kindled in me an awareness of the wisdom passed down through all the generations of my family tree. Soon after, I developed a song in an all-night ceremony that began, "Oh Grandmothers, sweeten our way," which went on to include descriptions of the many wise and loving behaviors I associated with my own grandmom. As I sang, I had vivid memories of her hands, how they moved through space, worked pie dough, patted me gently on the knee, touched my hair. My recollections brought a gut-level realization of the breadth and depth of the woman I am, beyond social definition.

This excerpt from *Women's Rituals* further expresses the need to recover our heritage:

Woman, remember. You have the memory living deep in your mind, in your blood, in your lifegiving darkness. Reach down to it and bring it forth.

Remember the time before men began to count time. Remember when woman was the world, and the world was woman. Remember when every mother established her clan, guided her children, set the standards of behavior for her lovers, and owned the home place to be passed down to her daughters. Remember when the Mother's laws forbade man to do violence to others, especially to women and children. Remember when rape was unknown, because every sexual encounter was by woman's choice. Remember when men dared not claim the right to control any aspect of women's economic, political, sexual, or reproductive activities, but honored all women for bringing forth and nurturing the human race. . . .

Remember that woman alone . . . had the right to decree wise laws for the benefit of future generations. Remember that woman alone knew the mysteries of life and death, of healing and cursing. Remember the shrines established by the primal ancestresses. Remember the great temples where priestesses dwelt, helping their people. Remember that the world was at peace, because men were forbidden to kill. . . .

Realize . . . that the real foundation of human life is Woman. Remember your Goddess.

Woman, remember.[6]

We embody the Matriarch when we are fully present, fully in our power. We stand strong for all of life, we hold the line. Added to this, flexibility and resourcefulness are essential to the Matriarch's feminine ecology. Looking for ways to connect others that their efforts may be mutually reinforcing instead of competitive and wasteful, expending only that energy which must be expended, and incorporating the cycles of nature into our lives rather than fighting against them, we ready ourselves to step into the role of Priestess.

CHAPTER 7

The Blood Sister and the Priestess

The Blood Sister bears out the promise of the Maiden within a circle of support. Young women in their Blood Sister time bond to each other out of need; as a group, they chart their desires, their experiences of self-affirmation, their disappointments, and their dreams.

Blood Sisters invariably rebel against social restrictions of feminine power. They move in packs like she-wolves or lionesses to hunt excitement, hunt mates, hunt meaning and purpose for their lives. They rely on each other for the nerve to articulate their countercultural principles and beliefs. Blood Sisters sing the body electric, celebrating the female form in all its beauty and vitality with creative and inventive styles of dress and speech. Mutual reinforcement of ideals gives Blood Sisters the courage to move out in the world and make their mark; they help each other individuate and thus prepare for one-on-one bonding in the forthcoming Lover stage. A young woman, age twenty-one, states:

> "Most of my friends jumped into sex too innocently, and then realized the guy they'd chosen was an idiot. You start out thinking all guys are nice, then decide you won't be taken advantage of again. I tell virgins to wait, and hone in on what they really want. You find you don't want this and don't want that by learning from your girlfriends' good and bad decisions. I think the time of Blood Sister is that of puppy love, of infatuation. Losing your virginity doesn't make you a Lover—that comes with increased self-esteem, independence, and confidence."

Whether sexually active or not, the Blood Sister is as yet unpledged to a partner. Her pledge is to the process of maturation; she vigorously attempts to revamp sex-role expectations so that she may do and be want she wants. We all remember the classic "blood brothers" act of childhood, cutting our fingers and mixing blood with another. This is a powerful metaphor for Blood Sisters' commingling their deepest selves that some unified force might be generated to fight archaic values.

For the Priestess, too, shared experience and vision are at the heart of exploring the unknown and ever more magnetic shadow side of existence. Both Blood Sister and Priestess discover the power of circling as a means to realize personal growth. Blood Sisters typically circle by phone or email, spreading news and seeking input in rounds of interaction. Going out in groups or meeting at the mall are classic examples of circling in the mid-teens. Later, exposure to feminist thought may lead Blood Sisters to expand the circle beyond their immediate peers, organizing for social change. But unlike the first wave of feminist organizers, they have moved beyond anger to firm insistence on their rights, in a spirit of celebration. As this young woman, twenty-one, relates:

> "To me, feminism means hanging out and bonding and celebrating ourselves. It doesn't mean male bashing; I don't agree with that. We just had Take Back the Night, and it was well attended by both men and women. I'm more into women's spirituality, learning more about myself, and learning to respect things I was never taught to respect about the Earth, nature, women's bodies, and our way of doing things.
>
> "As my friends and I get more involved with men, it gets harder to just hang out together. You know, we want to have our private time, get some wine or whatever, and the guys get real possessive. But our friendships keep growing anyway.
>
> "I think women's circles really help with this. And education— I'm a big advocate of education. If I do become a teacher, I'm going to teach women's spirituality, with books on the truth about the Inquisition, films like *The Burning Times,* all that. I want to help young women find a positive female image."

Every woman fortunate enough to have had a good course in women's studies or prepatriarchal history remembers the turning point of realizing, with her blinders at last removed, that the struggle of women to own their power is of global significance. Another woman, age twenty-four, recalls:

> "During my Maiden time, I was never told I was powerful or beautiful or unique—I was a witch and a bitch and useless. I grew up in a group home and was considered no better than anyone else, probably worse than most.

"College opened up a weave of social activism for me, a chance to connect with other women my age who were getting fired up about things. Joining a women's circle gave me a sense of control and self-esteem. It prompted me to take leadership roles, to say things I was afraid to say before.

"I think finding your power as a Blood Sister gives you the strength not to take so much crap during the Lover phase. Women who don't key into this element end up in more subservient positions, I think."

Not surprisingly, women in their Blood Sister stage become the most loving confidantes, and may experience same-sex intimacy for the first time. Many of the young women we interviewed told of feeling deep love for a particular woman at this time of their lives, with bonding based largely on comfort and self-affirmation:

"I had a close friend in college. We did everything together—long conversations, drives through the country near campus, trips back home. We cared very deeply for one another; we were together every day. One night, she called me and asked me to her apartment, which was not unusual, but when I got there she had candles lit and was wearing this sheer, lacy nightgown and she took me to her bedroom. I was surprised and frightened—I wasn't ready for this and didn't want to ruin our friendship, so I played innocent and we just talked. But somehow we stayed close—I actually think this incident and the way we handled it deepened our connection. That avenue of possibility, even though we never actualized it, created this tenderness between us, kind of like a secret bond."

Another woman, now in her forties, remembers:

"My best friend, Nancy, and I had been traveling back and forth across the country for a couple of years. This was the late sixties, and we were heady with 'bad girl' mystique and wildness. We had weathered various boyfriend traumas together and were very close. No one in the world knew me like she did. We were often affectionate with one another, but had never crossed the line to being overtly sexual.

"One night we saw Mick Jagger and the Rolling Stones in Boston Garden. Jagger was at his androgynous peak—throwing roses to the audience, tossing his scarf, and seeming to give permission to explore the hidden parts of ourselves. The heat of the performance and the message was so clear, we could barely contain ourselves on the way home. That night, our love for each other did cross the line. When we first kissed, it was tentative and we giggled out of nervousness, but then it got serious. I remember the wonder of feeling her body so much like my own—all familiar territory, so I knew exactly what to do. Very different than making love with a boyfriend and always worrying about his reaction or my performance. It freed me to feel more pleasure in my body than I ever had before.

"We made love over the next year and then our lives went separate ways. We both went on to have families of our own and we lost contact. But I am truly grateful for that window of time in my life when this sort of experience was possible."

When a woman moves to the nurturing phase, she tends to seek a larger circle of support from her community, particularly if she has children. As the years go by, her circle may expand or contract according to need. Once she becomes a Priestess, though, circling is no longer optional; it is her prime means of discerning her identity and purpose apart from family obligations. The circle has always been a classic female symbol, representing the womb and monthly cycling. Perhaps no one has spoken more eloquently on the meaning of the circle than the Native American Black Elk:

You have noticed that everything an Indian does goes in a circle, and that is because the Power of the World always works in circles, and that everything tries to be round. In the old days when we were a strong and happy people, all our power came from the sacred hoop of the nation and so long as the hoop was unbroken, the people flourished. The flowering tree was the living center of the hoop, and the circle of the four quarters nourished it. The east gave peace and light, the south gave warmth, the west gave rain, and the north with its cold and mighty wind gave strength and endurance. . . .

Everything the Power of the World does is in a circle. The sky is round and I have heard the earth is round and so are all the stars. The wind in its greatest power whirls. Birds make their nests in circles. The sun comes forth and goes down again in a circle. The moon does the same, and both are round. Even the seasons form a great circle in their changing, and always come back again to where they were. The life of a man is a circle from childhood to childhood, and so it is in everything where power moves.[1]

The need for circling unites Blood Sister and Priestess, although they are opposite in lunar aspect. The Blood Sister's moon is rising—more light than dark, she is surging toward the peak of her fertility and the height of her preoccupation with the ways of the world. But the Priestess's moon is waning—more dark than light, she tracks the undercurrents of her fate and is drawn ever deeper into honing her transpersonal self. In fact, every woman we interviewed who spoke of the Priestess stage linked it to a descent experience deeper than any she had undergone before. A few women descended intentionally by choosing to vision quest, relocate, surrender some former occupation or primary relationship, or relinquish a major addiction—as did Sumerian goddess Inanna, who went purposely to the underworld for self-renewal. This impulse also recalls the tarot image of the Hanged One, who deliberately turns herself upside down for self-initiation (as did Odin to receive the runes). The *I Ching* bears similar imagery in the hexagram of the Cauldron, which is represented by a ceremonial vessel over-turned so stagnating contents may be emptied out. This account from a woman, age forty-one, illustrates:

> "Several years ago, I went on a vision quest for twelve days, including four days of fasting, and five of telling our stories to the others in the group. When I went on this quest I knew I wasn't going for a vision per se, but to find some way to clean out all the parts of myself—not just my defects, but my most beloved aspects too.
>
> "The day before I began my fast, I went out to greet the sun and walked up this ridge that overlooked the whole valley, and the sun came up behind me and to the right of me and below me, but I was in shadow. I felt bereft and isolated, and then it was like the Goddess came in with her whole entourage and the entire valley became feminine. She said to me, 'You have been in my service for many lifetimes, and now your service to me in this way is done. I am sending you out into the world of men as an ambassador.' She was with me for the rest of my quest, teaching me, showing me the spectrum of the human condition, both the wonderful and the horrible."

And another account from a woman, age sixty:

> "I've been sober for almost ten years now. It took me seven of those years to figure out that I did not know how everything was put together, how people related. . . . It was a truly baffling period for me. I kept telling a friend, 'I just don't understand what's going on,' and some time later she said, 'You really don't know—you really are just learning about this, aren't you?' Yes, I was—being a

drunk for thirty-five years is a long time to avoid reality. I had to grow up all over again, starting back when I was sixteen, and in just ten years, work all the way up to where I am now. I had to go through the psychological, emotional, and intellectual things of every stage I missed, moving through the years one by one, reconstructing my life. My father was an alcoholic and my mother was in denial, so I was tossed continually from the negative to the positive, with nothing confirmed as far as my selfhood was concerned.

"In the first year of getting sober, the mind is mush. Literally— I couldn't carry on a conversation, something would shut down or evaporate. It was really weird; I just could not conduct myself in any kind of normal, linear way. Then I had this terrifying, absolutely terrifying experience of dried-up faith, like dropping through a black hole with no end, and there's never going to be any end, there's never going to be anything any different, there is no God, there is nothing to look forward to, and there is no spirit in the world. I had never experienced a crisis like this as a drunk, because as a drunk you can always rationalize things away or look at them in this magical, mystical, fairy-tale kind of fashion. I remember driving through Manhattan Beach and thinking there was nothing else but this, and it was terror, sheer terror. You know that Norwegian painting, *The Scream*? It was like that, and it lasted for days. Then I don't know what happened . . . probably fatigue . . . the terror was totally exhausting and then some survival instinct kicked in to make me want to believe in something, so I opened to the next possibility and took the leap.

"There was a spiritual dimension involved here, because despite the years I had been a drunk I was on the spiritual path. When I got sober I recovered not the peripheral aspects of the spirit, but the basic premise of the spirit. I came back to certain realizations I'd had as a drunk, but now I was establishing their foundations in real life."

For other women, the onset of descent is equally terrifying but entirely unexpected. It's not as if the Matriarch decides one fine day when all is going smoothly that it's time to take on her toughest, unresolved personal issues, nor is it a matter of simple weariness with the ways of the world that leads her to surrender material concerns. No, the descent as Priestess involves both loss of control and the demise of one's cherished stability, often due to an abrupt twist of fate.

"When it came time for my journey through the underworld, I went kicking and screaming. It was not an easy journey and I didn't go willingly; all the circumstances in my life got scattered into chaos and confusion. I went to England for what was to be a two-week holiday, and I didn't come back for a year. This was not my choice—I had a business and everything went under—I just lost my capacity to have any control. I like keeping my life in order, making choices and planning ahead, but every time I'd try to get organized, something would happen and I wouldn't be able to do what I expected. I had a total loss of faith because of this, and dropped into deep despair that everything I had believed in—the Medicine Path, the Goddess, Buddha, everything—was gone from my life. I became a complete nihilist; I felt totally alone and had no sense of the universe supporting me. When I got to the place of utter alienation from Spirit, that was just the pit, the bottom. The image I had of myself was of being on a large, black sea, madly flailing around like a many-armed goddess, every arm flailing on the surface of the water as I tried to stay afloat. Finally, in the midst of this panic, I called for help and said, 'What is this about and what can I do? This is taking a lot of energy, trying to stay afloat.' I couldn't sleep, and no matter what I tried to do during the day, I was psychically flailing. And this voice just came and said, 'Surrender, just drown, just let go and drown.' I stopped flailing and I let myself drown . . . and I drowned but I didn't die. I sank into this sea of peace, calmness, serenity—no, serenity is too strong—it didn't have the positive energy serenity has, but there was nothing negative about it. It was emptiness, and it wasn't taking any energy anymore and it was all right; I could just be there in this emptiness. It wasn't blissful but I could sleep, and immediately the energetics of my life shifted and started supporting me again. But if I tried to jump in with both feet, pick up the ball and run with it, I immediately got smashed back down. A month would go by and I'd think, 'Surely I can start being actively engaged in this process,' but nope, I'd be wrong . . . and this went on for nine months. My natural tendency is to bob back up and start running, but the challenge was not to emerge too soon from the underworld. Making the descent is a process, being in the underworld is a process, and making the ascent, slowly coming back is a process too, and if you short circuit any step along the way, you're going to have to go though the journey again. I had one such journey around the age of twenty-eight, another when I was nineteen, and you know, once a decade is enough for me [laughs]. I'm an optimist; I enjoy feeling good and I like to see myself as doing fine, so to see myself crumble and to have all my friends realize that I was crumbling was very painful. I got great support from my women friends, who were really there for me— they just kept telling me that it was okay, I didn't have to be so proud, I could fall apart, I didn't have to be the strong one, the together one. I get that mirrored to me a lot that I'm the strong one, and I've liked it, so to be completely crippled was extremely uncomfortable and embarrassing for me. I just had to keep telling myself, 'I'm not going to try to pick up the pieces, I'm not going to pretend I'm on top of this or working with this in any kind of way; I'm just completely at the mercy of this journey I'm on.'

"I think for some women, the trick is to emerge again at all. As we experience a descent into the underworld, the challenge is not to get stuck there for the rest of our lives or a decade of our lives, but to be present to what the process is about and move with it at an appropriate rate of speed, not ahead or behind, just present each day, each moment. The confusion comes when you realize that something has to die. I'm not suicidal by nature, it's contrary to everything I am, but in my despair, as I started to come out of it, I could see how women kill themselves—Virginia Woolf, Sylvia Plath—it's an error in logical typing, knowing that something desperately wants to die and confusing it with yourself, your physical being, rather than the part of you that just needs to transform."

This report defies fantasies of aging without a hitch, just doing what we do better and better, giving and taking as we please while becoming old and wise. Instead, it seems that in order to know and exercise real wisdom, we must first be taken to some outer reach, some distant shore far from our usual identity. To return to the myth of Inanna—at the deepest point on her journey to the underworld she met the goddess of the Great Below, Ereshkigal, who hung her body on a hook to rot. She struggled to keep body and soul together but was ultimately reborn by grace. If we wish to successfully undertake such a journey, we too must yield to what Richard Moss terms "transparency" by "releasing into dimensions that are broader than those reflected to us through the content of our experiences."[2]

Is there any way to prepare for this leap of faith into the darkness? The nature of the Matriarch's harvest will largely determine her willingness as Priestess to give in and go beyond what she has known. The more she feels satiated with experience, the more she has reckoned with her mistakes throughout the years, the more she has carried the pain of failure and found some way to transform it, the more likely she will be to believe that anything is possible and so take her leap of faith with relative ease. If the harvest has been

bitter or incomplete, faith may be difficult to come by. Yet by definition, faith is based not on proof but on devotion: enduring fidelity
to what one is bound to by a pledge. In sisterhood, our pledge is to
support one another in living life to the fullest extent possible. Whatever mistakes or transgressions or omissions we may have made, open
disclosure to our peers and receptivity to their feedback can help us
yield to life's hardest lessons. Positive experiences of bonding to
other women in the Blood Sister stage make it much easier to accept
support at this critical juncture as Priestess.

The Star card of the tarot bears the message that redemption
of one's life is always possible, and, in this regard, shows the blessed
healing potential of sisterhood. In the Motherpeace deck, Karen
Vogel's image includes a hollow in the earth, in which a woman
sits immersed in water up to her breasts. Pink flowers float in the
pool, symbolizing love. Bathed in starlight and night rain, the
woman awaits her sisters, who will gather around to bathe her, sing
to her, and reaffirm her beauty. Vicki Noble further elaborates on
these images:

> The idea of cosmic power reaching down and blessing our earthly
> lives is as old as rain. Like the pre-Columbian water pitcher and
> washbowl, the receiver of spirit is an open vessel and represents
> the archetypal feminine. . . . Immersion in water is an ancient heal-
> ing practice, and the power of mineral waters or hot springs
> cleanses and purifies the body and soul. Pain releases and fear lets
> go, opening the pores to love.[3]

Purity and purification link Blood Sister and Priestess together. In
the Blood Sister stage, there is purity of intent, a desire to be one's
genuine self in the outer world, to draw upon the blunt, unfettered
truth of one's peers. Virginal in their approach to life, Blood
Sisters uphold their purity by seeking genuine realization of their

ideals and desires, sexual or otherwise. For the Priestess, purification is a release from all the disappointments, misadventures, and blunders of the past, or of any experience that may have tainted her ability to know and show compassionate love. Christian images of purification usually involve the element of fire chastening the flesh, separating body from spirit. In contrast, the sacred feminine finds purification in the reunion of body and spirit, in the restoration of wholeness and sweet simplicity.

Note that compassionate love must not be confused with indulgence. Even goddesses representing qualities of mercy must be sought out with clear intent. Traditionally, Kuan Yin is approached with the deepest concentration and surrender of self, and the White Tara, through patience and dedication. The Priestess's experience of descent renders her pure enough to be with her sisters in nonsentimental ways that engender selfless enterprise and service.

"I feel like I'm finally old enough chronologically to be who I am, and not to be embarrassed by my power, by my shamanic inclinations. I no longer care whether people really like me or not, and although I have a broad network of friends, I feel like there's no time for lies or unnecessary niceties about things that are off. We can now begin to speak the truth, and we owe it to one another. I feel that my friends owe it to me to tell me when I'm off or out of it, and my friends have given me permission to speak that way to them. I relish this; it has been a real liberation for me. We've pushed our sisterly relationships to a whole other level where we have an incredible amount of fun together. And we're not tedious with one another—there's no room for being tedious, or whiny.

"So many women I work with say they'd like to show their Priestess side more, but they get the message from their women friends that it's best to suppress it. I tell them to get new friends.

If your women friends aren't supporting you being in your power and being as outrageous as you need to be, if they're intimidated or jealous or feel that they have to compete with you, get a new circle of friends. There are a bunch of women out there who support one another fully in being their most magnificent, radiant selves, and aren't freaked out by one another's beauty or whatever gifts each one may have.

"I think there's been a shift for many women recently. There's a line—quite a moveable line—but a line being drawn by women who identify themselves as healthy, versus women who say, 'I'm still healing,' or, 'I'll never be healed,' or, 'I identify myself as a blah-de-blah survivor of blah-de-blah.' More and more of the women who identify themselves as healthy have less and less patience with women who identify themselves as sick. The line is very permeable—you can move across it at any time. But there's a whole lot of women willing to move on in their lives—whether they've given up one year or ten years or three decades, they're done—and they don't want to hang out with grown women who are always in process, being narcissistic, repeating again and again the same traumas in relationships. We're all carrying various sorts of trauma, but it's where we place our identity that's crucial. For women that say, 'I'm trying to be healed and when I'm healed I'll do something good for the world,' forget it; just get on with your life. You don't have to place your primary identity with being raped (and I speak this from personal experience) or with being molested. It sounds cruel, but there is a time element in our lives; we have only so many decades. Do you want to go to your grave with your trauma as your primary identity or do you want to move on? I say, for the women who have moved on, we're really having a great time together [laughs], and it's very exciting and interesting. It's not inverted or convoluted in on ourselves—we have a whole lot of energy to put out in the world."

Based on love of one another, Priestesses come to realize that power indulged is the root of abuse, while power shared and blended with compassion works the miracle, speeds the healing, and is truly the pathway to wisdom. The union of power and loving compassion creates the experience of ecstasy—which yields the templates for work in the forthcoming Sorceress stage. Again, the seeds of this realization may be found in the Blood Sisterhood, as this woman, age twenty-two, observed:

> "The lessons I learned in the last few years were selflessness and doing no harm. I didn't have control over my emotions and actions before, but now I honor and respect the powers of the mind and manifestation. I take complete responsibility for my energy and what it brings, whether positive or negative. I see how healing actually works—visualization and suggestion shape energy and create our environment."

Another image in the Motherpeace Star card is an eagle, who represents the Priestess's psychic explorations and likewise serves as her guardian, protecting her from harm. The eagle signifies the spirit soaring through other realms and other dimensions, searching out information not readily available on the ground. Flying higher than any other bird, the Priestess-as-eagle reaches an elevation as dramatic as the depth of her former descent. In certain cultural traditions, the flight of an eagle above one's head is considered a call to shamanism. The eagle is also thought to be a messenger, bringing news and instructions from the night. In line with her darkening moon, night-borne wisdom is increasingly important to the Priestess. As she makes the transition to Sorceress, her challenge is to "download" this wisdom and embody it, wield it. Ultimately this means giving up the fight, allowing the changeover to be complete. Vicki Noble notes:

The Star is like Justice, but taken to a higher level. Now there is a conscious submission to Fate, a loving gift of the self to the spirit of life. No more unexpected karmic adjustments, no more confusion about what is right or wrong. Now the being gets in touch, through the body and the feelings, with how things are flowing and what the purpose of life is.[4]

Every woman we interviewed who considered herself in the Priestess stage spoke of this experience of getting in touch, finding life and self in sync. As one woman, age forty-eight, put it:

"The main difference between my Matriarch time and where I am now is that I am free of the struggle; I'm being used by the Mystery, and there aren't any shadowy places I'm trying to manage."

Another woman, age forty-five, noted:

"I have finally learned the art of being present. Before, I would be three steps ahead of myself, jumping the gun, but now I have some daily reminder to stay with what is and not to try to make it go any faster."

A woman in her early sixties recalls:

"I found out some time ago that an important check on how you're doing in life is to see if you're on time. Like if you're waiting for a package and you have to go someplace and the mailman comes right before you have to leave, this shows that you're not behind or ahead of your time track. And if you're not on time, just notice whether you're early or late.

"For the last decade, my life has been full of synchronicity. I'm about to move to New Orleans, I just bought a house there quite impulsively. The woman who is my partner in the deal told me the other day of a vivid dream she had some years ago that one day, she would be very happy at Versailles, and of course, she thought Europe. But this house we bought is on Versailles Boulevard! That's how it's been—things just seem to click."

A much more dramatic example of synchronicity is rendered in the following account from a woman, age forty-five:

"Several years ago, when my lover first came to live with me, I decided to do a rite for Pan—merry woodland goat-god, who my lover completely embodied—to thank him for our union. I did research and wrote several invocations. The ritual itself was very moving, with my lover enacting many aspects of Pan, his unbridled sexuality, his playfulness, his awe and respect for women.

"Several days later, I was driving down my driveway when I noticed something gleaming in the planter near the road. It was a brilliant February day; the sun was blinding on the snow. I picked from the planter a bloody mush encrusted in ice, and realized it was some kind of small horned animal skull, with much of the cartilage and fur still intact. Instead of being alarmed, I felt it was a thing of beauty, the small horns curved exquisitely. As far as how it got there, I didn't think twice because I have dogs, one part coyote and a skilled huntress, although it should have occurred to me that for the dogs to leave a kill in the planter box was a bit bizarre.

"I decided to dry the skull on a peg in my greenhouse. It seemed to have a large chunk of ice lodged inside where the spinal column had inserted. I left it alone and forgot about it, and then, on the second anniversary of my husband's death, I decided to go to the place where he died. As I gathered things to take with me, I passed through the greenhouse and absently picked up the skull, which was now bleached dry. As I turned it over, a beautiful quartz crystal tumbled from the vertebral hole and on to the floor.

"This occurred at a time of my life when I was still half in this reality and half in the other world, due to my husband's death. I assumed that this was a blessing, a magic gift from Pan for calling to him and reawakening the male principle in my life again. My family, on the other hand, wanted to track down the origins of this creature. They brought the skull to the Fish and Game Department for identification and were told that the animal was not indigenous to our area, and, in fact, they had no idea what it was.

"Some years later, after a long night of talking and exploring the Pan story with my new lover, we sat looking at the beauty of the skull and spontaneously turned it over, only to find in the bony structure the face of Pan, the Green Man. This too was a magical gift and foreshadowed, for both of us, lessons yet to be learned about the male principle and our relationship to it."

The synchronicity and prophetic dreaming characteristic of this stage have some basis in hormonal fluctuations. Generally, the Priestess time occurs in our mid-forties—those premenopausal years when we experience the most fertile of cycles, or conversely, wicked PMS. As we age, we skip ovulation occasionally, resulting in diminished progesterone levels. Progesterone moderates the effects of aldosterones, which are responsible for most premenstrual symptoms, so if progesterone levels are low these premenstrual symptoms are apt to go unchecked. The pituitary gland responds to these irregularities by sending out dramatic surges of follicle stimulating hormone (FSH) in an attempt to force ovulation. One woman spoke of being "wet to the knees" with fertile mucus in one such ovulatory period, as well as profoundly desirous of her lover and barely in ordinary reality. In researching women's hormones and their effects on the female psyche for my book *Women's Sexual Passages: Finding Pleasure and Intimacy at Every Stage of Life,* I found that extreme peaks of estrogen are associated not only with increased libido, but with vivid dreams, intuitive insights, and extrasensory perceptions.[5] This may account for the Priestess's ready ability to enter trance states, particularly while in ritual with her peers.

All the more reason, then, for a circle of protection. In the Motherpeace Star card, there are stones circling the perimeter of the pool in which the woman bathes, symbolizing her safety through containment. For any kind of ritual trance or healing work, the circle is "cast" by invoking the powers of cardinal points, the Four Directions of East, South, West, North, and their respective representatives, Maiden, Mother, Matriarch, Crone (or other ancestral guardians) for guidance and protection (see chapter 11 for more information). Carefully and deliberately casting the circle is essential for grounding the physical body so the spirit can travel freely and safely.

In the Waite tarot, the Hanged One is suspended by one foot only, the other leg free and crossed over the body. This is the cross within the circle: an image of containment and self-preservation. Any exploration of life's shadow side bears a certain degree of danger. The Priestess must learn, as was mentioned in an earlier account, to keep body and soul together so the ascent from darkness can be made safely. Poisonous and confounding revelations are everywhere along the way—the Priestess needs to know that such pitfalls exist, and must utilize the support of her sisters to circumvent them. She sees her way through the crack in the mirror, the portal that leads from ordinary to nonordinary reality—she is, in Native American tradition, Changing Woman. But until she learns to transmute that which is toxic, she is changed but not yet the changer, not yet a competent navigator of the way between worlds. She boldly sails upon the magical ship, but only as Sorceress will she take the wheel as pilot.

CHAPTER 8

The Lover and the Sorceress

The Lover and the Sorceress share a deep fascination with the power of love and the union of opposites. As was mentioned earlier by a woman in her Blood Sister years, sexual experience alone does not make a Lover. We must find the maturity to give and take, and sufficient self-respect to relate deeply to another without losing our identity. Male and female aspects—within and without—must be in complementary but egalitarian relationship. This is the key to hieros-gamos, the sacred marriage.

The Sorceress must likewise keep her masculine and feminine energies in harmony, that her wielding of power be for good and not ill. Thus her path becomes somewhat austere; every step she takes has significance. Through her descent as Priestess, she discovers a certain alignment and sense of timing that brings power to her life. If she veers off course occasionally, she will soon be drawn back; her choices are limited but her potency is great.

> "The way I see the Sorceress in me is that I finally know what to do—especially in tough situations, the right words come out of my mouth at the right time. Before, I used to clam up at the crucial moment; now it's like something gets into me, like a wave of energy and I rise to the occasion, I guess. And the higher the stakes, the better I am."

The Motherpeace image that most closely reflects the Sorceress is that of Temperance, the card of the shaman. Despite cultural connotations of self-denial, the core meanings of temperance—distilling or refining, as in tempering steel—are perfectly appropriate. For it is crucial to note that the Sorceress has crossed from the phase of power to that of wisdom. "No longer a novice," Vicki Noble tells us, "the Temperance shaman has come of age. Once having been involuntarily possessed by spirits, the shaman now understands and actively uses the process of 'raising the fire,' calling in the spirits. She is an open channel, cleansed and purified by past process, ready to handle tremendous forces and energies. She does not swing from one extreme to the other, but rides the wave in perfect union with it. . . . [S]he stays in what the Buddhists call the Middle Way, straight to the heart."[1]

We see this in the words of this woman, age forty-nine:

> "My experience as Priestess was service, service to an intelligence greater than mine, and I took my lead from it, I followed it. I crossed to Sorceress when I took that experience and embodied it, became it—the Goddess no longer lives outside of me and informs me. She is within me and I serve by acting her out, being her."

Being in wisdom is a change of focus. Acquisition of power is no longer at issue, declaration of power is no longer necessary. The Sorceress merges with power and draws upon it in all her activities. How does this change take place?

> "I think the ability to do sorcery comes from the loss of control as Priestess. Whatever agenda you've created for things being out of control or out of your hands is the dark spot you have to look into. Each person has a different experience of this—apocalyptic, euphoric, for some it's hell, for others, it's heaven, but either way it's disintegrating.
>
> "We have so many myths about dismemberment, fragmentation of ourselves, and the longing to reassemble parts of us that are disenfranchised. I'm reminded of the story 'La Loba' from *Women Who Run with the Wolves,* about an old woman, a wise woman, charged with finding bones and putting skeletons back together. She has found all the bones of a wolf but one in the left rear foot, and when she finally locates it, she stays up all night in ceremony before putting it in place. When she does, the wolf comes to life as a spirit-woman and leaves, smiling back over her shoulder. Finding the parts of ourselves most difficult to retrieve is trying and sometimes disgusting [laughs], but incorporating these is how we become whole, how we transform."

Bringing warring or scattered aspects of ourselves together is central to the process of ascent or return, whereby we change from Priestess to Sorceress. This is spiritual alchemy, wrought by inner fire. The water of the Priestess stage enables us to flow down to the depths, but the fire of the Sorceress kindles our reemergence, forges our reintegration, and brings us back to life.

How does this relate to the concerns of the Lover? Most young women long to give themselves to love and forge a consummate union that will generate new life. Unfortunately, this seldom involves the egalitarian pairing of complements. Instead we enact the battle of the sexes, with man's misguided quest for domination colluding with woman's submission and colliding with her rebellion. In order for the sacred marriage to take place, roles for each sex must be recast. In pagan tradition, man as lover was Pan, consort to the Goddess: virile, expressive, but always respectful of woman as the source of life. Although we see extremes of nihilistic and sadistic behavior patterns in some young men, others have embraced a Panlike model as described by this man, age twenty-six:

"I have a lot of faith in my generation. As much as people make fun of the older generation of men for looking for the 'inner wild man' and stuff, I see the result in me and my friends, who are a lot more respectful of women and sexuality. I also think it's because women—smart, strong women, including our mothers—were role models. The greatest lessons of Pan come to me by listening to women speak; even in quiet ways, they've taught me a lot.

"I completely relate to Pan and see the way he fit into the old religion, because it's really not a lot different from the way my life has developed. I was raised by women, mostly, and so I found a way through love of women to shape my personality. I wasn't raised by dominance; there wasn't the classic scenario of control issues. I never felt or saw sexism in my family, never felt a struggle between men and women. Because of this, I don't have to spend a lot of time in conflict—it has helped me to see what goes wrong in traditional relationships with women and men, and I don't buy into patriarchal structures set up by churches, the government, and business. Although I was raised by women, that didn't lower my opinion of men; I actually just saw everything as being equal, which makes me feel equally male and female, definitely an aspect of Pan.

"The number one principle of Pan is honesty. I've always been a straightforward, let's-talk-about-what's-going-on-here-

and-now, don't-repress-your-feelings kind of guy, and I see that even some of the most wonderful people in my life, with a little more honesty, could overcome major barriers they struggle with. You create Pan energy by constantly staying in touch and communicating, through love and demonstrative action, by speaking from the heart, even when you're wrong, and by being open to new lessons. That's the way you live it. Honesty, plus equality combined with love and sexuality, all of these working on all cylinders—that's the Pan energy.

"The other way you live it is by having a really fun time! I'm serious—by reminding yourself that hedonism, pleasure however you find it with no judgment attached, is really important. The pleasure principle is a big part of Pan—not letting yourself get trapped into some of the ways we've been patterned to believe that if it feels good, it's wrong, or if it's different, dismiss it. That's a big mistake.

"The most important way to get in touch with Pan is to stop trying to control women's sexuality. That's definitely hard for men to do! I don't know of many relationships where there is not some kind of control thing going on. It's difficult to get beyond, but if you keep reminding yourself . . . it's something you *learn* to do.

"My exposure to women's rituals, pagan ways, the history of what men have done to women, listening carefully to how women relate to pivotal people, all of this has bettered my character, improved my ability to understand relationships. I haven't followed just one religion or path or one way to be, but I've listened and seen and done a lot. All of that equals the song I am. It's like a jazz song, it's free of structure. I think Pan represents a spectrum of possibilities with nonjudgmental respect."

The challenge for any woman Lover is to own her power, to move from the idealism of the Blood Sister stage to realistic self-love, which is the only healthy basis for nurturing. The hard knocks and disappointments of earlier romantic entanglements help her purify and distill her essential self, which she (like the Sorceress) must find a way to honor in order to wield the forces of creation without personal annihilation. The Lover's signifying goddess is Aphrodite, known also as Marianne, the life giver who rises from the sea and stirs the fires of passion. Jean Bolen calls her the "alchemical goddess." She is lust, she is creativity, she is "at one with the union of opposites, constantly uniting, pansexual . . . the sexual goddess and death goddess all at once." But beyond all else, she is her own person, "almighty, irresistible."[2]

From a woman, age twenty-five:

"When I was younger I was quite promiscuous and wild. Sometimes I think I used sex to build my self-esteem—it was a substitute for love. I met an older man and tried the traditional female domestic role, 'librarian' by day, 'hooker' by night, but it didn't feel right. I read a lot, and I knew there was something more for me.

"Then I met a man who understood my ideas and took a genuine interest in how I felt. He knew and loved the experiences I'd gone through to get to where I was, he wasn't angry—I was completely comfortable talking with him about anything; I wasn't ashamed, didn't feel stupid or crazy. I had always thought I had to be quiet and accept the male ways, to serve. But I was completely honest with him from the very beginning, and he told me it was okay; he valued and loved me for my skills, intelligence, and individuality, which I had repressed. He is as much feminine as I am masculine, balanced. Real love creeps up on you—in every other phase of my life I was selfish, but when I fell in love I felt the exact opposite, I just wanted to give. I pay more attention to my health and well-being so I can give my best. As I get comfortable with our love, there is room for the more important things in life. I'm getting a better view of the big picture of my future, financially, physically, professionally, politically, spiritually.

Now everything I have ever done makes sense and has purpose; it has prepared me for what's coming and I can move forward."

The Lover's time is the late morning of the life cycle, moving toward high noon. Her sacred day is Beltane, which falls on May 1 when the earth is surging with new life and spring fever runs hot in the veins. Those who have heard of this holiday often associate it with wanton sexuality, involving mad coupling with any number of partners for purely hedonistic satisfaction. But the original intent of this celebration was to free the sexual energies of the community so that poor pairings might come undone and more fruitful unions be generated in service to the Goddess and the Earth. It is difficult for us to set aside our puritanical mores enough to understand that this ritual was performed in a passionate but sacred way, difficult to imagine a time when stepping outside one's pair bond meant not loss, but gain. Then again, not everyone did step outside; many resanctified their happy union and were satisfied. The true intent of Beltane was to give honor to the forces of creation and regeneration, to entwine the Maypole, the phallic shaft of life, with the ribbons of female fecundity.

For Lover and Sorceress alike, the specter of jealousy may rear its ugly head and threaten to destroy the most wonderful relationships. Many women entering the Sorceress stage identified jealousy as the prime motivation for their efforts to transmute the last vestiges of clinging, dependent love into love self-affirming and transcendent. Offering unconditional love to an adulterous partner may sound preposterous, but only by thoroughly understanding the male and female energies within each of us, the lusts and desires of each aspect, can we find our way out of the jealousy trap.

One woman, age fifty-two, speaks of her struggle to cope with an expanded relationship:

"I must admit that I've tried to create diversional energies between my man and his current intrigue. It's like changing the course of a powerful river with intention, but I'm trying to be very careful because I feel like I benefit from the river myself—the river is magic, the river is sex, sexual transcendence.

"I have some sense that our relationship has spaciousness in it, but for me to continue as his lover, he can't go much farther. I use my intention to blur the edges of our sexual triangle, to soften my fear and let it go. I actually think being a Sorceress is about learning to be in spaciousness by yourself. I almost made that choice permanent when we were separated for a while, but even now that we're back together I have not stopped choosing myself, and the spaciousness to be broad-minded. I feel safe there, like my alignment is not in question—I actually feel safer in the big space, getting rid of the trappings of the old Lover archetype."

It is useful in this regard to compare the Waite tarot cards of Devil and Lovers. Both feature male and female in union with each other, but the Lovers card shows a woman looking aloft, connected to the Divine while the man looks at her adoringly, whereas the Devil card shows partners focused only on themselves, not even looking at each other, chained and bound. Vicki Noble calls the Devil "Denying the Spirit." Her commentary notes the dualism created when Pan was reconfigured as Satan by patriarchal religions.

In a more positive light, the Devil card may be viewed as a call to come to terms with our shadow side, the denied aspect that haunts, restricts, and controls our reactions to those we love. The charge of the Sorceress is to differentiate "power over" from "power with," to learn to be inclusive in thought and deed, to flex personal boundaries, to take a broad view. It is crucial, however, that this effort be reciprocal among intimate partners, and that neither take advantage of the other.

The Sorceress's signifying goddess is Medusa, who represents the double-edged sword of women's power, the beautiful and the terrible, the ever-present threat of power's abuse. In some representations she was veiled; lifting the veil brought knowledge of death and the future. She was accordingly linked to various menstrual taboos—to meet her glance was to know the mystery of her magic blood, which could create or destroy life.

The Sorceress's holy day of Samhain falls on November 1. Note the proximity to our Halloween, which means literally, hallowed evening. The Mexican counterpart is the Day of the Dead on November 2, when ancestors are remembered on family altars, and are visited and fed at their gravesites. Beltane celebrates fertility and the act of conception; Samhain honors opposite forces of death and regeneration. Contemporary Halloween celebrations barely acknowledge death; we do recognize the witch, but our cultural characterization falls short of her true essence and power. The word *witch* is derived from the Anglo-Saxon *wicce* meaning seer or diviner. What does the witch divine at Samhain? Plenty, as Barbara Ardinger reminds us: "Although the door between the worlds of the living and the dead is ajar on all four quarter days, it's open widest on Samhain."[3] In pagan traditions, this is the Witches' New Year.

The Sorceress's moon is the final crescent, on the boundary between light and darkness. And she may find herself at yet another threshold, that of menopause. If so, erratic cycles and hormone surges can cause emotional and physical reactions so extreme that she sometimes feels near madness, on the brink of supreme creativity and ruthless destruction simultaneously. As her fertility passes away, she must transmute procreative energies to something else. Passion is one of her allies; she is Shakti woman, using sexual energy to initiate change. In her lovemaking she aims for resonance, not ease, and often takes giant leaps in the bedroom that reveal hidden aspects of her subconscious.

Remember that the Sorceress, if menopausal, steps out of the monthly cycle and likewise out of time. Less and less bound by physical rhythms, she takes an overview of life that clarifies her duties and responsibilities. Beyond her experiences of synchronicity as Priestess, the Sorceress perceives the spiritual superstructure in which these occur. She then enacts, in real time, events she has already foreseen.

One woman described this experience as "being in a prayer and working with it." Along these lines, menopause experts Christiane Northrup and Mona Schultz are currently engaged in research suggesting that the hormonal changes concomitant with this transition may actually precipitate transcendent, even visionary experiences. They found that levels of follicle stimulating hormone (FSH) and luteinizing hormone (LH), which prompt ovulation and conception, were extraordinarily high in menopausal women—up to a thousand times higher than at any other point in the life cycle. This made little sense, for why would the body produce these substances at a time when they could serve no purpose? Then they found evidence to suggest that in postmenopausal women, FSH and LH serve as neurotransmitters in the right hemisphere of the brain, in centers associated with creativity and intuition.[4]

The power of the Sorceress would seem much less obtuse or farfetched if we had a practical definition of alchemy in our culture. One reason we do not is that conventional Christianity has sought to suppress this information—after all, women are expected to submit to the "will of God" and seek refuge in male authority figures that actively discredit feminine power and magic. Thus the Sorceress is a controversial and relatively untapped figure in our society.

Alchemy is the art and science of transformation, based on principles of unification and, in the personal realm, self-healing.

Although of ancient derivation—*Al Khemeia* is Arabic for "matter of Egypt," where alchemy was supposedly invented—the practice became popular in Europe around the time of the Inquisition.[5] It is strongly linked to Celtic magical traditions, based on sexual and ecological harmony. The precise nature of alchemical experimentation remains something of a mystery, but surviving texts and writings, steeped in sexual allegory and symbolism, provide a clue. Constant references are made to alchemical procedures as "copulations" and "marriages." There has been some speculation that in a time when science was highly suspect, sexual and mystical imagery might have been used to marginalize and veil laboratory experiments. But British authority Alan Bleakley disagrees. "Although riddled with obscurities," he concedes, "the vast and complex literature of medieval alchemy is describing fundamental and real changes in the human body . . . that is seen as the container for transforming the psyche."[6]

Old plates both picture and describe a series of steps in the process of alchemical transformation, involving the union of man and woman. The initial stage of *philosophorum* has images of king and queen standing face to face, "identified with their separateness" yet in relationship. *Rosarium* pictures the two seated in a tub together, the water symbolic of the immersion in unconscious life which happens when we are deeply in love and communicate our dreams and visions to one another; Bleakley describes this stage as that of dialogue with the contrasexual archetype, when man and woman respectively make contact with anima and animus. The *convinctio sive* portrays sexual union, the conjunction. The process then comes full circle back to *philosophorum,* but with a new image of a single body with two heads, half male, half female—the androgynous self, reborn in command of opposing elements.

We have already discussed the importance of egalitarian self-love, or *philosophorum,* in approaching the opposite sex (or one's complement, regardless of gender). The stage of *rosarium* is worth exploring further, as it reveals the context necessary for sexual union to generate alchemical results. Without a commitment to go deep down, to contact our most basic fears and desires, sexual union will be compromising and unfulfilling, temporal and temporary. We must search out the shadow, the irretrievable aspects, the unresolved traumas that are carried in our bodies, often as weakness or disease. Once raised to consciousness, this shadow material is less likely to be projected on our loved ones as blame, suppression, even violence.

As one woman, age fifty-four, relates:

"So much of the time in relationships where love is involved or chemistry is involved, there's no real intention established in the beginning. And if not, when you get to a certain point—the chemistry has gone to a very sophisticated level but the intention hasn't been made clear—then a whole lot of compromising takes place.

"I still have this primitive lover in me, and part of my work as Sorceress is to transcend the narrow confines of romantic structure, or modernize it . . . maybe I just want to modernize it. There is so much baggage, a cultural clothesline of values I keep dragging around that heavily reinforces old behavior patterns. I've got so much melding in my primary relationship that I really want to change."

Old alchemical writings teach:

The substance that harbors the divine secret is everywhere, including the human body. It can be had for the asking and can be found anywhere, even in the most loathsome filth.[7]

The shadow is vulnerability, known in old Celtic legends as the "wound that does not heal," or what Bleakley refers to as menstrual wisdom:

> If the wound is left as an openness in character, a place where feeling and value speak directly, rather than closed over prematurely, then we may engage with the shadow through this wound, and in this, energy is released for creative application.[8]

For a woman, contacting her animus may mean enlivening the Pan energy deep inside her, engaging the "wild horned one" within and without, allowing herself to become focused and intent, joyous and playful. Experience with blood bonding or entrainment helps the Sorceress explore her animus with feedback and support. (At the same time, if her partner is male, he needs to get in sync with his feminine aspect.)

The *convinctio* step may be performed in actual sexual union, or in a more amorphous blending of male and female aspects within oneself. The key is to consciously recognize the third element being created—that which is rendered by the combination of the red and the white, the blood and the semen, the salt and the sulfur, variously called yab-yum, the healing waters of the *vesica pisces,* or the mercury of alchemical texts. The third element forms a third body or sacred container sometimes referred to as the philosopher's stone, or pot of gold at the end of the rainbow. Bleakley describes this "rainbow body" or "peacock's tail" as a fanning out of feelings: rich, colorful, and new. The alchemical symbol is the double pelican vessel wherein animus and anima begin to relate, and whereby inner and outer aspects of oneself become luminous.

Giving oneself over to *convinctio* may be the only real antidote for jealousy. For the third element is not only the product of alchemical union, but its catalyst as well. In order to face jealousy squarely, we must draw upon the sacred container, the big space of the subconscious, and come to know the invisible partner, the animus within.

Many of us mistakenly believe that to come to terms with male and female elements means to fuse them so that they lose their singularity. Bleakley compares the dynamic relationship of masculine and feminine to a guitar string stretched just so—if drawn too tight or left too loose, beautiful music cannot be made.[9] If opposite aspects are isolated, there is little or no charge between them; if they are melded too tightly, they become inert. Understanding this dynamic is the key to transcendence that creates the crack in the mirror, the way between worlds.

The Celestine Prophecy addresses this issue as a need to move beyond codependent relationships. Author James Redfield explains that as new lovers, we commonly (and mistakenly) identify our loved one as the ultimate source of joy, meanwhile neglecting our own self-development. When love fades from lack of nourishment, we increasingly demand, or may even attempt to force from our lover, the good feeling we miss. Acting as if half of a whole, and counting on our loved one to complete us, we enact a deficit, codependent model of relationship opposite that of true love, which can only be realized by "accessing this opposite sex energy in ourselves," learning to complete the circle on our own.[10]

Dynamic harmony between masculine and feminine energies is what generates the final form of *philosophorum,* in which a single body blends both male and female aspects. But keep in mind that the figure pictured in old alchemical drawings has two distinct sides, with separate heads and gender characteristics on either side of the body. Contrary to popular belief, the most transcendent mental states are associated with optimal activity of both right and left sides of the brain, objective and subjective aspects blending to create "interhemispheric coherence." Quantum physicist Eugene Wagner calls this "conservation of parity," a preservation of opposites that leads to creative insight.[11]

The final stage of *philosophorum* is suggested by the rebus symbol of androgyne, and also the goddess Sophia, who has red blood and white milk streaming from her breasts. Many creation myths figure the first humans as androgynous. The Hindus, Chinese Taoists, Persians, and early Jews all portrayed male and female as originally united in a bisexual body. The Greek Zeus supposedly envied these beings for their eternal bliss and tore a piece of clay out of the female part, which he then attached to the male: "That is why," the myth concludes, "women have an orifice that bleeds, and men have a loose dangling appendage that seems not to belong to them but always craves to return to the female body it came from."[12]

Sex returns us to this original, blissful state of union. Tantrism seeks to recreate the androgyne through prolonged sexual contact with limited movement. Certain techniques shared by Tantra, Kundalini, and other spiritual disciplines also seek the *philosophorum* state, and can be used either in partnership or individually.

When the Sorceress steps outside of time, she transcends gender attributes as well. Her body changes dramatically, certain armoring is surrendered, her physical rhythms are less personal and more universal. As she becomes adept, she is apt to feel more energy running through her system than she has ever known before. Healer Richard Moss describes this experience as follows:

> Every cell can be alive and vibrating as if one was electrical or indescribably blissful, and this seems to fluctuate of its own accord until there is a gradual stabilization. Basic to this is an inner kind of balance that cannot be described and must just be learned moment to moment . . . if one comes into harmony with the current, the sense of strength and vitality can be nearly superhuman.[13]

On the other hand:

> Physical symptoms such as tremor, weakness, extreme sensitivity to heat and cold, muscle spasms may occur . . . even when there is inner peace, the initial energy can simply be too much for the body—something like putting too much current through a wire.[14]

This may lead to emotional and mental instability, or feelings of insanity as related by this woman, age forty-eight, in her story of "Crazy Woman":

> "What I experienced was having the energy of the earth come through my body. It was very physical; it would shake me. It would shake and open, it roared and channeled a voice that many times had no words, but sound. It was *her* speaking and I knew that. She would not say—I would get an image, because words were hard. So sacred I couldn't utter a word to anybody, except a few women that were with me at these times.
>
> "At some point, I realized that for me to complete my path and challenge my life, I would have to go farther, and ask Crazy Woman to come in. We did a ritual on the dark of the moon and asked her to come. Right prior to that, I think maybe to prepare me, an owl landed in the field with us and came down on my shoulder. I thought, 'If the owl has come, maybe I really need to be prepared for Crazy Woman when she comes in.' Boy, did she come in! She is not easy, a very, very challenging partner to work with. She has a lot of pain to work through, she'll drive you nuts. She embodies the bag ladies on the street, all the crazy people out there, all the pain they have. When there is war, she is there. Our fear of her does not help; it makes her work more difficult. Then she becomes angry; she will whip you up.
>
> "Two mistakes I have made with her. One was when I asked her to come in—I didn't protect myself enough—I should have asked Kuan Yin to be present and embrace me. And later, when

I thought my work with her was done, I decided to burn her mask. The mask was black with snakes coming out, kind of like Medusa. We placed it on the fire, and it came *alive* with flame coming from the eyes, the mouth, and then she became immensely more powerful. I went through months of spiritual pummeling—my house burned to the ground, I was sued, and there was death. She would come and haunt me in my dreams—I tell you, she will *whip you up!*

"After that, I realized I hadn't done anything to get rid of her. Once she is with you, I realize now, you have to own her, she will never go away. Now she is my ally, and I will forever honor her. She gives me incredible strength—divine madness. It has been a few years now—I don't call her very loud. I'm humble when she comes, and I work when she needs work to be done, and I'm not afraid. I work with pride; I stand with my gifts."

The process of working in mystical relationship with a guide is another form of alchemy. This account makes abundantly clear that even though our Sorceress work is solitary, we still need a circle of protection, and at all times must be grounded in our practice. For one woman, this involved a new approach to ritual:

"I feel like my work—and I'm in the baby stages of the Sorceress—is practicing ritual, doing it on my own, not going by the books or the material that's out there. I want to be eclectic, to pull from my day-to-day experience, from nature and life around me. Like in the sixties, when we created our own religions, we can create our own rituals with materials at hand. The power of traditional religions like Catholicism revolves around getting people to practice ritual on a regular basis. Familiarity with the ritual process is a great strength, a great power—it involves magic.

"It is my intention to practice ritual in a conscious way, so it eventually integrates into my daily life. It's not about discipline—I don't think the Sorceress could be that way—it's got to be fluid, but you have to develop a certain degree of skill in order to be fluid. The most important thing, I think, that a Sorceress can do is to set aside integrative time, reflective time as part of her work—that's really what ritual does, it gets you focused and hopefully provides you with free space and time that you have created for yourself. And on that level you become a master of time—you can take a little capsule of time and light your candles and incense and use the simplest artifacts. It's about being on time, but not in the sense of punctuality. It's more about pacing, giving priority to daily life."

Artistic expression can be another vehicle for grounding. Aleister Crowley interprets the Temperance card as Art. In indigenous cultures, art is considered not so much a talent as an avenue of expression, available to all. In the folk-art tradition, art serves dual functions of self-revelation and community inspiration. Here is what one contemporary artist had to say about her work:

"After a period of great change in my personal life, I started a series of palm tree drawings, all very surface, from my textile design background—patterning, patterning—and then I tried them on larger paper, but they just looked wrong. It's like they couldn't get bigger from the outside—I had to go inside and enlarge the patterns (duh!). I used a buildup of mixed media—many layers of paint, oil pastel, tissue paper, Chinese funeral paper, watercolor—and added symbols, hieroglyphics to create these cellular images, expressing my own cellular memories. When it came time to show them, I titled them, 'Women Weave Patterns.'

"As a Sorceress, I am looking at my life; it is a life examined, and I have a focus, my art. I've always thought of art as a healing force and I assume, because it is a healing process for me as my energy goes into a piece, that when people have the piece around them, they'll feel that too.

"I can't censor what I create anymore; it's who I am, and I must be authentic, it's all I can do. Every day, I wake up in the morning and say to myself, 'Pay attention, be present, open your eyes to see.' And sometimes you have to say, this is not the time to do this work, or that. I'm happy with what I'm creating now, because I gave it the time. It's a matter of attention—the elements are there if I am. When I'm grounded, things just snap and pop, and when I'm not, I don't get it. I do tarot daily now, and I pick grounded friends, eat well, and get bodywork when I need it. I have certain bad habits I'm committed to breaking through— I want transformation."

Part of the task for Lover and Sorceress alike is to make manifest. In order to cross to the stage of Mother, the Lover activates the alchemy of sexual union to generate the third element or love body, be it a child or some core creative endeavor. The Sorceress manifests the marriage of alchemical forces within herself, and, dancing in ecstatic alignment, begins to reweave society. The spiritual superstructure becomes cultural as the Sorceress crosses to Cronehood.

CHAPTER 9

The Mother and the Crone

Both Mother and Crone engage in caretaking. The Mother nurtures her young, or some brainchild or creative endeavor, while the Crone, in her wisdom, nurtures society. These are basic, natural roles for women, yet neither comes easy in this culture. For instead of being sought out and honored for her seasoned perspective, the Crone is relegated to obscurity, guilty of the crime of aging. And the Mother has the overwhelming task of caring for children, partner, career, and self in relative isolation.

Here we return to the subject of grounding. Recall how the Sorceress finds this within herself, as is appropriate in her darkening moon, a time of introversion. But the Lover, focusing increasingly on the outer world as her rising moon dictates, seeks support from society to ground herself for the tasks of motherhood, only to find the help she needs to be virtually nonexistent. No wonder many women postpone starting families or forgo having children altogether, so grim is the prospect of struggling single-handedly with such weighty responsibilities.

Lack of social support makes the Blood Mystery of childbirth critically important for a positive transition to motherhood. If the Mother feels transformed and empowered by her birth experience, she may be able to forge the strength within herself to handle the complexities of her new role. Postpartum challenges of sleep deprivation, lack of privacy, and newborn crying jags drive many women near to madness, but those who have experienced birth as a personal triumph speak of drawing on their memories of labor, thinking, "If I can go through that, I can do anything." I have noticed that women who fall in love with themselves while giving birth more readily give love to their babies and partners, particularly when the going gets rough. Women deprived of menarche rites (or otherwise deep connection to the body prior to labor) often find that birth brings sweet integration and unprecedented self-esteem. A positive encounter with the mystery of creation not only brings a baby but rebirth to the Mother, which is how it is meant to be.

Of all the Blood Mysteries, childbirth most involves descent. Perhaps this is because the Mother's moon is full, at an extreme requiring its opposite for balance. The Mother finds the polarity of darkness in the descent of birth, a descent so dramatic that women often feel their lives to be on the line, as all vestiges of control and identity must be surrendered and swept aside. This *petite mort* ("little death") of childbirth is reflected in the Mother's holy time of Summer Solstice when, in the midst of long and brilliant days, darkness returns and begins to increase.

"Childbirth classes taught me to steel myself through contractions so I coped all right, but after twenty-six hours of labor my midwife said, 'You're stopping it, you're not letting it happen,' and threatened to take me to the hospital. Then it came to me to just let go—I was getting through labor instead of opening up to it—and as soon as I let go, everything happened. This was hard for me to do, because I'm a real control person. And even though I knew this in my head, the same thing happened again with my second and third births. I'd try to do what I thought I needed to, and then my midwife would say, 'Just let go.' Just let go?? I wanted to haul off and hit her—just let go!! Then that moment again, and dammit, she was right.

"With having kids, I became much softer. I'm more myself around my kids than anyone else. You just have to relax and let things take their natural course with children—you can't force them to do anything. Most of my good emotional memories come from being a mother. I'm really able to be a child again myself, in ways I wasn't able to in childhood."

As mentioned earlier, medications and interventions commonly used in hospital birth greatly interfere with this potential for rebirth. Worst of all is prescheduled cesarean section—here, the Mystery is avoided altogether. And yet, it is both curious and wondrous that, in spite of fairly sophisticated medical knowledge of pregnancy, we still do not know what makes labor start. This is akin to our inability to predict the precise configuration of factors that will bring us (or anyone) to death's door.

To deny the mysterious aspects of birth is to retard the metamorphosis of motherhood. The descent aspect enables women to recontact the deepest places and darkest fears within themselves and rally their core resources, which in turn leads to superhuman strength and ecstasy with ascent. Early in my work with birth, I recognized the two primary stages of labor as metaphors for death and rebirth. The first stage of cervical dilation calls for total surrender, letting go of the body, dissolving personal boundaries until, at the peak of transition, we feel barely in the earthly realm. The second stage of bearing down is heralded by a call back into the body, which leads ultimately to the powerful, orgasmic release of delivery.

But our culture has so sterilized and stylized birth that we miss these mythic dimensions altogether, and somehow think we're the better for it. Nearly 80 percent of births today occur under epidural anesthesia, which numbs from the waist down. Hailed as the "Cadillac of anesthesia," the epidural reduces birth to a spectator sport, devoid not only of the agony but the ecstasy of natural delivery. Many birth practitioners (myself included) observe that women who receive epidurals not only miss the pushing urge (which often necessitates forceps or vacuum extraction of the baby), but more critically, exhibit fewer of the spontaneous, genetically encoded bonding behaviors normal for new mothers. Instead, they look to those around them to tell them what to do. This observation is corroborated by research on birthing ewes, who exhibited severely impaired bonding behaviors when peridural (milder in effect than epidural) anesthesia was used, particularly in first births and for extended periods.[1] Certain of these behaviors, such as establishing eye contact with the newborn and methodically stroking its body, are meant to firm up the alliance between a mother and her offspring enough to ensure its survival. In the animal kingdom, impaired bonding almost always leads to maternal rejection of the newborn, resulting in death. It appears that our mechanized approach to the Blood Mystery of birth is potentially disabling for women, children, family, and culture.

One woman describes her experience:

"I gave birth the first time back in the early seventies, in what I would call the 'dark ages of childbirth.' Actually, I'd witnessed a home birth during my pregnancy, and wanted to do it this way myself. But there were no midwives around back then, so I asked the woman whose birth I'd witnessed if she would assist me. As fate would have it, I went into labor a month early when my friend was out of town. I went back and forth on what to do, but really felt I had no choice—I had to go to the hospital. There I had every intervention used at the time, including buccal pitocin, which forced my contractions into a nonstop, excruciatingly painful pattern for two-and-a-half hours. My hands were tied down, I had a huge episiotomy, my son was taken away, the hospital had no rooming-in, and the experience was truly a nightmare—except for the moment of birth itself, which was definitely the high point of my life.

"The next time I gave birth, I found midwives and again planned to birth at home. But this time I knew how to prepare: how far into myself I'd have to go to get through the pain, exactly what kind of support and privacy I'd need. Now *this* experience was one of the most exquisite, ecstatic experiences I'd ever known. As I gently pushed my daughter out, slowly and easily so I wouldn't tear, I heard my midwives mumble, 'Oh, if only we had this on tape!' I could feel my daughter's body moving through me, every detail as she emerged. Talk about the orgasm of delivery!

"When I compare this to my first birth, and how I felt minimized, demeaned, even abused by hospital policy, I wish I could go back and do it over again—oh, how many times I've wished this I can't count. But you only get one chance with birth, one chance to get that transcendence and to get your relationship with the baby off to a good start. If it's not good, it affects your confidence as a mother, and I went through incredible anger and lots of guilt for a long time after that first experience. I wish someone—my mother, a friend, anyone—had told me the truth about birth, what it really feels like and how important it really is."

THE BIRTHINGWAY

The Birthingway, which has its roots in Native American tradition, is a rite to prepare the mother-to-be to surrender to the mysteries of labor and birth. It is a powerful ceremony honoring the pregnant woman's strength and beauty as a life-bringer. This tradition may have been the prototype for our much diluted and sanitized baby shower.

Birth rituals are intended to help parents to accept a new person into their midst, but they also strengthen the ties that bind us together in community. In the Sudan, each pregnant woman is honored in a ceremony similar to that of Native American tradition. Her hair is hennaed, braided, and scented; she wears a special bracelet and leather thong around her waist for protection; and she lies on a ceremonial mat of palm leaf stems. Her relatives then gather around to rub her belly with handfuls of millet porridge—vitamin-rich and symbolic of regeneration. In the Mansi tradition, women assist the expectant mother by ritual preparation of birch-bark cradles, special coverlets of swan skin, and pillows of deer fur twice the size of the mother's hand; once these are ready, they begin work on a reed mattress on which the new mother will sit and sleep for a certain number of days following her child's birth.[2] Regardless of cultural specifics, the common purpose of prenatal ceremony is to empower the mother as her time draws near and to replace fear with affirmations of her sacredness as the gateway for new life.

Birthingways of today are basically gatherings of the mother's closest women friends and relatives, who bring gifts to honor her and her baby. They may wish to create ritual space by smudging with sage or cedar, or may simply choose to sit in a circle and talk, sharing words of wisdom regarding the challenges of motherhood, or perhaps a favorite anecdote regarding birth or child rearing. The mother's hair may then be combed and adorned with feathers, ribbons, and shells, her crown bedecked with flowers. Some mothers save these ornaments and use them to make mobiles to hang above the crib. The mother's feet may also be bathed in herbal teas and rubbed dry with cornmeal (once known as the Santo Domingo foot rub, this feels heavenly). Bathing and rubbing the mother's feet signifies the wish that she will success-fully walk the holy path of labor and birth.

All the women in the circle may then unite by lightly loop-ing a length of red yarn around their wrists one at a time, to symbolize the umbilical cord connection each had to her own mother. A bowl of red-stained eggs (dyed in beet juice and tra-ditional at Birthingways) can then be passed around the circle, and each woman in turn may speak three blessings: one for the mother, one for the baby, and one for the global community of women. The mother may also be given gifts of poetry and song. Sometimes she is presented with a bundle or pouch of sacred objects.

When it is time to open the circle, the red yarn is cut so that each woman can keep a bracelet around her wrist to hold the mother in her thoughts until she has her baby. The eggs blessed by the circle are usually buried outside in a special place, where the placenta might later be buried with a fruit tree or rosebush planted above it. (Women who birth in hospital can, by the way, request that their placenta be given to them to take home.)

It is imperative in creating these rites that we stay flexible, letting the personality of the prospective mother be the basis for our design. A simple format involves a gathering for the purpose of making a birth garment for her to wear during labor, such as an oversized T-shirt decorated with fabric pens, stitchery, sequins, and so on. As they make the garment, the women can sing or tell stories about birthing. At the same time, they may also wish to make a small garment for the baby. Or they could gather to make a quilt, each woman creating a square in advance, and then assembling them.

Another simple gesture is the Apache tradition of present-ing the mother with a basket cornucopia full of fruits, candy,

> nuts, and money, to symbolize abundance in the four life stages of infancy, childhood, adulthood, and old age.
>
> Whatever form it takes, feasting and levity always follow the ceremony. At this point, men may also wish to join the party. This is not to say that the father can't have his own ritual celebration—perhaps earlier, when the mother was circling with the women, his male friends and relations might have taken him aside to offer their own anecdotes and words of wisdom regarding parental responsibilities. But because childbirth takes place in the woman's body, it is crucial that the Birthingway be centered on her. As the ceremony concludes, she should feel deeply blessed by her loved ones, infused with courage and love.
>
> —C. LEONARD

We similarly disable young women seeking to mother a creative urge or enterprise by discouraging the self-exploration, however painful or risky, necessary to conceive and bring projects to fruition. Many an office memo with some innovative suggestion for improving company policy has gone unsent, torn to shreds by the author who stops herself, saying, "How dare I?" And with recent trends of corporate downsizing, it has become increasingly difficult for women to find the courage—let alone the support—to strike out on their own.

Too frequently, women fall into the booby trap of nurturing. Forever fulfilling others' needs and expectations to the exclusion of their own, they get stuck in demeaning, self-effacing behaviors. A woman in her fifties reflects:

> "It is nearly impossible not to get stuck in mothering in our society. That's certainly the role that the culture prefers, as far as I can tell. Women's basic and very good impulse to mother children has been so exploited by the patriarchy that they end up being mother

to grown men, who are free to behave like children and become very boring. It's a major cause of dissension between men and women, this exploitation—there's such a pull to keep us locked into that place.

"To break out of being defined as a nurturer, a woman has to commit to her own life, and doing that is scary—choosing yourself instead of someone else is really a frightening thing to do, like you're being a bad girl. But even as a mother, you have to make a commitment to your own life. And I don't think that can be done without a circle of sisters, where you learn to feel good and wonderful about yourself as you see yourself reflected in the eyes of women that you love very much—it helps you decide you are worth it, that your own life really must come first."

Women in their Crone years face similar risks of exploitation. Instead of being granted influential social positions commensurate with their wisdom, Crones of today are often reduced to menial labor, if they are able to get work at all. In contrast, Crones in the early matrilineal cultures of the Middle East and Egypt dominated the healing arts, working as physicians, surgeons, and midwives. As scribes, they recorded for both temple and court, maintaining vital records and histories, setting up calendars and official tables of weights and measures, transcribing and editing scriptures, running libraries.[3] Yet many Crones in our society live in poverty and isolation, and those that do not must struggle continuously to command mature and meaningful avenues of self-expression. For just as the Mother is bound by her moon's fullness to seek out the dark and fundamental side of life, the Crone, in her dark moon time, needs the light of worldly involvement. Her time is Winter Solstice, when light returns to overcome the darkness.

In many indigenous cultures, Crones have been revered for their Blood Mystery of menopause. By virtue of retaining their "wise blood," with all its magical and visionary properties, they are considered ready to lead society. But we degrade this process to a medical problem that must be remedied with various procedures and drugs, much like childbirth. Just as the specter of cesarean section looms for the expectant Mother, the prospect of hysterectomy is never far from the Crone. And just as every expectant mother must carefully consider not only physical but psychological risks of procedures and medications in labor, so must every menopausal woman consider the risks of hormone replacement therapy—not an easy thing to do, in the face of hard-sell advertising from our pharmaceutical industry.

How does the Crone resist being marginalized—how can she stay strong? She may draw strength from the sense of timing and appropriateness she learned through temperance as Sorceress. Slowly, gently, she reweaves her identity apart from the cycle of reproduction.

"I'm a baby Crone, not a full-fledged Crone for sure—but I've pretty well completed my menopause, I'm beginning to get my energy back, and I'm not feeling the childlike things I felt earlier in my passage. The emotional swings were very much like adolescence—I would feel things explosively, and tears came very easily. For me, this was all part of seeing my attachment to my body, and learning just what my body is and isn't. For instance, my libido went way down, and I've always had a very strong sex drive—it was just like falling off a cliff. I had sworn that I would be vibrantly sexual till my dying day, and when I discovered how much of that urge was really physiological and driven by hormones, I felt a little bit of . . . almost embarrassment at my presumption, thinking that I knew myself and realizing that what I had identified as self was so much physical. At that point, a lot of things started falling away, attachment to being in relationship and to the feeling of protection

I'd had by having another person around. I began to see my strength as coming from my own centeredness, centeredness in Spirit. We are all one and we're all alone; we split up into many pieces to entertain each other, to entertain ourselves.

"I think it's easier as Crone to be entertained by your foibles and those of others because by this time, you've seen things come and go and a lot of them are beginning to repeat—you see the patterns so much better because you have a length of time behind you for seeing what the larger cycles are, so you can laugh along, take and enjoy; let life come and go both at the same time."

As a mediator between inner and outer worlds, the Crone discerns her profound responsibility to the larger organism, Gaia. To do this she must draw ever deeper into solitude, at the same time becoming translucent so that her experience of the depths shines through:

"An important piece of this is that you no longer believe, in an ego-related way, that you are the be-all and end-all, the source, the doer. You identify with a much more universal force and allow it to move you—for you are the only manifestation of the divine who can do what you do, and by surrendering to what that is and getting out of the way, putting all the ego stuff and doubt out of the way, you become capable of living in the most beautiful, graceful, efficient, effortless way possible."

Two tarot cards express the Crone's duality: the World and the Hermit. Vicki Noble retitles the Hermit as Crone, describing her as one who has "learned the power of energy retention—she can choose how to spend or store her energies."[4] The card's subtitle, "Turning Inward," speaks to the Crone's need to withdraw from life so that she may better know the Mystery, understand her dreams, and perceive forthcoming events. The Crone is the ultimate active listener, forever tracking the tone and timing of whoever or whatever speaks to her. According to Mary Daly, she "peers into the labyrinth beyond the foreground," so that she may move ever deeper into the core of being.[5] This is motivated not in small part by decreasing levels of vitality and physical strength: the simple process of aging leads to surrendering the inessential.

> "Paring down really begins with menopause, because at that point you so poignantly feel the traditional beauty you've carried, whatever that might have been, falling away, and the need to replace it with that real beauty from the inside. That is imperative or you and your image of yourself fall away too—and that's pretty sad. I think we women are really fortunate to have menopause as part of our life cycle, because it pushes us into a reckoning that I see men just floundering about with—they don't have any landmark, or watermark, by which to gauge, 'Oh, well, I'm aging and it's okay to let go.' Little things start to fall away—you can't do such fine needlework as before, you can't hear quite as well and have to ask to have things repeated, or ask for help moving something heavy. All the things you have prided yourself on physically are just taken, pared, or given away, which is really preparation for the final transition of death. If you pay attention now and learn how to surrender the little things, you'll be able to let go of the important ones more gracefully when it's time."

The Crone also pares away deliberately, even harshly, that which alienates, confines, or unduly conditions her in any situation, any circumstance. For only by unraveling and deconstructing false, inauthentic parts of herself can she undertake her masterwork of weaving the largest and most complex tapestry imaginable—the Web of Life. The Crone's task of simultaneously reconstructing herself and society is what Noble calls "Casting the Circle." As she manifests results of deep inner work, the Crone brings to light (and finds balance for) her otherwise dark and solitary explorations.

One aspect of this process is simple truth telling, or what one woman referred to as reclaiming her voice:

"Claiming your voice is a big part of maturation, because when you're a mother guarding children and needing help with their protection and so on, there are times when you do shut up for the greater good. At menopause, there's so little left to lose that, well, if you're ever going to speak your true being, now is the time to start or your habits will just go to the grave with you. And so, at a time when on the street you're becoming invisible, you may as well speak up, be noticed for what you really are."

One of the benefits of truth telling is breaking up linear thought patterns, cause-and-effect imprints that hold us back in life. Remember that the Crone teaches by way of example, embodying wisdom rather than imparting it. When she speaks her truth, she instills wisdom in those around her and initiates cross-generational awareness. The Crone is mother to many, not in a nurturing sense but by providing a sophisticated point of reference within life's framework.

"In terms of my work, I'm certainly able to reach more deeply for the motivating energy that's inside and draw it out; I can see how patterns play themselves out and what makes things go one way or another, and link this to other affecting events, as part of a tapestry. Now I feel like I'm actively weaving the tapestry—I'm one of the Fates, rather than being at their mercy.

"But I'm still in transition, there are still parts of me being transformed where I'm not yet mistress of my fate. I definitely feel the difference between where that's so and where I'm in control or in my place, no longer casting about like, 'Should I be over there, or maybe somewhere else?' Right here is just fine, it really feels good to be here, to be me, and the more I find my place, the more I want to nurture it. The part of me that's going, 'Oh,

I don't really know what I'm doing, maybe I should be doing something different,' that part, I'm getting very impatient with— actually, I'm in the process of telling her to go fly a kite."

The paradox of surrender and control experienced in childbirth is relevant here. As Crones, women must likewise find a balance of taking in and letting go. For even as the Crone pares down her personal life she opens her arms to the world—opens them wide, wide as she can. As Sorceress, she danced with the fire inside of her; now she uses the steps she learned to dance with all the Earthly realm. Her dance incorporates the very substance of life—complex and variegated, strong and weak, beautiful and repugnant—that all may be woven in a pattern of unbounded integrity.

As regards her sexual nature, she survives the perimenopausal dip in testosterone and finds her libido well restored. In their research paper titled, "Sexuality in Aging: A Study of 106 Cultures," authors Niles Newton and Rhonda Winn note that in nearly all indigenous societies, postmenopausal women are the most fond of ribald humor, most likely to engage in suggestive dancing and dress, and in 70 percent of these societies, serve as sexual initiators of young men.[6] Apparently, the prevailing wisdom is that older women have the perspective and expertise to cultivate healthy sexuality in the next generation. In this, the Crone invokes Baubo, bawdy goddess of sexual wisdom and humor, she who displays her vulva in bold awareness of its power and sacredness.

The boldness of the Crone links to a deepening perception of her social responsibilities, as well as a desire to reweave cultural woes and misdeeds on the personal level. As this woman, age seventy, relates:

"I don't think about death—I just want to live for several more years; I want to see what's going to happen. When I can no longer do A, I do B. I have two artificial hips, one artificial shoulder, and one artificial knee—the athletic life I once had I no longer enjoy, so I'm learning how to use the computer, I'm taking classes in bridge, things that are substitutes for the fact that I can't go out and play tennis—I just substitute one thing for another. I think you can continue to grow as long as you're not complacent—the brain has a capacity for so much information, and there's an endless pool of material into which we can delve.

"Crone is a terrible word—if you called me a Crone, I'd be highly insulted. Although, in terms of contributing to the world, I've been interviewed by a bunch of people, I've done a lot, with a multiplicity of interests in areas that don't necessarily appear to be connected, and that intrigues people. I still think that when I play my saxophone, I become ageless—I play well, I sing quite well, and my husband and I work twenty jobs a year or more—there's an awful lot of the real me that comes out when I sit behind my horn. I've gotten better, I've honed down the kind of sound I want. We have a studio, and I'll be down at the house thinking, 'I don't want to do it; I don't want to blow,' but the minute I get up there, wow, I can do it. Some sort of energy is released; fatigue and body aches just go, they're not there anymore. That's what creativity does for me. And it's without boundary—I guess I could say the music comes through me.

"What's been hardest for me is being a woman in this society. All the things I wanted to do were thwarted because I was a woman, and that has really been rough. The idea of being a second-class citizen, simply by birth—that's been the tough stuff. To give you a clue—in grammar school I played in the band, I was the lead saxophone. When I went to high school I was prepared to go on, and Mr. Morton, my band teacher, said, 'Oh, you're a woman, you can't play in the band.' That really cut me to the quick. And then when I was in college, I majored in anthropology and wanted to go out on field trips and again, 'Oh, you can't go on field trips, you're a woman.' Those are the things that have really hurt, that have been the hardest for me. To this day, and to the day that I'm lying on that cold marble slab, I'll still be mad at Mr. Morton and the guys in anthro who told me 'No.'"

Incorporation of pain and suffering is critical to the Crone's work, and essential to her wisdom. Her alchemy is to transmute the substance of pain—ignorance, injustice, cruelty, violence, and abuse—to compassion and caring for all humankind. As Mary Daly says of Crones like herself, "We use the visitations of demons to come more deeply into touch with our powers/virtues . . . unweaving their deceptions, we name our Truth."[7] Thus the Crone becomes indomitable; her ruling goddess, Hecate, is the watcher at the crossroads who hears the cries of women in sad confusion and comes to their aid.

And so, the Crone becomes healer. Not only does she heal through social activism, but also one-on-one. She holds the big space in which others may become fully authentic, fully themselves. She discovers that once on the other side of menopause, all barriers to her healing and visionary abilities are more or less gone for good. The work of going deep inside, deep into the Mystery to bring forth healing tools and information is her right, her destiny, and her truth of being at this point in her life.

On a personal note: when I went through my menopause, I often felt like I was going crazy. I wanted to do it without drugs, although sometimes my intimates, particularly my husband, urged me to see a doctor. I'm not opposed to medical assistance per se, it's just that I felt that what was happening to me was so much more— I'd learned the truth about the power of the Blood Mysteries through my birth experiences, and so I trusted that menopause too had special secrets to reveal.

I was so right! Once my bleeding stopped, I found I could meditate, enter trance states, and communicate intuitively with my friends and family in ways I had only dreamed of before. Then, when I hadn't bled for almost a year, I suddenly got one last period and it was as if a curtain fell before my eyes—I could no longer see in this new, visionary way.

This experience gave me perspective on where I had been and where I now was, and gave me even more confidence in my healing abilities. In the months that followed, I began to teach other women how to find and use these abilities, and would occasionally be asked by one to do a private healing. I cannot put into words the power and beauty of these experiences, and the tremendous amount I've learned from each one. I'd honestly have to say that this experiential way of learning while in deep, sacred space has replaced my former penchant for book study—not only can I now know directly, but I learn even more when I practice one-on-one.

And there is a lot to learn in tangling with the great Web of Life! Things are not always what they seem, the best way is not necessarily the shortest, and humor can often move mountains when all else fails. This too is the wisdom of Hecate—that the clever are apt to survive. The Crone is like Hecate in that she learns shape-shifting—the art of changing one's appearance and identity at will in order to meet some challenging situation or to embody truth from a particular vantage point.

> "One thing I've learned is that people are nice to old ladies. I got stopped for speeding on the freeway; I was doing eighty-five. I think the state trooper who pulled me over was surprised when he saw me. He should have given me a ticket—I deserved it—but instead, he gave me a warning. I have this friend, she's at least as old as I am, maybe older, and we agreed that when it suits us, we'd play ditzy old ladies. Really, you can do wonders with that one.

"The Crone has a lot of power. Because at this point, you've endured everything life can hand out. And life can hand out some tough stuff. But you come back, and you survive. One bitter lesson I've learned is not to put up with any more bullshit. You see through people and the crap they try to hand you, and there comes a point in your life where you say, 'No more bullshit,' and just walk away from it.

"Now I have time to become involved in things I see are wrong and need to be fixed; I can finally do this work. My peers are doing the same. We're trying to make things better, not only for our age group, but for children and young people. In spite of what people think, old age is a time you can really get a lot done.

"I think the Crone has great dignity. She commands respect. I expect people to respect me. I know there are people who fear me [whispers] and I'm glad for that!"

To get things done in the world, Crones commonly band together. It is a little known fact that our constitution is an exact replica of the Iroquois model of leadership (with which Thomas Jefferson was most impressed) but for one critical omission—we left out the Council of Clan Mothers (or Grandmother Council), the backbone of tribal decision making throughout Native America. Imagine how different life would be if the Grandmothers were regularly consulted on all major environmental, economic, or political issues! And according to the Native American "law of right relationship," the Grandmothers also had the final say in setting right any social or political misdeed. For example, if a chief was not leading his tribe in such a way that the people had adequate food, water, and shelter, the Grandmothers saw to it that he was replaced. Or if in times of war, a chief instigated animosity to the point that the tribe's well-being was threatened, the Grandmothers would either redirect him or have him removed. The rule of thumb was that serious decisions should be made with the long view, justifiable for a minimum of seven generations![8]

Along these lines, here is what one modern-day Crone had to say regarding the responsibilities of women—and men—in society:

"I've been thinking a lot lately about what I call the four great mysteries—birth, death, sex, and food—and how these at one time were held by women, I'm sure of it, and how in each case they were usurped by the patriarchy and desacralized, exploited, and commercialized, and are now devoid of their sacred intention. The results, as anyone can see, are a disaster. I think that women need to start holding these again, which isn't saying that men can't approach these mysteries too, but is saying, 'It's through this door, and no other way.'

"I've also been thinking about sexuality, how sacred the womb is and that women should always be the custodian of this mystery. Not by talking, but by what they allow and what they initiate. I personally feel that intercourse is mostly for having babies, that it's a very small and limiting way to see sexuality. There's a whole, vast energy available if you don't get hung up on a phallocentric way of behaving. The Crone should be teaching this to the Daughter and the Maiden and the Blood Sister so they are empowered to hold the sacredness—this would put a big dent in rape, unwanted children, and all the other abominations in the sexual field.

"Since women relinquished the sacredness of life's mysteries (or had it terrorized out of them), they have fear of picking it back up again. I talk about this to women everywhere, and at first they are excited but then start worrying as they consider the implications. It's frightening to take charge again. It's precarious enough with one's partner, but even within ourselves it's really a struggle to recast our own patterns, and the more this involves sex and love, the deeper down you have to go, the more ingrained the fear, the darker it is. 'I will be alone, no one will love me like this, I'm not strong or smart enough, I'm nuts. What about my children, what's going to happen to them, I won't survive'—all those voices rise up, and the inner work has to be done so we can learn to live with them. If we run from the voices, we run right into the trap.

"It does come down to being willing to be alone, whatever it takes. Somewhere there has to be a willingness to lose it all. How do you really engage with your life in such a way that you're willing to lose everything in order to make your life good? That's what the Crone does—she risks it all."

THE CRONING RITE

> Ancient Queen of Wisdom
> Hecate, Cerridwen
> Old One—Come to Us!

This rite of passage is observed when a woman has completed menopause, with no bleeding for at least a year. The post-menopausal stage heralds the transition to a new life phase, when she is to be venerated for her life experience. It is a time of celebration. (If a woman has undergone premature menopause due to surgical or chemical intervention, rough guidelines place Cronehood at age fifty-six.)

Menopause honoring still occurs in nonindustrialized societies, but these rites are increasingly contaminated by patriarchal feelings of shame and disgust. Women must reclaim these rites, lest they be obliterated.

In the Seneca tradition, a woman entering perimenopause speaks with the Grandmothers of her tribe and chooses a subject to teach the young women of her community. Possible subjects might be the spirituality of dreams, animals, trees, or food. Or she may choose to address the challenges of maturation for women and children. After teaching for a year, she becomes a Grandmother and is revered as a wise one. When her menopause is finally completed, she is accorded the further honor of being allowed to select the chiefs of her tribe.

Older women of some Jewish congregations mark the transition from mother to elder by changing their names. In similar fashion, Native American women are often given new names at menopause by their chief.

The Croning Rite is designed around a standard format. The woman's female friends and relations gather to decorate the room, using evergreens, which signify immortality, or other boughs of winter classically representing the Crone. The circle is smudged and the Four Directions or four faces of the Goddess called in, particularly Hecate of the North, who represents the crossroads of life and immortality. The ceremony can begin with weaving a Mother-line: as a candle or other ceremonial object is passed around the circle, each woman speaks her name, and then that of her mother, grandmother, and great-grandmother, going back in her female lineage as far as she can remember. "I am Susan, daughter of Caroline, granddaughter of Rose, great-granddaughter of Violet."

The body of the rite can take various forms, from partying with ribald humor to giving gifts of acknowledgment. I recall the rite we held for a Crone midwife, who was retiring from active practice. Each midwife in attendance shared some memory of working with her, and as they told their stories they wove red, white, and black yarn, along with some special trinket, into a "story belt." Some of the stories were hilarious, but the result was a poignant ceremonial object of inestimable value. Or the women in the circle can take turns telling the Crone what it has meant to have her as a friend, or may ask her an important, personal question in hopes that she will provide wise counsel. Remember that this rite is not only a celebration, but also an initiation. According to Native American tradition, the Crone must pledge to use her energy in the service of caretaking and renew-ing life for All Our Relations.[9]

Another possibility is to place a cauldron of water in the mid-dle of the circle, from which each woman drinks in turn, saying, "I accept the wisdom of ages past." The Crone stands in the cen-ter and tells what she has learned in life, what wisdom she still needs, and what things she must yet do to fulfill her life's mission. The oldest woman present comes to her, dips water for her to drink, and says, "Take from the wisdom of the ages the means to fulfill your destiny," or "Shed the skin that has become too tight for you."[10] Then a pomegranate is traditionally given to the Crone—she is to ingest as many seeds as years she has lived, with as many blessings for continued fruitfulness in the years to come.

For the essential aspect of seclusion (found in numerous other rites, and symbolic of rebirth and reintegration), the Crone can conclude her rite privately, going alone to a three-way cross-roads where she offers food and prayer to Hecate:

> I have traveled the road from my mother's breast to
> Cronehood. Thank you, Hecate, for the good seasons
> past and the good seasons yet to come.[11]

The Crone must make her offering and not look back, to signify letting go of regrets while trusting what is yet to come. Mean-while, her "cronies" feast and make merry. They welcome her return with love and laughter, and they open the circle with a pledge of support for her in the crowning years of her life.

> Nascent rites can be enlarged and formalized. What is
> required is a small community of family and friends, some
> symbolic and traditional sources of inspiration, a clear for-
> mulation of the change involved and its significance—and
> courage.[12]

—C. LEONARD

Every Crone we interviewed spoke of being freed from her former identity through risk taking. Many felt that their experience of life had become so rich and variegated that they related less to Cronehood than to each and every point on the Circle. One woman spoke of getting up each morning and more or less pulling a stage from the pot, depending on her frame of mind. This ability to do virtually anything is one of the hallmarks of Cronehood.

> "I've finally realized I've got nothing to lose anymore. I can do exactly what I've always wanted to do, which is paint. Up until now, I discouraged myself by thinking of all the good painters already out there, and, after all, I've been a weaver all my life. But now I have this overwhelming relief at having gone through all the stages so I can finally be free to do what I want.
>
> "I've also decided that wisdom is 95 percent fatigue; you get so tired of dealing with inconsequential things that don't really matter that you just drop them from your psyche as not being worthy of attention anymore. Now you're focused; you're really honing in on what's important in your life. We've all heard it said that it's a pity youth is wasted on the young—because now, on the other side of life, you finally know what's really meaningful to you, there are no more deceptions. I just love getting older; if I could have done it sooner, I would have!"

This surrender to one's fate engenders faith, another attribute of Cronehood. Until we reach the stage of Sorceress, we have a tendency to discredit our life experience, to fail to recognize its relevance to our journey and to set it aside. But for women in their Crone years, faith is the key:

> "I believe in merry partings in life—don't hang on till the bitter end, let things be. I see people who will start a project—I've done it myself—and just hang on, go for the goal, tough it out, but

meanwhile all these doors around them are closing, it just doesn't work. I learned some time ago that if that happens, let it go—the universe is trying to tell you something—this is not the right direction, there's a better way. It really comes down to putting God first and the world second, trusting that there is a reason for everything. If you use your experiences along the road of life as signposts that say, 'Look at me, I've got something to tell you,' you can learn and move on. It may not be your choice, but it's what you need at that particular time, and it's all being handled by a higher power. Everything happens in its right order. It all counts, whether good or bad—we need our bad moments in order to grow; otherwise we'd not feel the need to search and would stagnate. I can look back over my life and just [laughs] ... I can see all these events just pulling and moving me like a chess piece. I no longer see myself as a failure if I don't reach a goal, because another door opens and moves me in a different direction and then click, click, click, I'm there! And once I'm there, I can see how I wasn't supposed to be elsewhere, as I might have thought. You listen to what your innards tell you, your intuition, and trust it, act upon it. You take the risk that you are doing the right thing. That's scary—taking risks always is—but you have to learn to trust."

This theme of learning to trust unites both Mother and Crone. The Mother finds she must trust her body to give birth, and so learns to trust her instincts in child rearing. The Crone must surrender her former identity in life, and so learns to trust her fate. By putting all her trust in life, the Crone becomes the Great Mother, caretaker of all.

Thus she forges an alchemy whereby she may transcend the personal and become the universal. To do her work, she will cross this boundary repeatedly. As Sorceress, she learned to maintain the integrity of opposing energies within herself and her intimate relationships; now, as Crone, she must hold creative tension between inner and outer worlds. Here again is the paradox of surrender and control. The Crone is so firmly rooted in life that she can be nowhere other than in her place, yet only by risking everything can she keep track of where her place really is. This is the ultimate lesson of loving deeply and letting go:

> "The Crone is a lot of inner work. I'm striving for serenity, but it's not easy, it's a lot of work. I'm trying to tie up loose ends, and bring closure to things I should have handled long ago. Hurts from childhood, and I think, 'It's time to let it go.' Easier said than done, but at least I try. That's what the Crone is all about— finding your own value system, evaluating your life, discovering that you did some really good things, and if you get rid of the garbage you've carried for years you can do a lot more.
>
> "My Croning Rite was the onset of coming into my wisdom. It spurred me into a great deal of growth. I feel I have been able to grow more in the last few years than I did in the first seventy. Really, so much growth—it's a powerful feeling."

By paring life down to the essentials, and doing the dance of herself that is effortless in the larger scheme of things, the Crone sows the seed of her own rebirth. She begins to weave a metaphysical cord, rather like the umbilical cord that holds fetus to mother, to link her to the Mother of All Things and carry her through the darkness of the death transition. In the next stage, the tiniest bit of light—the crescent moon—returns, as that which is dormant in the Crone becomes nascent in the Dark Mother and seeks the light of reanimation, even as earthly life is ending.

CHAPTER 10

The Midwife and the Dark Mother

The Midwife and the Dark Mother are gatekeepers—one of birth, one of death. The Midwife may literally be a birth assistant or may teach, enable, or facilitate whatever longs to take form in others. The Midwife brings forth what is essential; she lends a hand as life re-creates and renews itself. She nurtures, protects, and honors that which is fresh, innovative, new.

This work is a natural extension of lessons learned in birthing and mothering: that surrender is a source of power, and that staying in the moment brings wisdom. Sara Ruddick, author of *Maternal Thinking,* describes how motherhood transformed her intellectualism to more connected ways of being and knowing:

I found myself watching more carefully, listening with patience, absorbed by gestures, moods, and thoughts. The more I attended, the more deeply I cared. The domination of feeling by thought, which I had worked so hard to achieve, was breaking down. Instead of developing arguments that could bring my feelings to heel, I allowed feelings to inform my most abstract thinking.[1]

In mothering, we learn to pace ourselves to our children. The Midwife uses this same ability to pace herself to those beyond her own biological circle, encouraging them to be their own authorities, to claim their expertise and unique talents, and to speak their truth. Just as mothers are fascinated with their offspring and rejoice in their unfolding, Midwives are drawn to assisting others in the creative process, celebrating triumphs of the human spirit.

According to authors Mary Belenky, Blythe Clinchy, Nancy Goldberger, and Jill Tarule, "Parents who dialogue with their children are more likely to have children whose intellectual and ethical development proceeds rapidly and surely." In their groundbreaking book, *Women's Ways of Knowing,* they link this to a "midwife" style of teaching:

> Midwife teachers assist in the emergence of consciousness. They encourage their students to speak in their own active voices. The midwife teacher's first concern is to preserve the student's fragile, unborn thoughts, to see that they are born with their truths intact, that these truths do not turn into acceptable lies.[2]

In her work, the Midwife establishes a dialogue with client or student that is not only verbal but physical, emotional, and intuitive. Literally translated, midwife means "with woman." Facilitating others by connectedness, rather than teaching by rote, is the cornerstone of work in this stage. In contrast to the physician's penchant for clinical detachment, the Midwife sees her work as a passionate quest for knowledge in which she is on equal footing with whoever she assists. She does not deny her expertise or her responsibility, but knows she can learn something from everyone she serves.[3] This would be so much easier to convey if, as in the Dutch language, our verbs for teaching and learning were the same. An experienced educator relates:

"When I teach, I sit in a circle with my students. They are adults, and I have no illusions about knowing more than they do, except for my particular area of concentration. I find that the more truthful I am and the more candidly I share my own life struggles and accomplishments, the more my students open up to me and each other, and the more egalitarian the learning experience for all of us.

"After the first few years of teaching, you have a choice—you can more or less stick to your standard outline, or you can continually reinvent yourself in the context of your subject matter, take risks, find a way to bring your passion into it. This is the way for me—how I keep loving it, and keep the love flowing between me and my students.

"I've gotten pretty good at feeling the hesitations, fears, enthusiasms, and unspoken desires of my students, and seizing the moment to bring them to an accelerated level of learning. I also find I save a lot of time by connecting students who are in complementary process to one another—so much of learning has to do with self-assurance. Now, after fifteen years, I feel like I'm truly educating."

This method of incorporating (rather than denying) whatever occurs in the classroom is very much like apprenticeship, in which on-the-job situations are used to distill lessons in their moment of relevance. Storytelling is an important aspect of this approach:

"Birth stories are how midwives teach each other. There are stories that hold great lessons, told time and again. That's the oral tradition—you tell stories when it's appropriate for what's happening, instead of teaching in some linear way from a book."

In contrast, the conventional "banker-style" approach to teaching, which Paulo Freire characterizes as "dispensing knowledge top downwards to students viewed as empty vessels," retards the development of self-confidence and genuine ability.[4]

To return to the point made earlier about language, it is no accident that ours suggests a hierarchy in student/teacher relationships. Our language simply reflects the duality of dominant Christian beliefs, which polarize heaven and earth, mind and body. We have briefly touched on the effects of the witch hunts in Europe and the United States—now, we must look at how these persecutions of women were tied to the rise of both medical and teaching professions, and consider the continuing impact of the "burning times" on our ability to claim the wisdom of our bodies and share this freely with others.

Professionalism, or the takeover by a paid elite of services and functions people traditionally provided themselves, began in the sixteenth century, when the Catholic Church first sanctioned "experts" trained to oppose pagan spirituality. Although the Reformation destroyed Catholicism's monopoly on the expropriation of knowledge, it coexisted with the rise of a market economy in which men, who could pay for education and training, consolidated their power. Women, on the other hand, were barred from higher education.

Nevertheless, communities continued to generate their own healers, the midwives, particularly as physician-managed options proved both expensive and unsafe. Unlike physicians, midwives relied on preventative practices such as cleanliness, the use of herbs, and fostering their clients' strength through good nutrition. In some cases they dispensed pain relief and paid dearly for it—Anne Hutchinson was burned at the stake for the simple act of easing a birthing woman's pains with laudanum. But they forged ahead nonetheless, offering education and counseling on a variety of health and personal issues, much as they do today. Traditionally, midwives provided care for their communities from womb to tomb, treating a full spectrum of ailments and illnesses. Naturally, they honored women's Blood Mysteries and sought to incorporate them in the fabric of community life. No wonder the *Malleus Maleficarum,* handbook of the Inquisition, declared, "No one does more harm to the Catholic faith than do the midwives."[5]

The cost to society of midwifery's oppression has been great. Starhawk declares, "To destroy a culture's trust in its healers is to destroy that culture's trust in itself, to shatter its cohesive bonds and expose it to control from outside."[6] The struggle between midwives and the medical elite continues to this day—not only in the United States, where numerous trained and competent midwives have been put on trial for mere practice, but internationally, wherever the forces of medicine-for-profit encroach. Much more than a simple tussle over professional turf, this conflict reflects the greed of patriarchy, as Starhawk describes:

> As a woman, if my society withholds from me the approved knowledge about my body, and forces me to turn to men for care and help with the most female of experiences, I hear the clear message that I am incompetent, incapable of caring for myself. When women healers are downgraded and portrayed as filthy and malevolent, women as a group are forced to internalize a sense of shame, self-loathing, and fear of their own power.[7]

To overcome oppression, we need strength. Waite's tarot card of Strength portrays a woman gently closing a lion's mouth, with the figure-eight, double-helix symbol of eternal life, poised above her head. In Crowley's deck, she is Lust, riding a lion, drawing power from her knowledge of sexuality and regeneration. In the Mother-peace deck, she is "Mother Goddess . . . both a friend of Nature and a civilizing force," surrounded by animal totems, each with a particular power to share: the hare, lunar and subconscious illumination; the snake, visionary and transformative energy; the wolf, protection and strength through wildness; the spider, interconnectedness to all of life.[8]

The prime directive of the Strength card is contained in Vicki Noble's subtitle: "Finding Magical Helpers." The Midwife must enlist her allies, be they totem animals, oracles, or spiritual guides, in order to be strong and effective as gatekeeper of creation. As her moon begins to wane and incorporate darkness, she may struggle both to recognize and to trust nonlinear ways of knowing and the mysterious voices and images that arise unbeckoned from her subconscious. Yet this is precisely the work she must do—stand at the portal between worlds and learn to trust herself in that sacred place, even as she shows others the way.

From a midwife, age fifty-two:

> "I have always used my intuition—when something doesn't feel right, I look for physical indications or signals and proceed on that basis, but sometimes there are no physical signs—I just don't feel good about a situation and make a decision based on gut feeling. Over the years, I've learned to identify and separate my own stuff—my anxieties and personal problems—as the baggage I bring to a birth. I am very careful not to mix my stuff into this intuitive process."

Another woman in her twenties identified with the Midwife in her work at an abortion clinic:

"In my work at the clinic, I've had to overcome a lot of class and cultural bias. I've tried to hold to the belief that all women are but faces of the Goddess, but it's hard when you're hanging onto a woman with terrible hygiene or periodontal disease, and you have to midwife her through this traumatizing experience. I've built a class wall around myself and I've worked very hard for what I have, and I've also gotten into having the right clothes, acting in ways that separate me from my past. But when I'm helping women through abortion, none of this matters—women come in all shapes, colors, sizes, belief systems.

"Abortion is just one more aspect of a woman's life that's supposed to be shameful, one more stroke against us, one more thing men, religion, and society want to control. I'm continually frustrated that the women who are most in need are not the ones who get help. I feel that men just don't get it—you can pull them into the procedure room and think they're going to get it if they see their partner lying there in pain, in stirrups, but most of the time, they still don't get it. People aren't going to stop having sex—until we get sexuality out of the closet and start dealing with contraception, abortion will always be an issue. But we won't turn back—too many women have sacrificed their lives for that to happen."

By learning to overcome both inner and outer oppression, the Midwife reactivates her core identity and prepares for her forthcoming rebirth as Amazon. Her exploration of the boundary between this and other realities rekindles her wildness. I was recently asked to give a presentation on the topic of "Keeping Birth Normal," and was struck once again by how insidiously standardization and the quest for control has permeated this sacred Blood Rite. There is no such thing as normal birth—each is individual and nonconforming, and presents a spectrum of physical, emotional, and spiritual growth opportunities that is nothing less than extraordinary. In contrast, generic, reductionist views of birth make a travesty of the midwife's time-honored proficiencies and artistry.

However she assists or mentors, the Midwife must guard parameters of safety. But she should also encourage her clients or students to play their edges, experience deep currents of emotion, discover their own ways of transformation, and chart new creative territory. For themselves and others, Midwives are compelled to make the unseen visible and comprehensible, they recognize and validate gut instincts or other messages from the body and seek ways to translate these into tangible action and/or words.

In so doing, the Midwife discovers the interconnectedness of all life and knows the truth of the Gaia hypothesis. One woman we interviewed called this "the erotic field":

"When I'm out in the desert, I get time alone with myself and what I always discover is that I'm not alone, it's just an illusion, the whole universe is there with me. As I've come to see the universe as alive, I now believe that it's not only alive but friendly and supportive and there for me. If I just open my eyes and ears and pay attention, I have allies.

"This links to my expanding ideas about what relationship means. We tend to define it by the person we have sex with—that that is what's important—but if we took the whole idea of intercourse and even orgasm out of the picture, we could think about moving into a generally erotic field with people and life around us. By erotic, I mean deeply connected with all our senses. If we lived in that erotic field as much as we could, it really wouldn't matter who we were in there with—that's the field I love the most. I find it easiest to be there when I'm alone in nature—but if women really claimed the erotic field, they'd have something so much better to offer men than this little bitty orgasm thing we live out. If we could enter that erotic field as a people, think of the implications for the whole world, the natural world—we would be loath to destroy any part of it.

"Recently, someone I knew died, and I got the image of this vast surrendering. Talk about surrendering into eroticism—if you've been in the erotic field with the trees, plants, and animals, imagine dissolving into them consciously at the moment of death! I think the Dark Mother holds her arms wide for this dissolving, and we dissolve into Her. Watching my friend, I got a sense of how good it must feel to put it all down, let it go, and I imagine surrendering into something so huge, we don't even have a clue to what it is."

Here we see the connection between the work of Midwife and that of Dark Mother, in that both must access this erotic field for the challenging transitions of birth and death. To do this, each must get down to essentials; the Midwife distills her essential self through Motherhood, while the Dark Mother continues the paring away she began as Crone.

"What's happening to me now—I'm seventy-six, and I've worked all my life—is suddenly, in this last year, a gnawing feeling has hit me, 'Virginia, you've got to retire.' I still have my health, I still have my job, and I don't work for money; I work because I love what I do—and here comes this gnawing feeling, 'Virginia, it's time. Now's the time to leave your profession while you're still at your peak, when you can leave still loving it.' Along with that came a need to withdraw—I follow an Eastern path and work very well alone. I don't seem to need a lot of people, and I have felt the need for simplification, to get out of the world and more into meditation—I'm meditating two to three hours a day now, and I'd like to put in four to six hours a day. I'd like to simplify my life to where I don't have to be pulled out in the world. I'm not going to plays anymore, I'm not going to symphonies, and all these things were part of my love—I haven't been to a movie in awhile. So I think I'm moving into a time of being quiet, more in tune with the higher power and just getting myself ready for the transition of death. Now that may happen tomorrow, or that may take fifteen years, I don't know, but I do feel that it's coming and I want to be prepared spiritually to the very best of my ability, ready to make that transition. I have lots of friends and acquaintances who have potlucks and all, and I say, 'Don't ask me anymore, I don't want parties.' It takes my energy and pulls me out, and I want to be pulled in.

"Also, I'm leaving California for Idaho—we bought land there; I'll build with my children. I've never lived in snow, but I'm a winter person; I love gray days and I think the snow will enhance my desire for simplification, because I won't be able to get out and I'll have to utilize my time in a different way. I'm told it's very peaceful—that the mountains and trees look beautiful in the snow."

The season of both Crone and Dark Mother is winter, representing retreat, solitude, and the wisdom that comes from hibernation. Totem animals of this season include the bear, the owl, and the wolf, all of which signify perspective derived from simplification and emphasis on the inner life, spiritual flight. One woman, age seventy-three, described the increasing importance of her dreamtime:

"I think we can gain more from our dreams as we grow old, because they take the place of our active life. In my dreams I run, I walk, I jump, I play, I do all the things I can't do now in life, but in dreams they come naturally. I remember reading somewhere that when you reach a certain age, you should transfer your emphasis from your waking time to your sleeping time. And it is very true—in my dreams, there is nothing the matter with me, I'm perfectly whole. And that is very refreshing."

Winter is a season of latency, a period for nature to recover itself in preparation for spring's rebirth. Thus Dark Mothers typically reduce their worldly effects, deliberately cleaning out closets and cupboards, giving things away. Now in her late seventies, my mother has already assembled photograph and keepsake albums for my sister and me, in keeping with the traditional role of elder woman as family and cultural historian. Many women in this stage spoke of wanting to cut back their personal possessions and get their estates organized so that the anguish of doing so would not fall upon their children. This passage from a prayer written by Elizabeth Gray Vining illustrates:

> Help me to bring my work each day to an orderly state so that it will not be a burden for those who must fold it up and put it away when I am gone. Keep me ever aware and ever prepared for the summons.[9]

Not every Dark Mother experiences a gradual surrender of her former active existence. For some, the extraneous is cut away abruptly, due to catastrophic illness or disability. The goddess Kali, who represents the destroyer aspect of this stage, rends and separates the transitory from the eternal. Her countenance is fierce, her skin is black, she dances powerfully over her dead consort, Shiva, even as her yoni devours his lingam (penis). Kali, who stands at the edge of death and rebirth, represents the Great Mother as all consuming. The Greeks called her Atropos the Cutter, she who slashed away that which had outlived its usefulness and snipped the thread of every life. In Egypt she was known as Neith, the one beyond the veil whom no mortal could face.[10] Priestesses in Kali's service were known as Dakinis (or skywalkers) in Tantric tradition; their tasks included embracing and comforting the dying in their last moments, taking the last breath of the enlightened ones with the kiss of peace, preparing the bodies of the deceased, and conducting funeral rites. Though frequently gentle and benign, Dakinis could also be fierce in meting out violent or painful forms of death warranted by karma.[11]

Dark Mothers accept the destructive aspect of life because they know this is necessary for rebirth. Midwives likewise embrace the process of self-dissolution that precedes delivery. Gatekeeping requires being comfortable on either side of the portal, this world or that. Most women who do extensive work in Dark Mother or Midwife stages have also spent a good bit of time with the Transformer, learning about fear and courage, finding ways to accept and initiate change. Some women are drawn to these stages regardless of age, and find broad applications of lessons gleaned to diverse areas of life:

"I use the energy of the dark side, the Dark Mother, in my work with corporations. It has to do with making decisions based on a qualitative, innate understanding of people versus some analytical process or statistical data. Companies are choosing women more and more as advisors—they may rationalize with demographics and facts of women's buying power, but still they know there is something more, something they don't understand.

"When I first got into the business world, I thought men knew something I didn't, but now I see them almost as children and know how to work with them. I may know next to nothing about what they are discussing, yet I intuitively give advice they value. These men are missing something and I can see what it is— it's my awareness of who they are in their lives, it's very woman-centered knowledge. It's fun, because men know there is a void there too, and as you provide some women's knowledge in a male-based world, it feels right to both of you. It's not about being someone's mistress or lover or secretary, it's about being in your place and revealing the mysterious.

"The Athena archetype is important, as you use your brain and craft to deal with men, but you need to marry it to the Hecate/Kali part. People respond to someone who has the dark side alive in them—this is really my source of power, shedding light on the dark side. The dark side translates over age, sex, experience. It's Goddess realization. It gives me hope as I get older. If women tapped into their dark side, they would always be attractive.

"I use this to mentor people beneath me. I try to get back to the basics of relationship with mother love, as a tigress protecting her cubs. Sometimes I show the angry side of the Goddess which most women have been hesitant to call upon—the sacred bitch. It's important to be able to tap into that and not apologize for it."

One woman we interviewed, age forty-eight, and the mother of a seven-year-old son, placed herself in the Midwife stage but linked herself to the Dark Mother, particularly the Kali aspect:

"I see the Midwife as my guide in midwifing myself, my more mature self. For me, she is clearly opposite the Dark Mother, who is rest before transformation. The entity of Dark Mother is helping me make the transition to Amazon—she's a really powerful part of myself, one I'm just discovering. She represents my adult self who, like Kali, has all these arms, and she can fend off demons, hold a child, handle a job, care for herself while taking care of others and her tasks in the world. As Midwife, I've discovered that I'm a whole person in and of myself, a new thing for me. I don't feel so tentative, I feel power building in me, I'm more willing to take risks.

"My art therapy group has especially helped me to get comfortable with taking risks, discovering more about myself. It's helped me go into the dark—I've learned that the dark is something wonderful like a womb, a place of nurturing and safety. And there's this other side of the dark—the edge of fear, with lots of power and excitement—but it's not scary anymore, I actually look forward to it. I have this curiosity about the darkness that I never had before; I hunger for it, long for it.

"There are four of us in art therapy plus a facilitator, and we meet once a week. We start by casting a circle and creating safe space; then we decide if we want to have a verbal or drawing check-in. The drawing check-ins are much more to the point, they emerge spontaneously and more from the unconscious. What it's about is putting down on paper, really quickly, where we're at right now. Then we go around the circle and share what we see in our drawings. After this, we do some movement and guided meditation to focus on the work we're about to do. What comes out of the movement goes into our art; it comes out of our bodies into this nonverbal form that's so direct, so uncensored. It has nothing to do with art, really—it's just another way of communicating.

"Recently, my drawings have shifted—for a long time I was using black to represent depression, aloneness, victimization, despair, sadness, grief, and always some red for anger. Now I'm using green for growth, and the black has changed meaning to Amazon-warrior black, the wild Kali stuff.

"I've noticed in my group that we're all at the same point in our lives, a pivotal point where darkness turns from fear to revelation. We all had our kids late in life, so the Midwife stage is happening for us in midlife. When I first looked at the Circle of Life, I thought, 'Shouldn't I be a little further along than this?' No, I'm still in the nurturing phase. But I think my age gives this stage a different quality; it takes on greater depth."

Just as the Midwife came late to this woman, the Dark Mother may come early to those facing life-threatening or terminal illness.

It is not easy to come to terms with the prospect of death before one's time; a younger woman must draw upon the Midwife inside to aid her in the process of letting go. This account from a woman, age fifty-three, now recovering from a malignant brain tumor:

"When the doctors were talking about my prognosis and the need to be 'aggressive,' I kept thinking, 'It's not me that they're talking about—I'm going to live, I want to live.' It was so debilitating—at first, I was just numb, I couldn't think, I didn't know what to do. But a friend who was staying with me, an analyst, happened to know people who had recovered; he knew them by name, and he gave me a spark to believe in. Nobody else had been talking in terms of what I could do, that I had any choice in the matter, that at least I could live the life I have the way I wanted to live it, that I didn't have to live with the limiting fears of doctors, biopsies, and prognoses. I got really clear that I was in charge of my life. Somebody told me when I called for help, 'My dear, you are the driver of this bus, and you can make it!'—hopeful words I needed to soothe away the fear of the dark. Then I was able to say, 'I'm going to open myself to all the energies in the world—all kinds of energies there for healing.' I'd go out and stand under the moon and talk to the moon, talk to the trees, ask the trees questions when I went for a walk—and it occurred to me that *if I was quiet, the first thing that came to me was the answer.*

"But I realized that the doctors were there to help me too. I found doctors who were respectful of me as a person—caring, compassionate—and there is such a need for compassion when you suddenly feel like you've stepped out of life. You've stepped out of life and you don't know how to bridge the gap that separates you. Suddenly you're not who you were before—you can't do what you did before, or are afraid to try.

"Then I got that if I had inner peace, I could deal with anything, I'd have something to hold on to, something around me, something in me. People came along like angels with suggestions of things to try and do, with offerings. I do believe in miracles—as a child, I read the stories in the Old Testament, and I believed those. I was willing to accept that anything can happen, we don't have to be limited.

"Then I had a scan done that came out negative, but the doctors didn't believe it, so we took the next step in treatment. But I believed, and I asked myself in meditation if the treatments would hurt me. I was afraid of the treatments, but I got that it was okay to do them. I also had alternative treatments—in the middle of a Jin Shin treatment, I had a healing right there on the table and my fear disappeared. I heard something say, in words, 'I don't need this tumor anymore.' It was an incredible feeling. But it was a long wait before I saw the time when my 'inoperable' tumor was considered operable. I still have to keep working, keep on my toes, I can't be lax, ever.

"So many things helped me; I can't say what it was. The doctors say, 'Isn't modern medicine wonderful?' Yes, if you're not afraid of it, if it makes sense to utilize. One time my doctor said, 'You've worked so hard,' and I wondered if he meant all the meditation, visualizing, and praying. But they don't know about those things. I did a lot of crying too.

"To others facing death, I say, you don't know how long your life will be but you're still the driver of the bus, you're still in charge of what you have. If there is something you want to do that you never let yourself do, now's the time to do it. Go out in the sun, let its warmth come into you and know that you are beautiful, no matter what's happening to you. If there's anything you feel guilty about, well, forgive yourself. Picture yourself as a newborn baby—don't you love that baby? Beautiful little child that you were—hold that child in your arms. That beautiful little being is always in you, it's always been there, it's still you. Love that part of yourself, and don't stop loving it. Throw the things you might be angry about in the trash, throw away the things you feel guilty about. Put yourself in the light—the loving light.

"I really believe we have a connection to the divine, God, Spirit, Chi, whatever—there's really something there. Look at the things that happen unexpectedly that are so wonderful—they come to you. Just imagine leaning back into something that comforts and holds you. Lately I've gotten the picture of this very beautiful, big blue plush chair I can crawl up into, my divine chair—I'm utterly safe there."

Standing on either side of the portal, Dark Mothers are not only those who come close to dying, but also those who experience death by facilitating others through the process. It is a crossover role, as is midwifery (midwives often speak of being reborn in witnessing birth). Women who have helped the dying have their own special wisdom to share:

"I learned to assist death when my husband died. I was forty-nine. What's it like to lose your best friend, lover, workmate? It's kind of like helping birth, except it's killing you too. But you just keep saying, 'You're doing fine, great, just let go.' Finally, I told my husband, 'Look, you're the one who said that death was the greatest unknown journey—it's time.'

"How did I know it was time? Well, he wasn't there anymore, he couldn't speak—you know, it was time. As a woman, you know stuff like that. And with my friend recently, I didn't have to say that at all—he knew. His was the most amazing death—talk about a warrior; this was a warrior's death. He found out on Memorial Day that he had cancer of the liver, and he started right in organizing things for his family. He died August first. He was almost seventy, but he still had all these students, and a novel that he had not quite completed, which my friend and I put on the computer so he could see it all laid out. I think that's one of the main tasks—

helping the dying take care of unfinished business. He never actually told me he was dying; he told everyone else but me. And we really didn't talk about it—once in a while he would ask, 'Am I doing all right?' and I'd say, 'God, you're doing fabulously!' Really, he was a model on how to die. He died at home in his bed.

"As for me, I could only cope with these experiences by getting in the car and screaming, raging with my own death in losing those I loved. It was a necessary release, it helped me find ways to give again. There was no way to cry my own sadness as I sat with them, so I had to go away and scream for a while."

From another woman, age forty-nine:

"The Dark Mother I know a little something about, because I have a lot of Kali energy. When I first became aware of it in my thirties, I had trouble with it, because I didn't want to know that side, the destroyer, eliminator stuff. But I've danced with it a fair amount in my work as a midwife. And over the last five years, I've lost four close friends, with a fifth one on the way—the women all to cancer, the men to AIDS. So my one friend is battling breast cancer—we keep holding the possibility of a total miracle, but she's really far progressed.

"What I have experienced is the ecstatic depth of feeling that exists in the deathing process. After having midwifed five hundred births, I find that it is really the same process. The first woman I helped admitted to herself and her family that she was dying, and then she expected it to happen right away, which it didn't—like in birth, the stage of transition, where it might be five minutes, it might be five hours. And the unweaving of the body, how in birth the whole perineum's got to open and let the baby go, in death the whole body's got to let the soul go, and it holds onto it, just the way the perineum holds onto the baby. It won't let go too fast, 'cause too fast is dangerous. A beautiful, beautiful flow, and it's so intense—birth is intense in a way that's joyous, death in a way that's deeply sorrowful, but joyful in a way too. Not your run-of-the-mill kind of joy, it's not the run-of-the-mill kind of anything, it is an altered state to be with someone who's dying, who is conscious and present to their dying.

"For me, I drop into a much deeper place, I slow way down; my whole way of living moves at a snail's pace because there's so much to attend to, to notice, to appreciate, to participate in, and be involved in when a person's leaving that you just can't move at the usual rate; you can't be present with a person and moving that fast. So it's a practice, a spiritual practice of slowing waaay down, moving at the same rate they are or you miss it completely.

"As there is letting go, there is this unraveling, but not really a decrease in energy. I had this amazing experience of sitting with one woman in the night, in the quiet—what I saw was this angel of death, standing at the end of her bed, a masculine being. And he was gathering her in—she would release a part of her spirit, her life, her energy out the top of her head, and he would just gather it in, gather it in, gather it in, gather it in. Only the family was with her at the actual moment of death, but when I left she had just a little left and he had most of it, and he was so loving, a totally loving being, infinitely patient; he wasn't the least in a hurry—you know, like the perfect midwife, just listening to the women's body and her child's presence.

"The two men I helped each had an experience of going over a threshold when they died—that's what they believed would happen, and that's what we experienced. I really think it's like that with death, what you believe is what is created, before you go back to the Great Ocean."

THE DEATHINGWAY

Death is the final rite of passage in the women's Circle of Life. The Deathingway is a memorial ritual, to celebrate the life of the woman who has crossed over and remember all her gifts of beauty. It is a ritual of mourning and grieving, of keening and wailing in acknowledgment of the pain and separation of death. But it is also a ritual of hope and love and blessing, in the knowledge that all endings are followed by new beginnings.

Women and their loved ones are encouraged to plan and design their own death rites, ideally many years in advance. This is a startling concept in a culture such as ours, which seeks to deny death at any cost. But death is as inevitable and natural a process as birth, and so should be prepared for in much the same manner. Just as we attend childbirth preparation classes and practice breathing, relaxation, and other coping skills, we can prepare for death by learning comforting visualizations and breathing techniques. And just as we develop a birth plan describing the way we want our experience to take place, we can similarly devise a plan for conscious dying.

The intention of the death rite is to honor and encapsulate the phenomenon of death by separating it from ordinary life experience, so that its transformative power can be fully realized. Yet, as with birth, it is most desirable that the death process take place in familiar surroundings, at home if possible. For this reason, it is important that we create "living wills" or assign power of attorney to a loved one that knows our wishes regarding the use of life support or other heroic measures to extend our lives, and anything else we feel necessary to assure our freedom to exit life with dignity when it is time.

One ancient practice that might be included in the death rite is the soul kiss, otherwise known as the kiss of peace. In this, a younger person—perhaps a son or daughter, or a special woman friend trained in the art of supporting conscious death—deeply inhales the dying woman's final breath, as if to draw all her wisdom into herself. This was once a sacred practice among women healers, meant to ensure the preservation and transmission of Old Ways. Tradition has it that if the woman who shares this soul kiss is young and later becomes pregnant, she will bear a child carrying the essence and wisdom of the deceased.

> Arrayed in some new flesh disguise
> Another mother gives birth.
> With sturdier limbs and brighter brain
> The old soul takes the road again.[12]

An African practice of honoring the dead is the creation of a nine-day altar immediately after the moment of death. This is simply a consecrated space, filled with the woman's personal mementos, handiwork, photographs, favorite possessions, and so on. Here her loved ones can sit, remember her, and meditate on her contributions. If the Four Directions are called in, incense can be burned in the East, white candles can be lit in the South (and kept burning for the full nine days), a chalice of water or wine can be placed in the West, and some of her ashes or a special stone can be placed in the North. Flowers and a favored picture of her should be placed in the center. The nine-day vigil is believed to guide the woman's soul to its ultimate destination.

The purpose of the Deathingway is to give succor to the living. Thus there may be need for two memorial gatherings: one in church or community hall for loved ones most comfortable with a conventional setting and format; the other, a ritual designed by the woman herself, held in whatever setting she suggests and involving those closest to her. The public memorial service can include readings or music that reflect her personal tastes and preferences, being mindful to avoid dogma that is not part of her belief system. The main purpose of this gathering is to bring together all who have loved her to reminisce, share anecdotes and stories, and console one another at their loss.

The private ritual will probably involve her immediate family as well as those in her intimate circle. It can be eclectic and reflective of her unique spiritual practices, and should be held in some natural setting she loved. Her ashes may be sprinkled here; perhaps a group of wailers can help others unburden themselves of their sadness and express their grief. Scheduling this ritual near the new moon invokes energies of peace and reemergence.

Feasting should follow both of these gatherings. Foods should be fresh and green to signify new growth and renewal; drink should be abundant. These Rites of Release are also meant to celebrate life—music and laughter are to be encouraged.

A traditional Pueblo prayer tells us:

Hold on to what is good
even if it is a handful of earth.
Hold on to what you believe
even if it is a tree which stands by itself.
Hold on to what you must do
even if it is a long way from here.
Hold on to my hand
even when I have gone away from you.[13]

—C. LEONARD

If only we could embrace a healthy view of death such as this, we would free ourselves of the pathological fear of leaving the body that taints our day-to-day living. This fear leads us to try to control, sanitize, and medicate death much as we do birth; both are equally frightening in their intensity to a culture bereft of positive archetypes for these powerful transitions. It is so important to bring these rites back to the clan, the family—bring them back home. The data show that birth or death at home is no less safe or any more painful than in hospital; in fact, quite the opposite is true.

Overuse of technology in childbirth has been shown to contribute to increased anxiety, pain, and complications. And all of us have heard stories of, or have firsthand experience with, technological horrors that strip dignity from the dying.

In his best-selling book, *How We Die,* Sherwin B. Nuland observes:

> Everyone wants to know the details of dying, though few are willing to say so. . . . To most people, death remains a hidden secret, as eroticized as it is feared. We are irresistibly drawn by the very anxieties we find most terrifying; we are drawn to them by a primitive excitement that arises from flirtation with danger. Moths and flames, mankind and death—there is little difference.[14]

Nuland goes on to argue that death has little dignity in any setting, that any glory in dying must be found in the way one has lived. This is not the case in every culture. We have so desacralized death's mystery that we think only of what comes after—life on another plane divorced from this reality. We hope for salvation— but salvation from what? The desire to quickly leave this world behind springs from our dualistic way of living, our ruptured view of heaven and earth. In contrast, *The Tibetan Book of the Dead* presents an elaborate view of the death crossing that takes many days for the soul to complete.

What is beyond the veil, no one can tell; we do know that death is the inevitable reaper. On a biological level, death facilitates new life; they are interconnected. Again, from Nuland:

> Nature has a job to do. It does its job by the method most suited to each individual whom its powers have created. It has made this one susceptible to heart disease and that one to stroke and yet another to cancer, some after a long time on this earth and some

after a time much too brief, at least by our own reckoning. The animal economy has formed the circumstances by which each generation is to be succeeded by the next.

Mankind, for all its unique gifts, is just as much a part of the ecosystem as is any other zoological or botanical form, and nature does not distinguish. We die so that the world may continue to live. We have been given the miracle of life because trillions upon trillions of living things have prepared the way for us and then have died—in a sense, for us. . . . The tragedy of a single individual becomes, in the balance of natural things, the triumph of ongoing life.[15]

Resacralization of death demands that this biological view of transformation be extended to emotional and spiritual realms as well. In this regard, many women report communication with loved ones at the moment of death:

"I personally believe that love can be communicated even after death. My husband had been missing for several days and we didn't know why; we worried that he had been in a terrible accident. The anxiety of not knowing where or how he was, was unbearable. My mother had come to sit with me during the waiting, and I remember telling her that my love for him was so profound, that we were so psychically connected that I would know if he was dead, but that night I was sure he was still alive.

"The next morning I was quietly standing in the kitchen, looking out the window when a framed picture of him in an adjoining room fell off the wall, shattering explosively when it hit the floor. My mother ran down the stairs, saying she hoped that wasn't a bad sign. 'Yes it is . . . he's dead now,' I told her, 'and I need for you to leave right away.' What I did next was very instinctive. I went up to our balcony, took off all my clothes, and sat very still in the sun, breathing very slowly until I was utterly calm. Then I heard him say my name, gently, clearly. I *definitely* heard him—I was not hysterical, not hallucinating. And the way he said that one word said volumes to me. He said it calmly, peacefully, letting me know that he was all right, and was where he should be. Then I felt him physically leave me, like his spirit flowed out of me.

"I found out later that this incident occurred at the exact moment of his death. This bittersweet truth of his leaving gave me the courage to be strong, to go on with my life."

If we live consciously and deliberately, we grow ever wiser and more spiritually aware even as our bodies age and deteriorate. Surely death must involve some transmutation of our psychological growth, our realizations—it is only logical to expect the incorporation of all we have become in the death transition. But does this lead to reincarnation—or does the soul dissolve into the Oversoul/higher intelligence—or do we simply go home to the Mother? Whatever we believe, we are part of the evolution of human-kind, compost for life's continuation. Endings are invariably followed by new beginnings; why, then, should death of the body lead to anything less than rebirth? *Life* is the eternal state—death, a necessary stage in its renewal.

No one we interviewed expressed such views more eloquently than this woman, age ninety:

"I feel calm, sure, like at last I know what life is all about, where it's going. If you read in the obituary column tomorrow that I departed, know that it was with great expectancy. Peter Pan, in a tough moment when he was trapped on a rock with water encroaching and it looked like he might drown, threw back his head and said, 'To die must be an awfully big adventure!' That's how I feel—I haven't the slightest idea what it will be like, but I'm eager. It's too bad we avoid death. Just as the sun is going down in the room right now, we soon won't have that lovely light on the wall—but there will be another light.

"Thoreau is one of my favorite people; he said, 'Natural death, like natural birth, is a thing of inherent beauty.' It's simply a matter of going on, releasing so impending life can come. I feel a completeness and simplicity in me. I've been a religious person in a way, but for the last five years or so, I've felt a closeness with the reality of my being. I have no need to denominationalize myself. I don't belong to any church—that was a stage in my life, but right now the whole thing is between me and God, between me and life. I think that whatever happens at death is going to be based on my thinking, the strength of what my philosophy has done for me and what I've done in life.

"As for reincarnation, I don't really get into rooting around for past lives—this life is enough already! But I do believe the soul goes on to be reborn—not as me, but as my essence. I think the essence of what we are now connects up with other essences after death. That would certainly help to explain how we so rapidly connect with certain people in life, without having to go through all the trial stages of friendship.

"After this essence of me has gone on . . . well, I've just learned that almost all my organs can be used, if it happens quickly enough—my eyes, my heart (which happens to be a very strong heart)—and I'm terribly excited [giggles], it makes me look forward to being dead. Life just moves us out of the way, so more life can come."

In the end, we return to the Transformer. And having known her numerous times already, our last descent in life should be somewhat familiar. We know our fears and quirks with regard to letting go, our own best passageways to her presence. Even so, what happens at the death crossing cannot be put into words. What *results* is the miracle of life recreating itself—the Transformer as Destroyer is herself transformed to Creatrix, and life begins anew. Transformation upon transformation upon transformation, a spiral turning ever back around; this is the Great Mystery, that which we cannot comprehend on the Earthly plane.

And so, the Dark Mother's flickering light becomes bright again in the Daughter, and life surges forth once more. As a birthing woman delivers herself, her groans a cry between thighs, so death delivers itself to life in exquisite power and beauty. This is the stuff we are made of—the blood, the breath, the body of the Great Mother. We are She, and She is us.

If we honor and trust in our archetypes, we will find momentum and power in the Deep Feminine unprecedented at any point on this Earth. This is our chance to explore the great mysteries, the pleasures and joys of womanhood with our mothers, daughters, sisters, lovers, and friends as never before. The time is right, the choice is ours.

CHAPTER 11

Creating Your Own Circle

To truly bring the information on the thirteen archetypes of women to life, we must share it with one another. Women's circling together is the most natural thing in the world; most of us did it as little girls when we got together to play games, tell stories, have sleepovers, giggle, and carry on. But in the teen years, circling may take on a new note and become cliquish, as we are programmed to compete for the attentions of young men. Who has the prettiest hair, the nicest clothes, the best body? Most of us have rather painful memories of being cast out from one circle or another in junior high or high school. Perhaps this is the root of many women's distrust of circling.

We must also consider our deep history. Some of us have subconscious memories, genetically encoded, of the Inquisition in

Europe, or of the witch trials in the United States, or of the slave trade from Africa, or of Indian suttee, and so on. During the Inquisition, women who had once circled together under the light of the moon were forbidden to do so; soon, all gatherings of women were suspect and became clandestine. Thus circling became synonymous with danger.

In recent decades, women's gatherings have been marginalized as coffee klatches; gossip sessions; "consciousness-raising" groups; silly little meetings focused on clothes, diets, and relationship woes. But there are so many essential ways women have circled through the ages—to weave, to do the washing, to plant, to harvest, to quilt.

"Growing up a lonely child in the South, my 'aunties' (related mostly by marriage and headed up by Aunt Tommie) formed a female wisdom circle into which I was initiated from age seven to my mid-teens. These ladies held certain things very dear—a gracious life style, their families, their men, and their concept of what it means to be a Southern female. Some of my best-remembered teachings came in the form of homilies, such as:

- 'If you don't take care of yourself, who will?'
- 'A woman who doesn't take care of herself [physical condition and appearance included] is the worst kind of fool.'
- 'If you want to have friends you have to be a friend.' [Meaning, among other things, that you take a sweet or covered dish to any friend at the first sign of calamity.]
- 'The Lord helps those [especially women] who help themselves.'

"With a few adaptations to fit my heart, these nuggets have been most helpful. The sense of camaraderie and belonging I felt in my auntie circle made it possible for me to have many, many friends in my adult life, which has been a great blessing!"

Women have also joined forces at critical social junctures, to help each other prepare for marriage or birth, or to prepare the body of a loved one for burial or cremation. Numerous indigenous societies relied on women's councils for decision making, such as the Council of the Clan Mothers in Native American culture. And from what we can glean of ancient Egyptian, Sumerian, African, and Celtic cultures (to name a few), women also gathered regularly to create ritual and weave magic. As Jean Bolen says:

> Whatever once existed and then was not allowed still exists in the collective unconscious or morphic field, waiting to be brought back into consciousness. It is not about needing to "reinvent the wheel" but about remembering it. The respect for the sacred feminine and its expression through women elders, priestesses, or oracles may be excised from patriarchal history, forbidden, and then forgotten, but once the process of remembering begins, it is like uncovering a blocked spring that was once a holy well.[1]

Woman's propensity for circling may be partly linked to brain evolution. In primordial times, her ability to remain alert while simultaneously paying attention to several tasks was essential to rearing her young in relatively threatening circumstances. With a baby on her hip, other children clamoring for her attention, food preparation underway, and some wild beast scuffling outside the door, woman became expert at diffusing her attention, at multitasking for survival. Man, on the other hand, had to stay highly focused, single-minded while hunting or defending himself or his kin. Over time, this led to significant differences in male and female brain structure and function.

Unique to females is a thickening of structures that connect the right and left sides of the brain—the corpus callosum and anterior commissure—which enables us to readily switch from hemisphere to hemisphere.[2] In 50 percent of women, the prefrontal cortex is also thicker than in men. This part of the brain houses "control centers" that govern behavior; in the male, functions are highly specialized, "lateralized" according to hemisphere, but in the female, functions are diffused, replicated on both sides of the brain. An outstanding example regards the emotional centers, which in women are found in both hemispheres but in men are located on the right side only. If we consider that men have verbal centers in the left hemisphere only, we begin to see a biological basis for the difficulty men may have in expressing their feelings.[3] That men also show a decided preference for the left side of the brain (associated with linear thinking) is hardly surprising, whereas women regularly access both hemispheres. Since the right side of the brain has more connections with the body than does the left, women also have greater access to body-based wisdom when thinking and speaking than do men.[4]

Neurobiology not only explains women's ability to multitask but their quest for multiplicity. Women want the big picture; they are endlessly fascinated by how things connect and interrelate. As an example, consider our usual approach to problem solving—we strive to be inclusive, to incorporate as many factors as possible, even seeking conflicting viewpoints in order to get to the heart of the matter and distill the deep truth. We encircle our area of inquiry before moving to the center for a solution. This is what author Helen Fisher has termed "web thinking."[5]

Women's aptitude for contextual, holistic thinking has led to high expectations of their male partners, particularly in terms of complex communication. But in light of the research, these expectations seem quite unrealistic. Again, consider men's approach to problem solving—they break things down, categorize then add up factors methodically, bricklayer-style. No wonder that when men and women try to solve problems together, men are at a loss to understand why women bring in so many "unrelated" factors and can't "get to the point," while women can't understand why men must be so "controlling," so "tight-lipped" about talking things through.

If there is one piece of information I would give to a woman about to marry the man of her dreams, it would be to avoid the mistake of trying to turn him into a female confidante. I would estimate that 90 percent of the complaints I hear from women about their male partners are rooted in having made this mistake, and then suffering the consequences of frustration, disappointment, and loneliness.

This is why circling with other women is imperative. It is not optional. Not only is it critical for our personal welfare and development, but for the larger community. We know the truth about interconnection; we are tuned into it from childhood. We realize, whether we acknowledge it or not, that if one of our friends is not okay, or if something is out of order in our family, that the circle is broken—our well-being is inextricably connected to those around us and we are part of the Web of Life. Yes, culture exploits women in this regard and would make us codependent at every turn, but this is no reason not to circle.

As renowned author Alice Walker states:

> I have been part of a circle for three years. It is one of the most important connections of my life. One reason the circle is so powerful is that it is informed, in fact, shaped by the Grandmother Spirit. The spirit of impartiality, equality, equanimity. Of nurturing but also of fierceness. It has no use for hierarchy. Or patriarchy. It tolerates violence against itself for a while, but will sooner or later rise to defend itself. This is the spirit of the Earth itself.[6]

The circle is an antidote for the loneliness, separation, and isolation endemic to our society, where rugged individualism has evolved to make it increasingly possible to survive without physically interacting with others. Technology now lets us bypass interpersonal dynamics: we pump our own gas, bank with automatic tellers, watch television or play video games in solitude, and order out for our food. No wonder we feel alone with our problems, and that no one can relate to us. One woman we interviewed bitingly observed, "Our society seems to take pride in inventing new ways for people to have less and less to do with each other."

In contrast, an experienced circle participant had this to say:

"I am part of a circle of eight women, we have been meeting for eighteen years. We have crossed many thresholds with one another, celebrating and grieving life passages together. Children have been born, come to puberty, married, and divorced while we brought all our feelings and questions to each other. We know we will be present when each of us dies. The steady hum of history and trust supports us as a community. We have become sisters, laughed, cried, explored, and discovered together.

"We have also reached out to the community in many ways. We recently produced several Councils on Aging, to help women find their way into beautiful and powerful elderhood. We have also done dramatic readings of the remarkable book *The Vagina Monologues* as an offering to the community."

So why do women hesitate? Some are afraid of the raw power that can be generated in circling. However, the most common fear of those who have not circled is that they will get stuck in the dogma of the group and will lose their individuality, or will be drawn into behavior with which they don't agree. Then, if they quit, they may be ridiculed, shunned, or made grist for the local gossip mill. This points up the essential differences between the circle and a clique—a clique is exclusive, based on forced commonality and unquestioning loyalty, a closed group; but the circle is open, changeable in nature as the individuals that comprise it, a living, dynamic body. The clique suffocates individuality, but the circle promotes healthy relationships in which authenticity is treasured. As Sedonia Cahill, coauthor of *Wisdom Circles: A Guide to Self-Discovery and Community Building in Small Groups,* told us:

> "The circle is made rich by the synergy of all the talents and insights of each individual. As soon as trust has been established, we bring to the circle not only our physical bodies, but also our fears, childhood issues, personal preferences, skills, and foibles. We show up, fully present in all our diversity, willing to respond, to be truthful, to be present for others, to dive deep, and to stay awake. The intensity of such focused attention invites the spirit world to participate in our process. Everything becomes sacred within the time and space of a circle."[7]

Fortunately, there are time-honored guidelines to help our circles realize this vision. The structure of the circle is no accident; it is a metaphor for intent. In a traditional classroom, rows of chairs face the front, and anyone except the teacher can leave without affecting the dynamics very much. Frequently, the students sit but the teacher stands, to further place the locus of power on the teacher. But in the circle, leadership is egalitarian, power is equally shared. The circle breaks down old paradigms of student/teacher; it changes the hierarchical system where one person knows and speaks and others merely listen. In the circle, each voice is as valuable as every other voice. Each participant holds a place, and if anyone leaves, a gap occurs that must be filled for the circle to be complete:

> "The dynamic of sharing power in a circle is strong and delicate at the same time. Each participant must hold her thread with integrity. Each has the choice to let go and dive in with the rest.

Even one woman hesitating at the edge of the abyss can keep all the others from fully experiencing a sense of community and the feminine field."[8]

Setting Up a Circle

The practicalities of setting up a circle can be simply categorized into who, what, where, when, and how.

Who should be part of the circle? How many women are needed to make a circle complete? As for who should participate, the key is really intention, which ties to the second question of what the group is to be about. But beyond any specific focus, the deeper intention to which all circle members must commit is to be fully present in the group, to be truthful, and to hold the space for everyone else to do the same.

I have been in contact with many women's circles over the last fifteen years, and have found it somewhat surprising that participants in the most enduring circles are not necessarily the best of friends, and may in fact lead very different lives and socialize very little with each other outside the circle. Perhaps the lack of day-to-day contact makes it easier to keep a clean emotional slate, so when the circle does meet, participants can more readily get down to the subject at hand. Diversity in the circle is important for yet another reason; it can trigger a deeper level of learning than might be possible in a group of women more alike, with concomitant lessons in humility, empathy, and compassion.

As for group size, most groups limit themselves to eight women, certainly no more than ten. You can start a circle with as few as three. Keep in mind that whatever topic you discuss or activity you undertake will involve input from every member, and this should not feel rushed or become tedious due to sheer numbers.

What will your group be about? Here it is important to set an intention. You may decide you are together primarily for support, or for fun and play, or for deep exploration through ritual, or for community service, or ideally, for a combination of all the above. Circles should revolve around group needs; for example, one woman spoke of circling with a small group of five women who called themselves alternately the "Hot Potatoes," the "Fried Potatoes," or the "Wild Yams," with the express purpose of sharing postmenopausal wisdom.

Circles can serve numerous functions, as this woman explained:

"There have been several circles over the years that we organized to explore particular issues, and then dissolved when their relevance to us had ended. There was the Heart Lodge, which was a married couples circle that ended for me when my third marriage ended, and the Spider Lodge, a woman's circle exploring new models of power. There was Sky Mother's Basket, a place where women and men came together to share deep and sometimes scary truths about gender, and there was Sisters of Medusa, women learning to be strong with their truth. All of them have been valuable, in one way or another, to everyone who participated."

In general, a circle that combines a round of check-in with either topics for discussion or creative activities, peppered with occasional field trips and community service projects, will find balance and ample opportunity for each participant to express known talents and discover new ones.

Here are some sample topics for discussion:

- Mother-lines—our female relatives, matrilineal heritage, anecdotes.
- Our sexual histories, first orgasm!
- Our histories with money.

- Stories of how we were born.
- Stories about our menarches.
- What we do and don't tell our children.
- Vanity and beauty issues.
- Games we played as girls.
- Creativity.
- Addictions.
- Power issues.
- Holistic ways of coping with menopause.
- How we envision our death—our death plan and crossing-over ceremony.

And here are some sample activities:

- Make collages on a particular theme.
- Decorate papier-mâché boxes on a given theme—a yoni box, a fertility box, a menstrual box.
- Create Blood Rites to honor participants or their loved ones.
- Create ritual celebrations to honor participants' birthdays.
- Create ritual celebrations to honor change-of-season and cross-quarter days.
- Enact various goddesses (one per meeting), each participant taking a turn.
- Make dolls to express participants' wild selves, crone selves, maiden selves, and so on.
- Do massage or aromatherapy for each other.
- Try belly dancing (hire an instructor if necessary).
- Have a drumming or singing circle.
- Do mask making, in honor of the season or a landmark of maturation, and so on.

For community service:

- Put on a benefit—a play, musical performance, or lecture event.
- Donate time to a youth or elder facility.
- Create a publication—a calendar or cookbook, for example.

And for field trips and outings:

- Art exhibit or theater piece on women's issues.
- Camping trips.
- Night circles or bonfires.
- Sleepovers.
- Parties and events where partners or family are invited.

These are merely suggestions to get a group started. Or perhaps one of these themes or activities will constitute your circle's central focus. Once you decide what your circle will be about, you can give yourselves a name.

Where should your circle meet? You can meet at any participant's home, then rotate from one home to the next. An advantage of rotating is that it distributes the burdens of preparation and cleanup more fairly, and keeps the energy fresh. Rotating location may also involve rotating the task of facilitation, which can help keep power evenly distributed while inspiring each participant to get more deeply involved in circle dynamics. The role of facilitation may also involve the responsibility of generating the topic or activity for the meeting—it all depends on how your circle wants to work together.

Or it may be that someone clearly has the most suitable location for gathering and this becomes your permanent base. Wherever you decide to meet, you'll need privacy and quiet to really go deep, so other family members should either be in a different part of the home or out of the house entirely, and all phones and answering machines should be turned off. You'll also need adequate space to comfortably sit in a circle, with a central area for setting up an altar.

Decisions about **when** a circle will meet are very important. Will the group meet by day or night? Night meetings may be more convenient, or may be the only option for women with standard work schedules. But daytime meetings are such a pleasure— everyone is fresh, time flows more leisurely, a midday meal can be fully enjoyed, and the women who make their contributions late in the meeting don't have to worry about their sisters nodding out on them! Day meetings might be scheduled from 10 A.M. to 3 P.M.; night meetings work best if they begin with a meal around 5 P.M. and end no later than 10 P.M. (Sharing meals makes time for casual talk so that circle discussions can be more focused.)

And then there is the thorny issue of scheduling. There are several ways to set this up: either circle participants pick a regular meeting day or night—for example, the first Monday of every month—or they schedule as they go. The latter is often messy and time-consuming. One thing is certain—if scheduling is done meeting-to-meeting, it should definitely take place before the circle is adjourned!

Depending on the desires and beliefs of circle members, meetings may also be scheduled to honor the changing seasons or cross-quarter days. Or the group may want to meet regularly at a certain lunar phase, full or new moon. And when a circle has been meeting for a while, it can be stimulating to change the routine.

As regards format and structure, the **how** aspect of circling will be fully addressed in the forthcoming section. But it is worth mentioning at this point how important it is to put procedures in place for changing meeting dates or topics, for admitting new members or handling disputes. Too many circles learn this the hard way, with clumsiness and hurt feelings. Lack of clarity on these matters can actually make or break a group, so they should be addressed as soon as the group feels cohesive enough to do so.

Here are several cardinal rules of circling:

- Whatever is said or done in the circle stays in the circle.
- No triangulation—no gossiping among circle members about another woman in the circle.
- The same goes for problems or complaints regarding the circle—they should be brought to the circle, and in a timely way.
- Personal crises always come first—the circle will set everything aside to help a circle sister in need.

The Format–Casting the Circle

"Casting" the circle simply means that you follow certain steps to create an atmosphere around your work that makes it special, or what some would call sacred. The following steps are of Celtic derivation, but are found in numerous other spiritual traditions, including Buddhism and Christianity. These steps are meant as guidelines, and the suggestions for enacting each are open to reinterpretation. Ultimately, the format is optional, but it may be helpful to your circle as a point of reference, and in critical situations, can be counted on to work.

Before casting the circle, begin by arranging the seating and creating an altar. Lay down a large and beautiful scarf, rug, or other cloth. Then arrange candles, one in each cardinal direction—East, South, West, and North—and one in the center. Place some beautiful and meaningful objects on the cloth, like goddess statues or other sacred items. Make sure to represent the four elements: water, earth, air, and fire, by having a little of each on the altar. (Water can be held in a bowl or chalice, earth can be represented by a stone or crystal, air is suggested by bird feathers, and fire, by candlelight.) Just go all out, and make your altar as beautiful and evocative as possible.

The steps for casting the circle are:

1. Purification.
2. Invocation.
3. Stating the intention.
4. Raising the energy.
5. Transformation—the body of the rite.
6. Integration.
7. Closing (some call the last step "opening the circle" because it serves to unwind the energy from group focus).

The first step, **purification,** involves tools for helping each woman in the circle set aside her daily concerns. In my circle, we generally begin by sounding a Tibetan bell, which helps us relax and center. Then we smudge in the Native American tradition, that is, we burn a combination of herbs in an abalone shell and let the smoke waft over each of us in turn. Dried sage is considered the herb of wisdom and is traditional for its purifying properties; cedar is sometimes added to induce spiritual vision.

To speed the smudge on its way, we use a smudge fan, made of long bird feathers bound together and attached to a handle. In Native American tradition, the fan is a way to dispense "feather medicine," or the properties characteristic of the bird whose feathers comprise the fan. When using the fan, we try to use our spiritual vision, our "other eyes" to see tension, blocks, or negativity around the woman we are smudging, which we sweep away and replace with the positive energies of love. Smudging is primarily meant to cleanse the aura of the recipient.

We generally pass the task of smudging around the circle—I smudge the woman on my left and hand the smudge and fan to her, then she smudges the woman on her left, and on around until the process is complete (the last smudger should also smudge the altar before putting out the smudge). Alternatively, one woman can do all the smudging, then rotate the task to another woman at the next meeting.

The next step, **invocation,** involves calling on the powers that be to come join the circle. There are numerous ways to do this. One is for each woman to light a candle and invoke a quality, like peace, courage, compassion, or levity. She may also call on her ancestors or a personal spirit guide. This sets the circle between the worlds.

The more traditional way is to call in the Four Directions: East, South, West, and North. (Note that in the Northern Hemisphere, we call in the directions in a clockwise fashion, but in the Southern Hemisphere they are called in counter-clockwise—East, North, West, and South.) In the Northern Hemisphere, East represents spring and the Maiden, South represents summer and the Mother, West represents fall and the Matriarch, and North represents winter and the Crone. (In the Southern Hemisphere, North and South are reversed.)

Each direction is thought to represent certain qualities and has a specific color and natural element associated with it. In the Northern Hemisphere, the East represents illumination, rebirth, inspiration, flight of the spirit, and is associated with the color yellow and the element of air. The South represents love, family, security, stability, and is associated with the color red and the element of fire. The West represents introspection, maturation, deep emotion, mystery, and is associated with dark blue or black and the element of water. The North represents antiquity, the wisdom of the ages, the ancestors, Grandmothers and Grandfathers, and is associated with the color white and the element of earth.

To the Four Directions some add three more: Below, Above, and Center. The direction of Below represents all forces of support, all subconscious forces, the underworld. The direction of Above represents the heavens, the universe, the forces of expansion. The direction of Center represents the center of all, the Cauldron/Transformer, the Creatrix, the Goddess of Change.

Following are some examples of how one might call in each of the directions.

For the East:

> "Oh guardian spirits of the East, place of the Maiden, of springtime, of hope and inspiration, place where spirit flies, where winged-ones show the way, come be with us in the circle, illuminate our hearts, let us play and be joyous together."

For the South:

> "Oh guardians of the South, place of the Mother, place of children and family, of the good red road home, of the wild coyote, of passion and play, bring sweetness to our work today, fill our hearts with love and trust."

For the West:

> "Oh guardians of the West, strong women of the West, place of the Matriarch, of the water creatures, the wise whales with their deep, encoded wisdom, place of the black bear, of still waters, the deep pool, open our hearts to our soul's story, let wisdom flow between us today."

For the North:

> "Spirits of the North, Grandmothers of the North, place of the wise Crones, the white bear, White Buffalo Calf Woman, please bring us your wisdom, let us feel our antiquity and know the truth of our work here on Earth, oh Ancient Ones, come hold us and help us today."

For Below:

> "Oh spirits and entities of the great Below, the underworld, ground of our being, dark hidden places, forces subconscious, come and support our work today, help us find deep truth and hidden meaning."

For Above:

> "Oh forces of the heavens, skywalkers, angels and allies of the vast Above, guide and inform our work today, enlighten us, show us our place in the great Cosmic Order, in the Web of Life."

And for Center:

> "To the Center, the womb of the Great Mother, safe-haven within and without, home beyond home, bring us peace, bring us transformation, give us trust in the forces of growth and change."

How to begin? Start in the East, and simply have the woman sitting nearest that spot light a candle, stand, and turn to face east for her invocation. Then continue on to the next direction and next person.

The most important aspect of the invocation is sincerity, true prayerfulness in speaking from the heart. A simple, respectful chant to acknowledge the Grandmother in each of the Four Directions will suffice. Learn about the directions, then just let the words flow.

The next step, **stating the intention,** or what the group has gathered to accomplish, serves to focus everyone fully on the work at hand.

Then comes **raising the energy,** which usually involves singing, drumming, rattling, or chanting to loosen body and mind and bring everyone together. Too bad so many women are inhibited at the throat, inhibited in speaking their truth, and thus inhibited in raising their voices in song! Raising the energy can take some patience, but there is definitely a point when the group can feel that everyone is connected and the circle has gelled. Now transformation is set to begin.

The meaning of the next step, **transformation** (and the body of the rite), depends on what the group has planned. Basically, the circle goes about the business of doing what it has gathered to do, whether discussion of a particular topic or planned activity. But before getting to either of these, many circles like to have a brief period of check-in, where each woman can tell a bit of what is happening in her personal life (this can also be done before the circle is cast, perhaps with tea or with a meal). Then again, when a circle has not met for a while or big changes have happened for several participants, check-in may constitute the entire meeting.

The challenge inherent in check-in is not only to keep ourselves from using more than our fair share of time (and many circles do designate a timekeeper to avoid this pitfall), but to hold firmly to truth telling rather than processing. What is the difference between the two? Truth telling springs from the heart; it happens if we lead from the honest place deep inside us, rather than leading from our heads.

Usually there is a talking object used in the circle—a stone, a stick, or perhaps a small goddess figure. Whoever holds it is free to speak, and while doing so, should receive the undivided attention of all who are present. Not only do we speak from the heart, but listen the same way. Sedonia Cahill explains:

"Listening in circle takes on new meaning. Witnessing is deep listening that involves the body in the listening process. As we hear stories, we refrain from rescuing, care taking, or interrupting the flow of the process. As we clear away more of our own issues we can be more fully present with each other. We learn to witness ourselves too, honoring our feelings, being open to examining our patterns, exaggerations, blind spots, and the places where we remain stuck. We witness each other's guilt, shame, regrets, and secrets, all the veils that keep us from seeing ourselves in our awesome human beauty.

"The women who surround us in circle become mirrors, showing us various parts of ourselves, and we in turn provide mirrors for them. This 'circle of mirrors' gives us the opportunity to see whatever we are discussing in a larger and more expansive way. If we speak and listen open-heartedly, we begin to understand that we are all in this together, that we each have a part of the answer, and that we are weaving together a new story that is more holistic than the fragmented one we have been living. To know and experience this is to participate in the healing process."⁹

The willingness to listen deeply and nonjudgmentally is wisdom embodied by the Chinese goddess of compassion, Kuan Yin, whose name means "She Who Hearkens to the Cries of the World." She is known in Tibet as Tara, in Japan as Kannon, and in Vietnam as Quan Am. Others honor Mother Mary, or Guadalupe. You may wish to find a statue or picture of one of these for the center of your circle.

Once check-in is complete, we move on to the body of the rite, which may involve any of the topics listed above, or perhaps trance journeying or other healing work. This is the Work, where the intensity of our focus increases exponentially.

"This past Samhain we focused on weaving our strength with the Afghan women to help them reclaim their lost voices. This process was profound and very powerful. Our voices rose spontaneously and built to the most incredible sound—not exactly a scream but a sound so primal and so *loud* that it literally knocked some of us over—as we unleashed our support for the Afghan women.

"Immediately after this, we grounded by kneeling down and placing our hands firmly on the Earth, sending the energy back to the Mother for healing. We stayed like this until our breathing slowed and we felt more or less normal. (Whenever we go wild like this in circle, we find that if we skip the grounding we become very irritable later on—much to the dismay of our partners.)

"Then we went around the circle for another round, and as we chanted together, we each made a commitment to a personal act that would help prevent further gender-cide: the oppression, imprisonment, or torture of women by religious extremists. Almost immediately after this rite, we were thrilled to hear that the Afghan women's liberation organization, RAWA, had made huge political inroads!"

When the body of the rite is completed, the phase of **integration** helps prepare the circle to close. In this, participants once again pass the talking object and truth-tell about what they have gleaned from their experience, what gifts they will take with them, or any vows they wish to make. They may also offer words of acknowledgment or thanks, either to themselves or to the group.

Closing begins with a brief grounding practice, which can be as simple as a few moments of quiet and deep breathing to the sound of the Tibetan bell or chime. At this, the circle unwinds itself. The woman who was last to call in a direction goes first; she stands, offers words of thanks to the forces and guardians she asked to be present, then blows out her candle. The process continues until the first direction to be called is finally released. The circle is now both closed and open, and participants can talk, laugh, and celebrate!

This circling format can be used to create various kinds of ceremonies. What exactly is the difference between a ritual and a ceremony? In the description above, one of the rituals used was smudging, and yet another was passing the talking object. Taken together, ritual elements constitute ceremony. Known also as rites, ceremonies may be conducted in honor of marriage, of the birth of a child, of the Blood Mysteries, or of seasonal changes and cross-quarter days.

Circle participants themselves best express the long-term benefits of circling. One, who worked in women's health and had a large volume of clients, said that if the women she cared for would just get together and circle, they would have the answers to questions they sometimes had to wait days or weeks to bring to her attention. Another said that what she loved most about her circle was how everyone went deep, and said that this had changed her life because she now brought this depth to her other relationships. Another said the circle had helped her let go, "go wild," and really explore herself.

This brings up another aspect of what strengthens a circle—the willingness to explore the dark, shadow side of ourselves, to go to our uncomfortable edges and stay there a while as we wait for insight. "The circle is not a place to go for a 'feel-good' experience," Cahill tells us, "but it is a safe place to do unsafe things, so we can practice becoming wild, express the inexpressible, drop into deep wordless places."[10]

As this woman, many years into circling, relates:

"Karen and I were extremely close when this crisis occurred between us. My husband and I were getting divorced and I was feeling suicidal—not that I was planning my death but I simply didn't want to be alive. I totally depended on Karen for support—we were inseparable

"But Karen's life was also overwhelming. Her house was on the market, and the two girls were still under five. Karen was growing more and more anxious; she was approaching the age her mother had been when she became seriously depressed and committed suicide. It was all too much. She stopped eating, sleeping, getting out of bed, being able to cope. Some would call what she experienced a nervous breakdown, but true to Karen's wisdom, she called it her breakthrough. And breakthrough she did. With the help of her friends, family, and therapy several days a week, she slowly came back to life.

"In her recovery process, one of the issues she needed to deal with was her relationship with me and my depression and talk of wanting to die. When her mother committed suicide, Karen felt guilty for not being able to save her, and I was triggering anxiety and fear in her with all of my stuff. Her therapist strongly recommended that she and I sever our ties until we could come around to a healthier relationship. Well, I didn't fare too well with this. My husband and Karen had been my best friends for fifteen years, and neither of them wanted to relate to me anymore. I felt abandoned and lost and hurt and angry and wondered what was wrong with me that my closest friends were leaving me.

"Karen and I went to a therapy session together to have a safe place to hear each other out. She really wanted me to understand that she didn't think there was anything wrong with me but that our relationship was unhealthy and she needed space from me indefinitely. I appreciated her efforts but I was bitter.

"So this is where our Sister Circle saved us. We were both committed to the circle and neither of us ever missed a meeting. The other women in the circle sat with us for a long time trying to give us space not too feel too awkward being in close proximity. Holding the talking stick and knowing that we would each have a safe place to share what was going on for us gave me permission to be authentic, as our circle has always done. So when I was feeling horrible, I knew that the circle was an appropriate place to talk about it, that I would be heard. Our circle sisters tried to help us keep things in perspective and depersonalize what was going on between us, reassuring us that this was a healthy and necessary period in our friendship, albeit painful. They always acknowledged our friendship as special, and I think they were as shocked as us by this whole turn of events. So, we were all kind of in it together, trying to hold a safe place for one another. And each month, although I had thoughts of skipping circle for fear of facing Karen and feeling heartbroken, I persevered because I knew it was the only place that she and I could be in the same room together, share intimacy, and stay connected.

"As time went on we both got healthier, both within ourselves and in our lives. The circle held the space for our descent into darkness . . . our sisters gave us courage, they witnessed, validated, and believed in us. Precious and sacred sisters!"

The sense of security that comes from knowing that circle sisters can be counted on in an emergency is undoubtedly one of the greatest boons of circling. This account illustrates this point in a most powerful way:

"I meet with a group of five women, all in our fifties and sixties. Our bond is deep, and our explorations are often surprising and challenging and very sweet. This circle really calls me to myself.

"In this circle is a woman whose eighteen-year-old daughter was murdered in cold blood by an intruder. Our circle was in place to support her. In the face of such unspeakable tragedy, we dropped everything to listen to her and help with the tasks at hand. A couple of us went with her to prepare her daughter's body for cremation, and sometimes my ears still ring with her cry of disbelief and utter pain upon first glimpsing it. We helped make arrangements for a farewell ceremony. For years after the event, we sat with her in her process of grieving and slowly healing. Our circle was strong enough to hold her and her grief, and at the same time it was made stronger by our intense involvement with her and each other around that tragedy."

This depth of commitment is rare among women unrelated by blood. But to have a strong circle of women to fall back on makes so much sense. Particularly in a horrific situation, other family members may be virtually immobile, too shocked and grief-stricken to take care of immediate details, let alone each other. Women's support of one another centers in the circle, but extends to create community. And this is precisely what the Circle of Life is all about—the community of women, in which each of us holds an essential place.

Afterword

Writing this book was truly a journey into the unknown—a journey that could hardly be described as a purely intellectual pursuit. Little did we know when we began how far we would have to stretch to grasp the meaning of each archetype, and how our interviews would challenge our preconceived notions. Separately and together, we had amazing experiences of discovery, synchronicity, glimpses of the future, visions of what our lives are all about.

There is great joy to be had in rediscovering these ancient archetypes, and in finding roles for ourselves that have substance and feel natural. But there may also be some stress and discomfort in changing our lives to make room for these expanded roles. I have made a habit of issuing a disclaimer at the start of my workshops that afterward participants may find their priorities in life shifting dramatically. Perhaps an intimate relationship is ripe for upheaval and must undergo deep transformation to feel right, or changes must be made in employment to find something that fits. Somehow we've gotten the idea that we can revolutionize our lives externally, without having to leave our emotional comfort zones. Nearer the truth is the contemporary idiom—no pain, no gain.

When seeds of change sprout and grow from deep inside us, transformation of our lives is far-reaching and often disorienting.

This is where a Circle of support—your own women's circle—really comes into play. In childbirth, we know that women traditionally surround the laboring mother, extending themselves body and soul that she might use them to transmute pain to pleasure. We had a similar experience of being carried along and enfolded by the wisdom of the women we interviewed, particularly when the subject matter was a bit over our heads. Again, we extend our gratitude to every voice in the Circle of Life—for as we saw ourselves in you, and in each of the archetypes, we felt deeper love and respect for women than we had ever known.

It is said of teaching that we teach whatever we wish to learn more about; the same is true of writing. Carol and I are grateful for having found this vast subject to contemplate and investigate. We know we will feel this project's reverberations in our lives for many years to come.

In closing, we ask that you use these archetypes to find compassion for women in all walks of life, regardless of your own opinions or beliefs. Rise above the divisiveness and competition bred in us by the patriarchy, and remember the simple choice of "power with" versus "power over." How does this translate to everyday life? If you have ever expressed the wild abandon of the Amazon, why fear or try to repress that energy when you see it rise in another woman? If you have known the grace of true connection as Lover, why pit yourself against another woman for passion's sake? If you have wielded the power of Sorceress, why judge (or begrudge) another woman doing the same? Or, if you have explored your domesticity as Mother, why belittle a woman holding to this as her prime identity? The true purpose of the Circle is to encourage women to unite, never to typecast or pigeonhole one another.

In fact, everyone we interviewed commented on the inclusive nature of the Circle. Over and over, women said they couldn't wait to hold this book in their hands—they felt it was important for women everywhere and that time was of the essence. This was personally gratifying for us as authors, but also made clear the sweeping changes taking place in women's awareness now, engendering new imperatives for connectedness and a spiritual framework that lends power and dignity to our lives. Clearly, it is up to us to shift social constructs that denigrate our mysteries and define us as less than beautiful and strong in our own right.

Mystery is magic—and women are hungry for the opportunity to work their "ordinary magic" as never before. Dancing through the Circle of Life, exploring each archetype to the fullest extent, is our heritage and our destiny. What power and what joy to perceive the grand pattern of our lives as women, and yet be possessed by the mystery of its unfolding!

APPENDIX

Which Archetype Are You?

Here's a short quiz to help you find your archetypal profile according to the thirteen archetypes in *The Circle of Life*. Have fun—and don't be overly sensitive! Answer for who you are now, not who you were in the past or who you aspire to be. Have pen and paper handy to keep track of your answers. Ready? Take a deep breath . . .

1. What physiological phase (Blood Mystery) are you in right now?

- Have not started menstruating yet. [D]
- Just started menstruating recently. [N]
- Having periods but have not given birth and have no intention of doing so in the near future. [B]
- Having periods and considering the possibility of having a child. [L]
- Have given birth to at least one child or major creative project. [M]
- Still have my moontides but am probably done with childbearing. [W]

- Love my bleeding times! [A]
- Almost too busy to notice, but some very intense PMS! [R]
- Periods are beginning to be erratic, either heavy and often, or irregular, spacing further apart. [P]
- Still appear to be dealing with the fallout from hormonal imbalances. [S]
- Have not bled for a number of years. [C]
- Can't remember what all the fuss was about in the first place. [K]

2. In a social situation you often find that you:

- Are rather oblivious to the social mores at a party. [D]
- Tend to hang out by yourself, as that is much more interesting than making small talk. [S]
- Are really interested in everyone there and just want to have a great time. [N]
- Make your opinions loudly known to everyone within earshot. [A]
- Find your posse of girlfriends and stay in a cluster gossiping. [B]
- Hang out with the men (women) being charming as hell. [L]
- Find the other women who have young children to share parenting tips. [M]
- Get involved in the thickest of political and environmental discussions. [W]
- Find one or two intelligent women to have a meaningful conversation with. [P]
- Are either the life of the party or are completely bored, depending on the caliber of the gathering. [R]
- Don't feel the need to socialize much in general. [C]
- At this point, *life* is the party! [K]

3. In regards to a sexual partner, you gravitate toward:

- That special someone. [L]
- Having a partner hasn't occurred to you yet. [D]
- Someone considerably younger than yourself. [A]
- "I've had *many* partners and am not interested in that again!" [C]
- Someone who will help you take care of your child. [M]
- "I'm just getting used to being sexual with myself!" [N]
- "A loving partner would be great, but I'm more focused on serving others." [W]
- A partner who will share life's joys *and* responsibilities equally with you, male or female. [R]
- "Definitely my best friend in college, she's hot." [B]
- Having a partner again hasn't occurred to you for some time. [K]
- A playful Pan consort. [P]
- "I think I might scare away a serious lover right now." [S]

4. If people were to describe you, they most likely would say:

- "She's just so damn mouthy, I wish she'd grow up already." [A]
- "She really has matured into a fine leader, she gets things done." [R]
- "I wish she would realize how beautiful she truly is and not stress about how she looks." [N]
- "What a wonderful, creative, and independent child." [D]
- "Oh, she's going through her neo-feminist phase right now." [B]
- "She's so strong and elegant in her waning years." [K]
- "Her love for her children is so selfless and unconditional." [M]
- "People seek her out for her wise counsel." [C]

- "She's always picks the 'bad boys (girls),' but this new one looks like a keeper." [L]
- "Her intuition in caring for others is amazing." [W]
- "She's deeply into that women's spirituality thing." [P]
- "To tell you the truth, I think she's gone a little mad." [S]

5. If you were to describe yourself, how you feel in the present, you would say:

- "I picture myself running free on the beach, or in the forest." [D]
- "I find a lot of solace and nurturing by being in a formal circle with my close women friends." [P]
- "My world revolves around getting this life project off the ground." [M]
- "It feels like everything is falling into place for me to teach and be of service to others." [W]
- "I am really turned on by learning about true feminist thought." [B]
- "I have just filled out my living will." [K]
- "I feel as though I have reached a plateau where I am reaping the harvest of all my hard work." [R]
- "At work, men treat me like a dominatrix." [A]
- "My life is so rich and full and blessed." [L]
- "Truthfully? I'd rather be shopping." [N]
- "I'm a little in awe of the aging process." [C]
- "To tell you the truth, I think I've gone a little mad." [S]

6. What is the most important thing in your life?

- Myself. [S]
- How I look to others. [N]
- Recess. [D]
- My work for society. [C]
- My girlfriends. [B]
- Exploring my spiritual path with my close women friends. [P]
- My freedom. [A]
- Romance and passion with my mate. [L]
- My passion with life. [K]
- My children. [M]
- My career. [R]
- Teaching and sharing my knowledge. [W]

7. Which profession most appeals to you?

- Environmental activist. [B]
- Hospice worker. [K]
- Veterinarian or equestrian. [D]
- Nurse or psychotherapist. [W]
- Actress or singer. [L]
- Yoga teacher or the CEO of a socially conscious firm. [P]
- Shamanic Healer. [S]
- Restaurant owner or wine vintner. [R]
- President or matador. [A]
- Mediator. [C]
- Fashion designer or Olympic gold medal figure skater. [N]
- Landscaper. [M]

8. To best describe your favorite way to relax:

- Draw a long, hot bath scented with lavender oil and surrounded with candles. [P]
- Take a hike in the forest alone (or with someone you feel spiritually connected to). [S]
- Do some vigorous, marathon exercise activity. [A]
- Update your day planner and review your goals. [R]
- Sit alone in front of the fireplace in a cashmere throw, drinking a cappuccino and eating a croissant. [K]
- Unplug the phone and curl up in bed with a great book (for once, blissful solitude). [M]
- Veg out in front of the TV or surf the Internet. [D]
- Work with your hands, making Martha Stewart's latest creations. [W]
- Play Nancy Sinatra tunes for your friends and open a bottle of Gallo. [N]
- Wear black velvet, set a single rose in a vase on the table, and write a poem to him/her. [L]
- Create wickedly fattening foods for your girlfriends, with margaritas and definitely something chocolate for dessert. [B]
- Make dinner reservations. [C]

9. My style of decorating and housekeeping would best be described as:

- Simple, comfortable home, good for lounging and playing with children and pets, very low maintenance, washable slipcovers, framed pictures of family. [M]
- Classic, understated style that looks put-together but not fussy or trendy—English country, dark woods, silver, crystal vases. [C]

- A hodgepodge of furniture purchased at thrift stores without much thought or planning, fun retro seventies furniture. [B]
- A comfortable home that I feel confident in and know will make a positive impression—soft, luxurious fabrics, warm. [R]
- Artsy, somewhat eccentric, eclectic feel—plants, antiques, funky forties fabrics, sun-filled rooms. [S]
- Minimalist and efficient, no particular style—I'm paring down. [K]
- Interesting pieces from garage sales and Goodwill, constantly evolving look, making old things look fabulous by painting and reupholstering, rearranging to accommodate new things. [A]
- Fresh, quiet surroundings, Eastern influence, Zen-style with natural wood, deep, muted colors—the perfect Feng Shui setting. [P]
- Anything handmade, knickknacks, crafts projects I've done myself, needlepoint pillows, afghans, paintings, collages. [N]
- Old South or Victorian, lace and floral chintz, frilly canopy bed entwined with artificial flowers, stuffed animals. [D]
- American Country, straw baskets, collectibles, rustic tablecloths, piled-up pillows, easy to keep up. [W]
- Romantic, with fresh flowers in every room, Jacuzzi or sunken tub a focal point, focus on small details. [L]

10. What do you long for most in your life?

- Simplicity. [K]
- Being in charge of myself. [D]
- Female bonding, a true friend. [N]
- A loving mate. [B]
- Nurturing (a child, anything!). [L]
- Women's wisdom. [M]
- Recognition for my contributions. [W]
- Authority and autonomy. [A]

- Spiritual exploration and support. [R]
- Ways to wield power. [P]
- Wisdom. [S]
- Truth. [C]

SCORING

D If you scored predominantly D, refer to the Daughter archetype.

N If you scored predominantly N, refer to the Maiden archetype.

B If you scored predominantly B, refer to the Blood Sister archetype

L If you scored predominantly L, refer to the Lover archetype.

M If you scored predominantly M, refer to the Mother archetype.

W If you scored predominantly W, refer to the Midwife archetype.

A If you scored predominantly A, refer to the Amazon archetype.

R If you scored predominantly R, refer to the Matriarch archetype.

P If you scored predominantly P, refer to the Priestess archetype.

S If you scored predominantly S, refer to the Sorceress archetype.

C If you scored predominantly C, refer to the Crone archetype.

K If you scored predominantly K, refer to the Dark Mother archetype.

If you were all over the map and got a little of each, refer to the Transformer archetype.

$\mathcal{N}otes$

Preface

1. Jean Shinoda Bolen, *The Millionth Circle: How to Change Ourselves and the World* (Berkeley, Calif.: Conari Press, 1999).
2. Y. L. Michael, G. A. Colditz, E. Coakley, and I. Kawachi, "Health Behaviors, Social Networks, and Healthy Aging: Cross-Sectional Evidence from the Nurses' Health Study," *Qual Life Res* 8 (1999): 711–22.
3. S. E. Taylor, L. C. Klein, B. P. Lewis, T. L. Gruenewald, R. A. R. Gurung, and J. A. Updegraff, "Female Responses to Stress: Tend-and-Befriend, not Fight-or-Flight," *Psychological Review* 107, no. 3 (2000): 411–29.
4. Diedre Badejo, *Osun Seegesi: The Elegant Deity of Wealth, Power and Femininity* (Trenton, N.J.: Africa World Press, 1996), xvii.

Chapter 1: The Goddess and the Mystery

1. Jean Shinoda Bolen, *Goddessses in Everywoman* (San Francisco: HarperCollins, 1984), 1–4.
2. Joseph Campbell, *The Hero with a Thousand Faces,* 2d ed. (Princeton, N. J.: Princeton University Press, 1968), 19.
3. Jean Houston, *The Possible Human,* (Los Angeles: J. P. Tarcher, 1987).
4. Barbara Walker, *The Woman's Encyclopedia of Myths and Secrets* (New York: Harper & Row, 1988), 188.
5. Starhawk, *Spiral Dance* (San Francisco: Harper & Row, 1979), 170.

Chapter 2: The Thirteen Stages of Women's Lives

1. Barbara Ardinger, *A Woman's Book of Rituals and Celebrations* (San Rafael, Calif.: New World Library, 1992), 139.
2. Starhawk, *Spiral Dance,* 188.
3. Ibid., 189.
4. Walker, *Woman's Encyclopedia,* 629.
5. Ibid., 378.
6. Philip Rawson, *Erotic Art of the East* (New York: G. P. Putnam's Sons, 1968), 159.

Chapter 3: Blood Bonding

1. Walker, *Woman's Encyclopedia,* 635.
2. Ibid., 636.
3. Ibid., 637.
4. Phyllis Chesler, *About Men* (New York: Bantam, 1978), xx.
5. Dena Taylor, *Red Flower: Rethinking Menstruation* (Freedom, Calif.: Crossing Press, 1988). 49–50.
6. Paula Weideger, *Menstruation & Menopause* (New York: Alfred K. Knopf, 1975), 107.
7. Walker, *Woman's Encyclopedia,* 642.
8. Ibid., 643.
9. Ibid.
10. Ibid., 644.
11. Luisah Teish, *Jambalaya: The Natural Woman's Book of Personal Charms and Practical Rituals* (San Francisco: Harper & Row, 1985), 60.
12. Chesler, *About Men,* xx.
13. Taylor, *Red Flower,* 102.
14. Walker, *Woman's Encyclopedia,* 638.
15. Ibid., 639.
16. Brooke Medicine Eagle, "Women's Moontime—A Call to Power," *Shaman's Drum* 4 (spring 1986), 21.
17. Winnifred Cutler, *Love Cycles* (New York: Villard Books, 1991), 151.
18. Ibid.

19. Mickey Hart, *Drumming at the Edge of Magic* (San Francisco: Harper & Row, 1990), 121.
20. Judy Grahn, *Blood, Bread, and Roses* (Boston: Beacon Press, 1993), 44.
21. Ibid.
22. Penelope Shuttle and Peter Redgrove, *The Wise Wound* (New York: Richard Marek, 1978), 96.
23. Grahn, *Blood, Bread, and Roses,* 52.
24. Mary Jane Sherfey, *The Nature and Evolution of Female Sexuality* (New York: Random House, 1973), 52.
25. Shuttle and Redgrove, *Wise Wound,* 43.
26. Ibid., 4–5. `
27. Grahn, *Blood, Bread, and Roses,* 75.
28. Walker, *Woman's Encyclopedia,* 637.
29. Ibid., 1040.
30. Pam Keesey, ed., *Daughters of Darkness* (San Francisco: Cleis Press, 1993).
31. Alan Bleakley, *The Fruits of the Moon Tree* (London: Gateway Books, 1984), 252.
32. Ibid., 249.
33. Walker, *Woman's Encyclopedia,* 640–41.
34. Kathy Jones, *The Goddess of Glastonbury* (Glastonbury, England: Ariadne Publications, 1990), 30.
35. Walker, *Woman's Encyclopedia,* 644.

Chapter 4: The Role of the Transformer

1. Demetra George, *Mysteries of the Dark Moon: The Healing Power of the Dark Goddess* (New York: HarperCollins, 1992).
2. Clarissa Pinkola Estés, Ph.D., *Women Who Run with the Wolves* (New York: Random House, 1992), 11–12.
3. Carlos Castaneda, *The Teachings of Don Juan* (New York: Pocket Books, 1968), 82–87.
4. Teish, *Jambalaya,* 213.
5. Elizabeth Davis's notes from workshop: Helen Palmer, "Discrimination Between Projections and Accurate Intuitive Impressions," San Francisco, 1988.

6. Richard Wilhelm and Cary Baynes, *I Ching* (Princeton: Princeton University Press, 1950), 97–98.

7. Vicki Noble, *Motherpeace* (San Francisco: Harper & Row, 1983), 102.

8. Joan Halifax, *Shamanic Voices* (New York: Dutton, 1979), 4.

9. Jean Shinoda Bolen, interview in *Magical Blend* 44 (October 1994), 52–58.

10. Jamie Samms and David Carson, *Medicine Cards: The Discovery of Power Through the Ways of Animals* (Santa Fe: Bear and Co., 1988), 61.

11. Walker, *Woman's Encyclopedia,* 903–904.

12. J. C. Cooper, *An Illustrated Encyclopedia of Traditional Symbols* (London: Thames & Hudson, 1978), 129–30.

13. Bolen, interview in *Magical Blend,* 52–58.

14. Wilhelm and Baynes, *I Ching,* 98.

15. Walker, *Woman's Encyclopedia,* 150–51.

16. Ibid.

17. Noble, *Motherpeace,* 17.

18. Wilhelm and Baynes, *I Ching,* viii.

19. Ralph Blum, *The Book of Runes* (New York: St. Martin's Press, 1982), 31.

20. Ibid., 20.

21. Ed Buryn, *Vagabonding in the USA* (Berkeley, Calif.: And/Or Press, 1980), 4.

22. Walker, *Woman's Encyclopedia,* 973.

23. Noble, *Motherpeace,* 110.

24. Stanisloff Grof, *The Adventure of Self-Discovery* (Albany: State University of New York Press, 1988), 187–88.

Chapter 5: The Daughter and the Amazon

1. Walker, *Woman's Encyclopedia,* 475.

2. Noble, *Motherpeace,* 66.

3. Charlene Spretnak, *Lost Goddesses of Early Greece* (Boston: Beacon Press, 1984), 109–18.

4. Traditional by Doreen Valiente, adapted by Starhawk, *Spiral Dance,* 102–103.

5. Christine Downing, *The Goddess: Mythological Images of the Feminine* (New York: Crossroad Publishing, 1981).

6. Zsuzsanna E. Budapest, *The Grandmother of Time* (San Francisco: Harper & Row, 1989), 91.

Chapter 6: The Maiden and the Matriarch

1. David Cohen, ed., *The Circle of Life* (New York: HarperCollins, 1991), 64.
2. Ibid., 62.
3. Jane Ellen Harrison, *Themis: A Study of the Origins of Greek Religion* (London: The Merlin Press, 1963), 487.
4. Edward S. Gifford, Jr., *The Evil Eye* (New York: Macmillan, 1958), 55.
5. Budapest, *Grandmother of Time,* 155–56.
6. Barbara Walker, *Woman's Rituals* (San Francisco: Harper & Row, 1990), 184–85.

Chapter 7: The Blood Sister and the Priestess

1. John G. Neihardt, *Black Elk Speaks* (Lincoln: University of Nebraska Press, 1959), 168.
2. Richard Moss, *The I That Is We: Awakening to Higher Energies Through Unconditional Love* (Berkeley, Calif.: Celestial Arts, 1995), 47.
3. Noble, *Motherpeace,* 125.
4. Ibid.
5. Elizabeth Davis, *Women's Sexual Passages: Finding Pleasure and Intimacy at Every Stage of Life* (Alameda, Calif.: Hunter House, 2000).

Chapter 8: The Lover and the Sorceress

1. Noble, *Motherpeace,* 107.
2. Budapest, *Grandmother of Time,* 70.
3. Ardinger, *Woman's Book of Rituals,* 169.
4. Christiane Northrup, *The Wisdom of Menopause* (New York: Bantam Books, 2001), 49.
5. Walker, *Woman's Encyclopedia,* 18–20.
6. Bleakley, *Fruits of the Moon Tree,* 253.
7. Ibid., 16.
8. Ibid., 17.

9. Ibid., 181.

10. James Redfield, *The Celestine Prophecy* (New York: Warner Books, 1993), 194.

11. Bleakley, *Fruits of the Moon Tree,* 182.

12. Walker, *Woman's Encyclopedia,* 33.

13. Moss, *I That Is We,* 53.

14. Ibid.

Chapter 9: The Mother and the Crone

1. D. Krehbiel, F. Levy, P. Poindron, and M. J. Podhomme, "Peridural Anesthesia Disturbs Maternal Bonding in Primiparous and Multiparous Ewes," *Physiology and Behavior* 40 (1982): 463–72.

2. Cohen, *Circle of Life,* 4.

3. Barbara Walker, *The Crone* (San Francisco: Harper & Row, 1985), 31.

4. Noble, *Motherpeace,* 77.

5. Mary Daly, *Gyn/Ecology: The Metaethics of Radical Transformation* (Boston: Beacon Press, 1979), 390.

6. Niles Newton and Rhonda Winn, "Sexuality in Aging: A Study of 106 Cultures," *Archives of Sexual Behavior* II, no. 4 (1982).

7. Daly, *Gyn/Ecology,* 378.

8. Paula Underwood, "Clan Mothers in the Twenty-First Century," in *The Fabric of the Future,* ed. M. J. Ryan (Berkeley, Calif.: Conari Press, 1998), 158.

9. Brooke Medicine Eagle, *Buffalo Woman Comes Singing* (New York: Ballantine, 1991), 339.

10. Luisa Francia, *Dragontime* (New York: Ash Tree Publishing, 1988), 104–105.

11. Zsuzsanna E. Budapest, *Holy Book of Women's Mysteries* (Berkeley, CA: Wingbow Press, 1989), 86.

12. Barbara Meyerhoff, "By Means of Performance," in *Celebration: Studies in Festivity and Ritual,* ed. Victor Turner (Washington, D.C.: Smithsonian Institution Press, 1982), 88.

Chapter 10: The Midwife and the Dark Mother

1. Sara Ruddick, *Maternal Thinking* (New York: Plenum Press, 1980), 150–51.

2. Mary Belenky, Blythe Clinchy, Nancy Goldberger, and Jill Tarule, *Women's Ways of Knowing: The Development of Self, Voice and Mind* (New York: Basic Books, 1986), 218.

3. Elizabeth Davis, *Heart & Hands: A Midwife's Guide to Pregnancy and Birth* (Berkeley, Calif.: Celestial Arts, 1997).

4. Paulo Freire, *Pedagogy of the Oppressed* (New York: Seaview Publications), 68.

5. Heinrich Kramer and James Sprenger, *Malleus Maleficarum,* trans. Rev. Montague Summers (New York: Dover Publications, 1971), 66.

6. Starhawk, *Dreaming the Dark* (Boston: Beacon Press, 1982), 204.

7. Ibid., 204.

8. Noble, *Motherpeace,* 89.

9. Elizabeth Yates, *Call It Zest* (Brattleboro, Vt.: Stephen Greene Press, 1977), 89–90.

10. Walker, *Woman's Encyclopedia,* 492.

11. Ibid., 206.

12. Ed Fitch, *Magical Rites from the Crystal Well* (Saint Paul, Minn.: Llewellyn Publications, 1984), 139.

13. Cohen, *Circle of Life,* 277.

14. Sherwin Nuland, *How We Die* (New York: Vintage Books, 1995), xv.

15. Ibid., 262, 267.

Chapter 11: Creating Your Own Circle

1. Jean Shinoda Bolen, *Goddesses in Older Women: Archetypes in Women Over Fifty* (New York: HarperCollins, 2001), 179.

2. Laura Allen and Roger A. Gorski, "Sexual Dimorphism of the Anterior Commissure and the Massa Intermedia of the Human Brain," *Journal of Comparative Neurology* 312 (1991): 97–104. Laura Allen and Roger A. Gorski, "Sex Differences in the Corpus Callosum of the Living Human Being," *Journal of Neuroscience* 11, no. 4 (1991): 933–42.

3. Anne Moir and David Jessel, *Brain Sex* (New York: Carol Publishing Group, 1991), 46.

4. Christiane Northrup, *Women's Bodies, Women's Wisdom,* rev. ed. (New York: Bantam, 1999), 33.

5. Helen Fisher, *The First Sex: The Natural Talents of Women and How They Are Changing the World* (New York: Ballantine Books, 1999), 3.

6. Alice Walker, *Sent by Earth: A Message from the Grandmother Spirit* (New York: Seven Stories Press, 2001), 47.

7. Sedonia Cahill, interview by Elizabeth Davis, Guerneville, Calif., 2 December 1999.

8. Ibid.

9. Ibid.

10. Ibid.

About the Authors

photo by Suzanne Arms

ELIZABETH DAVIS, B.A., C.P.M.

A renowned expert on women's issues, Elizabeth Davis has been a midwife, women's health-care specialist, educator, and consultant for twenty-five years. She is internationally active in women's rights and lectures widely on midwifery, sexuality, and women's spirituality.

Elizabeth served as a representative to the Midwives' Alliance of North America for five years, and president of the Midwifery Education Accreditation Council for the United States. She is cofounder and director of the National Midwifery Institute, Inc., a three-year, MEAC accredited, apprenticeship-based midwifery program. She holds a degree in Holistic Maternity Care from Antioch University, and is certified by the North American Registry of Midwives.

Her books include the classic, *Heart & Hands: A Midwife's Guide to Pregnancy and Birth* (now in its third edition); *Energetic Pregnancy; Women's Intuition;* and *Women's Sexual Passages: Finding Pleasure and Intimacy at Every Stage of Life.* She is widely quoted in women's periodicals, and is a popular radio and television guest.

Elizabeth's hobbies are snorkeling, gardening, hiking, and metaphysical studies. Her passion is seeding women's circles, for which she is in frequent demand. Elizabeth lives in Sebastopol, California, and is the mother of three children.

photo by Jenn Star

CAROL LEONARD, B.S., N.H.C.M.

Carol Leonard, a foremother of the modern midwifery movement, is a New Hampshire Certified Midwife and has been practicing for twenty-five years. She was cofounder of the Midwives' Alliance of North America (MANA), serving one term as president. Her work to improve maternity care in Moscow during the Soviet era was featured on *20/20* and was written into *Congressional Record.* She was recently appointed first chairperson of the New Hampshire Midwifery Council and is also a member of the state Birth Center Rules & Regulations Review Committee.

Carol runs a birth center on her farm in New Hampshire called Longmeadow Farm Birthing Home, which was state licensed in September 2000. She is on the faculty of Birthwise Midwifery School in Bridgton, Maine, a nationally accredited program.

She recently finished writing an account of her midwifery practice, *Lady's Hands, Lion's Heart: Memoirs of a Radical Midwife,* which is now installed in the Margaret Sanger Archives at Smith College. Her hobbies are gardening, skiing, and fly-fishing. She raises medicinal herbs and free-range chickens and has three wild grandsons.

Index

A

Aging process, 173
Alchemy, 32, 152–57, 161
Al-Lat, 39
The Amazon (archetype)
    the Daughter as complement of,
        27, 84–85, 90–91, 93, 94–96
    details of, 84–89, 93, 94–96,
        99–101
    examples of, 86–88, 89, 91–94,
        100–101
    overview of, 27–28
Ananta the Infinite, 63
Ancestors, female, 121–22
Aphrodite, 23, 148
Archetypes. *See also individual*
    archetypes
    complementary, 16, 84
    definition of, 9
    determining your, 241–48
    importance of, 9
    individual characteristics of,
        18–37
Ardinger, Barbara, 151
Artemis, 89, 96
Astarte, 10

Athena, 95–96
Atropos the Cutter, 197
Autumnal equinox, 40, 103

B

Badejo, Diedre, xiv
Baubo, 175
Baynes, Cary, 72
Belenky, Mary, 188
Beltane, 22–23, 149, 151
Birth. *See* Childbirth
Birthingways, 167–69
Black Elk, 128
Bleakley, Alan, 50, 153, 155
Blood. *See also* Blood bonding;
    Blood Mysteries
    drinking, 39, 49–50
    fear of, 41–42, 43
    menstrual, 38–44, 48–49, 52–53
Blood bonding
    the Amazon and, 99
    to the Earth, 44–45
    the Matriarch and, 29
    meaning of, 38
    with men, 50–53
    with women, 45–46, 50